JEWISH IN AMERICA

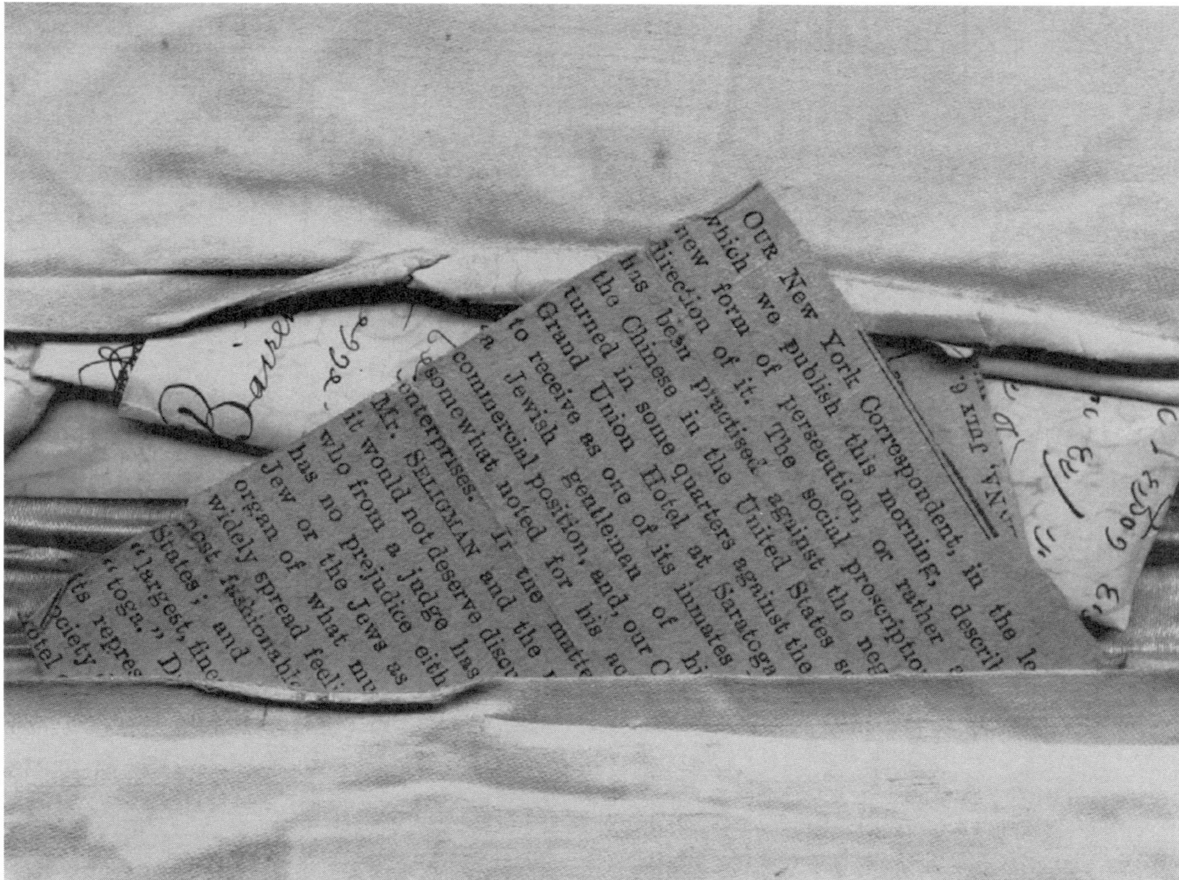

Joanne Leonard, *Scroll: Reel Family*, 2000 (detail)

JEWISH IN AMERICA

JONATHAN FREEDMAN AND SARA BLAIR

INTRODUCTION

In this volume, we gather a diverse set of responses to a seemingly simple question: What does it mean to be Jewish in America? But we also begin with a sense of the difficulty—fruitful, we hope, but nevertheless daunting—of any such inquiry. For if any question is more unanswerable than Crèvecoeur's famous interrogatory, "What is an American?" it may well be, "What is a Jewish-American?" Jews have, of course, been insistently part of the American scene for more than a century (and longer), but have in that time been described as subversive aliens and true-blue patriots; outsiders to the cultural dominant and insiders to the national narrative; quizzical critics of capitalism and masters of the economic universe; makers of high culture, wizards of mass culture, purveyors of the middlebrow.

Virtually every attempt at defining Jews and/or Jewishness has raised as many questions as it has provided answers. Jews, of course, are a group primarily organized by their relation to Judaism. But in what form? Conservative? Reform? Orthodox? Modern Orthodox? Reconstructionist? Ethical Culture? Add to the equation the notoriously lax attendance of even religiously identified Jews (as they are ritually reminded on the High Holidays), the fine old tradition of Jewish freethinking, and the widespread practice of intermarriage, and that way of answering the question looks—well, complicated. Judaism is an inevitable and ineradicable component of Jewish-American experience; but the form it takes, the expression it finds, and the meaning that is made of it are profoundly, even distinctively, various.

So too with many of the terms U.S. culture uses for categorizing populations, most notably the idiom of "race." Luckily, American Jews were never fully submitted to the process of racialization in the Nazi sense of the word (although the anti-Semitic productions of Henry Ford and the ravings of Father Coughlin should not be swept under the rug). But Jews were, beginning in the fin de siècle, catalogued according to typologies of racial identity in ways that testify to the unsettled if not ludicrous quality of the notion of "race" itself. Over the past 150 years, Jews have been variously classified as Black, "Oriental," "Levantine," "Semitic," or some debased mixture of all of the above; more recently and insistently, they have been defined as "white," a source of both privilege and embarrassment.

Perhaps, then, it's better to think of Jews in terms of the fuzzy idiom of ethnicity—a discourse, with its Whiggish narrative of assimilation and attendant tropes like "the melting pot," that was itself largely formed with reference to Jews. But here, too, problems proliferate. Recently, the Jewish-as-model-ethnic narrative has come under severe attack by Jewish as well as non-Jewish critics, some pointing to its occlusions and uses as an enabling logic (both vis-à-vis the Jewish community and as an implicit mode of comparison with other ethnic communities); others rebelling against it by proudly proclaiming their Jewish difference; still others quietly (or not so quietly) enacting it in their upward mobility and concomitant drift to the neoconservative—or just plain conservative—right. Analogously, cultural formations are often taken to be the defining characteristic of Jews, or more precisely Jewishness: but what culture, which formation? Jews have been called the People of the Book—not only the sacred ones parsed and interpreted in shul or study groups, but those interpreted and produced by the abundance of Jews who flooded into academe in the postwar period or those that compose the Great Tradition of Jewish-American writing (Malamud, Bellow, Roth, Paley) or, for that matter, those that compose the middlebrow canon of the same era (Fannie Hurst, Herman Wouk, Leon Uris). Yet Jews might also be—and have been—thought of as people of the Delicatessen, people of the Stock Market, people of the Silver Screen, and even, as late as the 1950s, people of the Gun.

Who, in such a welter of representations, defines the "real"—the representative, the archetypal—Jew? The labor organizer or the Wall Street broker? The Jewish Mother or the woman rabbi? Woody Allen or Mickey Cohen? The professor or the Princess? Rebbe Schneerson or the Klezmatics? In what social arenas is Jewish cultural identity forged? The kitchen? The shul? The

New York Review of Books? Seinfeld? In what sites should the Jewish-American experience be located? The Lower East Side? The Upper West Side? Boca Raton? How might Jewishness look different if its sites of reference were extended even further—and not merely to Europe (Old World of oppression or nostalgia or escape) and Israel (site of identification, skepticism, ambivalence), but, as Louis Simpson's autobiographical narrative included in these pages would suggest, to Jamaica? What happens if the timeline of Jewish history in the United States is similarly distended? Does that history look, as Stephen Whitfield asks, like the end of or an alternative to the exile that has traditionally served as a central, if not definitional, trope of Jewish identity? Or is Jewishness itself to be read (and valued) as a crucial integument of Diasporic identity, an entirely new expression of an age-old wandering, vagrant sensibility, itself not out of keeping with at least one tendency in American letters, that represented by the Bard of Vagabondage, Walt Whitman?

These questions press more insistently in the wake of the events we have come to call "September 11" and their tumultuous aftermath—the augmentation of the second Intifada, the wars in Afghanistan and Iraq. Against this backdrop, what can we make of the new conflation of the terms "Jew" and "American" circulating around the world via Al-Jazeera and the Internet? ("We have no hatred towards anyone, not even the Americans or Jews," writes one contributor to an on-line chat hosted by an American al-Qaeda supporter. "We just love to send them to hell where they belong in the eternal flames of fire.") Conjointly, the second Intifada produced an anguished set of responses among American Jews, some reaffirming a primal connection to the survival of the state of Israel, others feeling impelled by their ethical as well as political commitments to heightened sympathy with the Palestinian people. Setting aside, if they can be set aside, the geopolitical dynamics of these developments, they raise questions of the most acute moment: What kind of present and future is being dictated by and for Jews, Americans, Jewish-Americans, via world events that seem to be outside our control? What kinds of revisions do these hard facts enforce, as we come to terms with what now look like complacent assumptions that had governed our sense of the world for at least the past decade, if not longer? What new conditions of imaginative and experiential possibility do they close off—or create?

No wonder, then, that as we responded to the tidal wave of submissions for the journal that provided the basis of this volume, we came to think of our title as *Jewish—in America???*—as if the sheer improbability of the former could only be matched by the definitional multiplicity of the latter. And we have tried to honor this sense of the open-ended by aiming at as wide a response as possible. Thus we have assembled a collage of responses to these varied conundrums, drawn from writers, poets, memoirists, artists, historians, photographers, and observers of everyday life; from religiously identified Jews, thoroughly secular Jews, non-identified Jews, and non-Jews. We have also tried to pay special attention to works that attest to the diversity of Jewishnesses (generational, ideological, imaginative) in an equally, and increasingly, diverse America. Obviously, we have not been able to include work that would touch on every facet of this phenomenon. Indeed, to our deep regret, publication constraints prevented our inclusion of many of the contributions we accepted for the two-volume special issue of the *Michigan Quarterly Review* that served as the basis for this book. Here, we feature contributions from as many different parties as space permitted, work that we hope will offer not only a representative sampling of the imaginative and scholarly activity currently under way in and around the terrain of Jewishness, but testimony to its multifariousness. It is also, and no less importantly, our hope that these contributions will offer the reader as much pleasure and provocation as they provided us.

As we look over the volume, a few generalizations suggest themselves. The first is the open-ended quality of writing and art about Jews and Jewishness—the sense of definitional freedom, even free play, that so many of these texts exploit. Charles Bernstein's poem "Sign Under Test" is an exemplary instance. Although not a "Jewish" poem in any obvious way, it takes Jewishness as its very condition of possibility. Bernstein provocatively juxtaposes Talmudic motifs with playful, mass-cultural modalities of expression:

> A husband returns home to find a burning cigar in his ashtray. He soon discovers a man in the broom closet. "What are you

> doing here?"—"Everybody's got to be somewhere." [Henny Youngman]
>
> Rabbi Eliza asks, "When is a Jew no longer a Jew?"—"When the book is closed."

And Bernstein's ambit includes not only religious tradition and stand-up comedy, but also the highest of European high culture:

> "The world is everything that is the case." But the case is locked in the trunk of a stolen car.

What those three Jews, real and fictional—Henny Youngman, Ludwig Wittgenstein, and "Rabbi Eliza" (the last a product of Bernstein's own fertile imagination)—all share, it would seem, an acceptance of what is the case, the world in all its manifold imperfections. If that acknowledgment leads to a sense of enclosure (in the broom closet, the book, the trunk of a car), it also yields a recognition that even these bounded spaces contain infinite possibilities. Bernstein, the assimilated American Jewish poet, not only has all of these various authorities and the traditions they represent at his fingertips, but possesses the instincts of a master thief, stowing them away in the stolen vehicle of his art. His mingling of cultural registers is one that many of our contributors practice. John Limon constructs his Jewish identity—or perhaps it would be better to say his critique of thinking in ethnoracial terms that would include Jewishness—in a complex dialectic between the dialogue of Don Rickles and that of Shakespeare's Rosencrantz and Guildenstern as transmitted by (the only recently self-identified Jew) Tom Stoppard. So, too, virtually all of our commentators celebrate and privilege the mode of verbal dexterity. An expansive sense of the play of language, making and unmaking the world, informs Jacqueline Osherow's poetic fractals and Sharon Pomerantz's recording of the vagaries of the hustle and the hard sell. But what Bernstein encapsulates above all is the sense of possibilities that these discordant and delightful Jewish voices ("two Jews three opinions," as Alisa Solomon reminds us in another, more sober context) bring to the American cultural table—or is it what they take from that table? The last line of his poem—remarkably inviting not despite but rather because of the foreboding that every morning's newspaper only enhances—issues a powerful request: "Save the last chance for me."

As the final word of that final line suggests, the everything's-up-for-grabs aspect of Jewish-American imaginative expression is tied to the individualist quality of U.S. culture—thus the remarkable proliferation, in the submissions we received, of personal narratives. By way of highlighting the variety and intensity of the personal mode, we not only feature a large proportion of works of general interest; we also open the issue with a section devoted to a kaleidoscope of brief responses to questions about Jews, Judaism, and Jewishness in America, responses freed of even the loose strictures of the full-length memoir or nonfictional essay. In keeping with our sense of the admixture of the personal and the interpretive, of experience and commentary on that experience, we have entitled this section "Drashes," reflecting both the religious origins of the habit of interpreting in personal terms the texts and contexts that shape our experience and the quintessentially Jewish-American practice of adopting tradition to modern circumstances.

Still, as Bernstein's parting shot suggests, this very emphasis on the personal has a complicated relation to a tradition that has always striven to affirm collective predications of identity and the power of history. Even within the most accomplished moves to the autobiographical, we note, something larger is always at stake. Alisa Solomon's anguished recounting of her experience with the public theater in Lebanon moves directly into a powerful jeremiad against the American Jewish establishment's circle-the-wagons response to the second Intifada; we pair this with the meditations of a Jewish-American who has chosen to spend her life in Israel, Shira Wolosky, who muses on the same phenomena and reaches very different conclusions. Similarly, Pearl Abraham's movement away from her traditional Hasidic upbringing draws her toward an Emersonian individualism that in turn leads her back to a deeper understanding of her Hasidic roots. Leonard Barkan's look back at his own experience as a self-negating Jew turns on a reading of Shakespeare's *Merchant of Venice* in contemporary Venice, then turns toward a remarkable conclusion that offers a provocative recasting of both Jewish and queer identities. "In comparison" with negotiating the multiple emblems of Jewish experience he encounters on the ground or in memory, Barkan writes, "being gay seemed almost simple." The qualifier in that sentence testifies that he knows full well the staggering complexity of both the categories he is working with, and of their intersection. Our point is that this move from the personal through the Jewish to rethinking categories of identity is so common in our contributors that we might even be tempted to offer it as a defining quality of American Jewish imagination—if the very burden of that move weren't to call into question hard-and-fast definitions and resolutions of *anything*.

More affirmatively, we were struck, in looking over the materials submitted for this volume, by the recurrence of certain defining texts and experiences as reference points: the Torah and Talmud, of course (as evidenced implicitly throughout and explicitly in poetry like Osherow's and Daniel Mark Epstein's); the Yiddish and Ladino languages and the remarkable trove of imaginative responses they produced; the aforementioned canon of Jewish-American fiction and poetry written in English; and, inevitably, the Holocaust, which finds moving responses in a number of contributions. But equally striking were the presence of Shakespeare's *Merchant of Venice* and T. S. Eliot's anti-Semitic lyrics, with which many of our contributors found themselves in spirited dialogue; the performance art of stand-up comedians; and the photographic canon, to which, Sara Blair argues, Jews of various self-definitions have made a powerful contribution. All of which suggests to us that Jewish culture in America is creating a genuinely new archive—a powerful admixture of texts old and new, Jewish and gentile, sacred and secular, on which our writers and critics offer creative commentary and to which they make compelling response. Shaped in the American crucible of race and ethnicity, pushed and pulled by the American traditions of ahistorical and individualist thinking, empowered by a powerful sacramental and hermeneutic tradition yet challenged by that tradition's stunning variety of inflections, impelled to furious response by world crisis, these writers testify not only to the anguishing and joyous complexity of being Jewish in America, but to the creative energies such multiplicity generates.

Drashes

LEONARD BARKAN

MERCHANTS OF VENICE

The following is adapted from a work-in-progress of personal reflections entitled Satyr Square, *which chronicles my life in Italy as interwoven with experiences of art, literature, food, and wine. In several chapters, my life is set in parallel relations to particular art works, including* Don Giovanni, *a famous late antique bronze statue called the* Spinario, *and in the case of the following excerpt, which narrates experiences while teaching Shakespeare at the University of Venice*, The Merchant of Venice.

The Merchant of Venice has all the most delicious trappings of Shakespearean romantic comedy: true love whose course isn't running smooth; girls who dress up as boys; a real world vs. a green world; multiple interlocking plots. I'd venture to say it's the most poetical of all the plays, and yet it's all about money.

All three main characters are rich, and you can plot them according to some sort of primitive Samuelson. Portia is heiress to vast sums of old money, but its origins are mystified and, since her dead father's will prevents her from choosing her own mate, her wealth is blocked from free circulation in the modern world. Antonio, the merchant of the title, is one sort of economic alternative: a new-style, mercantilist entrepreneur, who is careful to diversify but still risks great sums on around-the-world import/export schemes. The other alternative is Shylock, whose riches are neither socked away in ancient privilege nor funding global productivity but rather operating in a closed circle of money-lending for interest.

No romance without finance. Portia's suitors have to identify correctly the relative value of gold, silver, and lead; and if they fail, they must go home and die unwed. The right answer is lead, not because it is the most (or least) valuable but because it involves the most *risk*, which is, of course, the core value of merchantry. That in itself is a luscious mix of ancient fairy tale and modern economic analysis. What is more bizarre in the gaining of Portia is that you have to spend a lot of money just to mount the expedition that crosses the water in order to compete for her. After all, what sets the plot in motion is that Bassanio needs even more money than he has already taken from Antonio in order to woo Portia; Antonio is temporarily illiquid; he borrows from Shylock on the expectation of future returns; the ships go astray; Shylock is left with a contract permitting him to take a pound of Antonio's flesh.

Have I left anything out? Oh, yes. Antonio, sad at the beginning of the play and solitary at the end, loves Bassanio enough to sacrifice his own fortune and his life, with nothing to show for it. And Shylock is a money-grubbing Jew, who delights in the prospect of shedding Christian blood and is punished in the comedy's happy ending by impoverishment and forced conversion. God, I love this play.

* * *

Once the fatal loan has been proposed, Shylock asks to meet with Antonio, and he is duly invited to dinner. "Yes," says Shylock, "to smell pork, to eat of the habitation which your prophet the Nazarite conjured the devil into: I will buy with you, sell with you, talk with you, walk with you, but I will not eat with you."

Around the time I was sixteen, I started pretending I wasn't a Jew, and I didn't really quite finish with this impersonation, or with the lying sub-routines that followed from it, until I was in my thirties. Among this circle of buried memories are images such as myself at age sixteen in lower Manhattan's St. Paul's Chapel, reassuring a Catholic woman who was terrified because she had unwittingly prayed in a Protestant church (with some censoring I recounted this to my then aged mother, who asked, "Did she know she was getting this advice from a Jew?"). Or, some years later, a vision in a dream on *erev* Good Friday, in which I witnessed the crucifixion—I noticed that the sweat on Christ's upper legs made them resemble a roast basted with olive oil—and I was given secret reassurances concerning death. And it provided, as comic relief to these melodramas, the weekly experience of New Haven's Christ Church, where stratospherically high Anglican rituals of holy water, Latin, incense, and confession were presided over by a nasal-voiced convert who looked like my uncle Irwin and was named Father Kibitz. Which afterlife is he now living?

* * *

Unlike Shakespeare, Ben Jonson's friend Thomas Coryat actually visited Venice, publishing a lengthy account, which he called *Crudities* "hastily gobled up in five Moneths travells," as the title page puts it. Everything fascinates Coryat: the *giro di ombre* in the Piazza San Marco; public torture; women performing on stage, a thing unheard of in England; vast and exotically stocked food markets, affording his first ever sight of a watermelon, as astonishing to him as the fact that in Venice great noblemen do their own grocery shopping.

But his fullest version of any human encounter takes place in the Ghetto. That dinner invitation which Shylock at first refuses would be quite impossible in real-life Venice, where the Jews, in a complicated politics of economic exploitation, interdependency, and containment, had been shut up onto a narrow island, which admitted neither entry nor exit at night. Coryat goes there in the daytime, and with a relatively open mind. He notes the beauty of the women and the riches of their dress; he is impressed by the zeal with which they keep the sabbath but offended that they don't show enough respect in the house of God to remove their hats; he notes the wealth they have gained through usury; he regrets not being able to witness a circumcision. He engages a rabbi in spirited theological argument concerning the status of Christ as Messiah. Tempers flare. Suddenly the rabbi has reinforcements: forty or fifty Jews surround Coryat menacingly, and he is saved only by the opportune appearance of the English ambassador, who rescues him in a boat.

* * *

It was easier for Coryat to cross the strait from Christian to Jewish Venice than it was for me. Over the years of my many visits to the city, I could never bring myself to take the ritual guided tour of the two beautiful and solemn little spaces, to be the kind of Jew who ignores the Doge's Palace in order to make *aliyah* among Shylock's people. My opportunity came with the visit of two American friends—a male couple, as it happens—of unimpeachably Christian credentials, one a Kentucky boy law professor, the other a WASP to the point of being nearly albino. When I was finally surrounded by suburban Americans with expensive clothes and moist but uncomprehending eyes, I spent the hour of the tour in an agony of self-cancellation, clinging to my two Christian friends as though their proximity would bleach and straighten my hair.

There were, to be sure, surprises. The grandest of the synagogues contained rows of gorgeously carved private pews, most of them with ancient brass nameplates. They bore names of the dead among which one could read the European diaspora in its most aristocratic form: Tullio Gomes de Silva; Emmanuele Levi y Lopez. But a little further along, on the same ornately fluted moulding, names of the living were pasted on with Scotch tape: Saul Schapiro; Arthur Lustgarden; Menachem Goldberg. The guide noticed immediately that my eye had strayed to these inscriptions. She anxiously interrupted her monologue to explain that of late a Lubavitcher group had taken up residence in the community. Her face was a study in pained impartiality.

After we finished the tour, I saw that the one large commercial space in the Ghetto Vecchio was occupied by a kind of supermarket of Schneerson paraphernalia, complete with a colossal photograph of the messianic candidate himself. Some things, I thought, never change. There's always someone trying to convert the Jews. I turned away from the Moshiach merchants to a much smaller commercial space, where a little grocery shop advertised *pane azzimo*. They handed me a dimpled rectangle that looked something like a very stale crumpet. It was as though anchorites had conveyed the specifications of matzos to Martians. I chewed on it while crossing the bridge that would lead me back to safety in Christian Venice just about where Coryat had escaped the rabbinical posse.

* * *

All that denial: was it the banality of being a Jewish boy in New York, of the stories of the old country that were just like everyone else's stories, all the utter normality of my peculiar microclimate, which appeared so far from the difference it really was? Perhaps that was it. Or else I was feeling some terrible and ancient sense of exclusion from the feast. "I will buy with you, sell with you, talk with you, walk with you, but I will not eat with you." I was never going to utter that sentence, never going to refuse an invitation to dinner. Being gay almost looked simple by comparison.

LOUIS SIMPSON

THE JEW'S HOUSE

> Inquire the Jew's house out, give him this deed,
> And let him sign it.
>
> *The Merchant of Venice*

My mother came from Russia. As a child she emigrated to New York with her family and worked in the garment district. There was work for extras in the movies, so she became an extra. She was chosen by Annette Kellerman to be one of her bathing beauties and traveled to Jamaica to make a movie. There she met a prominent lawyer, Aston Simpson. He was what the people there call "Jamaica white," a can of white paint with a dash of black.

They were married and lived in Kingston, at Cross Roads. They named their house Volyn, after Volhynia Province in Russia where our mother was born. She was a Jew and so, according to the rabbis, were her children, but neither my brother Herbert nor I knew anything of this. Our mother talked about her childhood in Russia, but not about her people being Jews.

Our father's family was Methodist but he himself had no religious affiliation—he was devoted to his profession, law. We lived as well-to-do people did in a British colony. Our parents gave lawn tennis parties. The guests drank whisky-and-sodas and smoked Player's Navy Cut cigarettes. Rosalind admired the English for their manners and "English accent." She played golf at the Liguanea Club, and every afternoon at four tea was brought by the maid and served on the veranda.

Our parents followed the British custom of sending their children to a boarding school. My brother went to Munro College, in the mountains a hundred miles west of Kingston. When I was old enough I went to Munro too. It wasn't a college but a school, modeled on British public schools. The masters were imported from Britain; we played cricket and attended Church of England chapel twice a day, with an extra long chapel on Sunday.

* * *

When my brother and I came home for the summer vacation our mother was absent. We were to stay with our father's relatives.

One day my father took me with him to look at a house he was thinking of buying. The house was still being built, with boards and nails lying about. My mother appeared suddenly. She was holding a revolver and pointing it at my father. He said, "Now, Rosalind." He walked across the room and took the revolver from her hand. She shrieked and fell on the floor, foaming at the mouth.

We were told that our mother had "gone back to America." No one told us why—there were things you didn't tell children. Some time later, when we were at school, we had a letter from our father saying that he was getting married again. Our Aunt May said that Amy Hall was a typewriter, and "Aston married her for her legs." In those days a typist was called a typewriter.

Our mother was at the Royal York Hotel in Toronto. She came back to Kingston to see us, and we stayed at the Manor House Hotel where the countryside began. There were tropical flowers and peacocks on the lawn. I played badminton with Herbert and went swimming in the pool at the Myrtle Bank Hotel in Kingston.

She cried when she had to leave us and go back to Toronto. She was in the beauty business, selling cosmetics.

Then she was living in New York, and traveling from place to place, representing Helena Rubenstein cosmetics. She wrote to us often. She traveled on buses and at night she stayed at a hotel. She was reading a lot. *The Bridge of San Luis Rey* was a fine novel. Sometimes she would send us a book. For Herbert who was five years older, *How to Win*

Friends and Influence People; for me, *Penrod and Sam* and *Tarzan and the Jewels of Opar.*

* * *

There were two boys at Munro who on certain days would wear a sort of cap—not really a cap, it was round and blue, and they would wear it even when they were eating in the dining room. This was because they were Jewish. But they went to chapel too like everyone else.

Some of the lessons in chapel were about the Jews. Their God sounded like the headmaster, "Wagger" Harrison, who taught Latin and came into the classroom with a stick. When he was angry his voice could be heard all over the school. If a boy hadn't done his prep, his homework, Harrison would tell him to bend over and then hit him with the stick.

My best friend, Peter Lopez, must have been a Jew—the name is Sephardic, but I don't think Peter was aware of this, any more than I knew that my mother was Jewish.

I sang in the choir and was assigned to read the lesson in chapel, the first boy in the history of the school to do so—the lessons had always been read by the masters. After I did this other boys were allowed to read the lessons too.

I took and passed the Cambridge Higher Schools exam in one year instead of the usual two. It was thought that I might win a scholarship to Oxford. But scholarships always went to a boy in science, not for reading poetry and novels. I was not awarded a scholarship. I took the exam again the next year with the same result.

My father unexpectedly died, leaving his estate to his typewriter, and only a few hundred pounds each to my brother and me. The day after the funeral our stepmother sent us packing. He had not left any money to send me to a university. I once heard him say that he knew of men who went abroad, to a university. They took up a life of dissipation.

I received a letter from my mother asking if I would like to come to New York for the summer and see the World's Fair. There was no future for me in Jamaica. I left the island and did not go back.

* * *

I was a student at Columbia College, living in one of the dormitories. On Friday night I would take the subway to New Lots to have supper with my grandmother and my mother's sisters. The one man in the family, a pharmacist, might also be there. My mother was usually absent—she was selling cosmetics in Central and South America.

The sisters talked about what happened that week at work. My uncle the pharmacist had seen Al Jolson come into the drugstore. He went over and spoke to him. Al bought a pair of nail scissors. I ventured to make a joke. They smiled at me. I was at Columbia College, they explained to a visitor.

The family name was Marantz. My Aunt Ruth had changed her name from Marantz to Manners—there was an Englishwoman, Lady Manners, whose face appeared in ads for soap. Ruth had been a singer, a "chanteuse," on cruise ships plying to South America. Now she was the receptionist at a beauty salon. Annette ran a theatrical agency—she found work for actors. Another sister was a secretary on Wall Street.

There was nothing about the New York relatives that would have made anyone think they were Jews. My grandmother was a religious woman. When she visited one of my aunts she would take the bacon out of the refrigerator and throw it in the garbage.

On the weekend when students went home I would eat by myself in an automat or cafeteria. I took long walks on Riverside Drive—no danger of being mugged in those days. I went to a movie at Times Square, preferably a foreign movie.

When war came my grandmother feared for the lives of her relatives in Russia. I knew nothing about the religion of the Jews and had nothing in common with the men in black coats and hats I had seen walking on Kingston Avenue. I did not speak their language. But on further thought I did have something in common with the people with a beard and hair hanging down the sides of their face. The Germans would call me a Jew. They would like to knock my teeth out and put me behind barbed wire.

Then America entered the war. I could either register for the draft or go back to Jamaica. I did not hesitate. I wanted to be an American—this truly was the land of opportunity . . . and liberty. In Jamaica they were always afraid of what people might think. If you were offered a glass of ginger ale you were supposed to say, "No, thanks." Not until the third time it was offered did you say, "Yes, thanks."

I preferred American writing: Mark Twain, Dreiser, Hemingway, Saroyan. I wanted to get rid of my English accent as much as some Americans wanted to have one.

I was drafted and wound up in the 327th Glider Infantry, a regiment of the 101st Airborne Division. On D-Day the sixth of June I was on Utah Beach in Normandy. I saw combat in France, Holland, Belgium at Bastogne, and Germany until the end of the war. I had an infantryman's war, wet and cold, being shelled or shot at, but I never doubted that this war had to be fought.

My feelings about the war in Vietnam would be different—it was a lie from the start. I took part in protests against the war in Vietnam.

I didn't feel good about this. There were people, Americans, who seized the opportunity to heap opprobrium on the United States. At a meeting in Philadelphia to protest against the war a poet got up on the platform, pointed to the American flag, and said, "Get that rag out of here." I loved my adoptive country and wanted nothing to do with such people. The French, who have lived through bloody divisions of their country, and yet still love it, have a word for such people. The word sounds like what they are: "canaille."

Many of my early poems had been imitations of English poetry—some of them good imitations . . . the English liked them. But I was making a discovery of America, and one day, with the help of Whitman's idea of a Muse "installed amid the kitchenware," I found my voice—poetry of the life I saw around me.

The war in Vietnam put a stop to thinking about the life around me. My poems had been, however muted, a celebration. There was nothing these days to celebrate.

But I had to write, it is my nature. I thought of a subject that was far removed from the war in Vietnam—stories my mother told about her childhood in Russia. I would make poems of her stories.

* * *

In Russia when Rosalind was a child she slept in the cellar, on chairs pushed together. There were rats in the cellar, running across the floor. If the chairs slid apart she would fall on the rats. She slept with her hands clenched, not moving.

Rats brought the typhus that killed her sister Lisa. She had the sickness too, but there were other children, and her mother could not give her the attention she needed. She would have died but for a woman who came and took care of her.

When she was convalescent they sent her to Odessa to stay with relatives. She walked by the sea and looked at the ships, the naval officers in white, the ladies on the esplanade in their fine dresses. She bought some plums with her last kopecks to take back to the family. But the journey by train was long and the plums were beginning to spoil. She ate them one by one, crying as she ate.

The child who slept across chairs, keeping still while she slept so as not to fall on the rats, would have a life that sounded like a novel. But I was not the one to write it. When I saw my mother in some restaurant in Manhattan—she was on a flying visit—she talked about bolivars and dollars, a theme that interested me not at all.

In the nineteen-forties her business took her to Caracas. No one in New York knew anything about Venezuela. Caracas was growing rapidly, a hustling, modern town. Rosalind broke her journey short, flew back to New York, and made a contract with Helena Rubenstein that gave her exclusive rights to sell cosmetics in Venezuela.

She bought a building in Caracas. She had to carry the boxes of cosmetics upstairs herself with the help of a woman. There was a tree of historic interest that was protected by the State. It was blocking the view of her building from the street. She arranged for a colonel in the Venezuelan army to come at night with a crew of convicts and cut down the tree. The name "Helena Rubenstein" was now visible. People even thought that *she* was Helena Rubenstein.

When the business in Venezuela was flourishing Rubenstein tried to break the contract and take away the business, but Rosalind hired the best lawyers in New York to fight Rubenstein, and held onto the contract.

In the nineteen-sixties she retired from business, married

again, and moved with her husband to his country, Italy. She bought a villa in Lucca, at San Alessio—not just a villa, a palazzo. It came with twenty-eight acres of vine-growing Tuscan soil. She was proud of her palazzo and named it Villa Rosalinda.

I see her sitting on the lawn, beneath the pines. Renato is absent in Rome, on some business he has to do for his brother, the Engineer. When Renato returns he will take Rosalind to dinner at Tito's, the best restaurant in Lucca.

She is thinking . . . remembering something that was said long ago, and the face of the person saying it. The faces of her sisters Ruth and Annette . . . her brother Joe. These faces and voices are her life.

* * *

What is it to be Jewish? In January of 1942 the Germans held a conference at Wannsee, outside Berlin, to plan the extermination of the Jews. One of the participants questioned the description of Jews as a subhuman species. There were Jews, he said, who were highly intelligent and had moral values. Exceptions could be made. The officer in charge of the conference put a stop to this kind of talk. "Anyone who behaves like a Jew," he said, "*is* a Jew."

Do I behave like a Jew? What would Jewish behavior be? There is a feeling I have that I think may be Jewish. I have lived in America most of my life, and would not want to live anywhere else—a week or two in France is enough. But there are times when I feel like a stranger in America. It is a feeling that a child of the Wilderness might have. A child of the Diaspora. We are born into the world—it isn't *us*. We would feel a bit strange wherever we were.

So we move to another place. Is there anything typically Jewish about this? Americans of all kinds, not only Jews, are famous for moving: Swedes, Germans, Poles, Irish, Italians. Nineteenth-century visitors to America remarked on the American propensity for moving. From a cabin in Kentucky to a house in Springfield, Illinois. And all those covered wagons.

I recently bought an old house and had it renovated. I tore my quadriceps carrying boxes of books upstairs in a hurry—a water pipe burst in the basement and was killing my books.

The leg was painful and I had to use a walker. I hope this is the last time I have to move, but I have moved too often to think I have come to the end of it.

Millions of people have no thought of moving. Some are not merely content to be where they are and living as they do, but positively happy. I see in the *Times* that the new Maserati sells for eighty to ninety thousand dollars. It's a bargain: the Ferrari starts at a hundred and thirty. There are men who would ask for nothing more of life than to own one of these. And the learned astronomer for whom night is an ever-deepening wonder, star upon star, galaxy after galaxy, *ad infinitum*—who could say that such a man isn't happy?

But there are others who are unsatisfied, for whom the life they have isn't enough, no kind of life would be enough. The psychiatrist would say that such feelings are due to the circumstances of one's early life. Take me for example. When I was a child my mother disappeared—one day she was there, the next she wasn't, and no one told me why. In the years that followed I missed having a mother and did not understand that I missed her.

I could not talk about my feelings—I had no language for what I was feeling. No one had given me any language.

Who would I have talked to? Not my father—he never talked about his feelings, he had only contempt for that kind of talk. He was angry with my brother because he had failed his law exams. And our stepmother complained about Herbert to his father. None of her tales were true. Meals at our house took place in silence.

During the vacations I would usually be alone. Herbert was with his father at the office. I had a friend next door, Neville Alexander, who would go swimming with me, or we would play ping-pong, but I would as soon go to the pool by myself. I preferred to be alone. I would take along a book. One by Joseph Conrad would be fine. While I read about a ship at sea palms would be swaying and waves breaking on the shore below.

I was in the sixth form at school and had passed my exams. Outside of class I could do as I liked . . . lie beneath the willows with a book. The words I read in solitude were as real as life—in fact more real. They were not just a commentary on life but a life in itself, more intense and meaningful than the life of every day. The stories and poems I read were a kind of magic—they transformed the world.

Jews are said to be "people of the word." I see a boy with a big nose and glasses hunched owlishly over a book. An anti-Semitic stereotype. Then I think of all the people who are not Jews, yet who love words as much as any Jew. And all the famous writers—was Chekhov Jewish? Not if it is a matter of one's parentage. But his sympathy for misfits and losers, his love for all sorts of human beings. . . .

Anyone who behaves like a Jew *is* a Jew. The Germans would have known Chekhov for a Jew. You are a Jew if they think you are.

* * *

There are times when circumstances are favorable to meditation. During the war I would walk with a message from the company to battalion and back. I walked in a field that was littered with the dead. I walked in a forest that was covered with snow, a landscape ringed with fire. Scenes such as these seem to have a significance that is larger than life.

The Sermon on the Mount sums up my religion. I do not know whether my parents had me baptized—so I had myself baptized. I go to church on Sunday, and say the prayers and sing the hymns that we had in school.

The people who are never satisfied, never at peace . . . the psychologist would say that it is because they are unable to love. On the contrary, it is because they love so much, because they believe in God and are still in a wilderness, following a pillar of cloud by day and a pillar of fire by night.

The Jew's house has walls and a roof, but it might as well be a tent.

RICHARD KOSTELANETZ

SEPHARDIC CULTURE AND ME

In memory of my friend Diane Dietchman Tong (1943–1998), an independent scholar who wrote her M. A. thesis on the Judeo-Spanish language commonly called Ladino.

There is a rumor in my family that when I was born in 1940 my parents thought about sending out a card that would read, "Now we present our son Dick, one part kike, some other parts spic." Politically correct before everyone else, so avant-garde were they, my parents decided instead to print a more conventional announcement of my arrival.

One continuing source of identity confusion, at least for me, is that Latinos in New York hear my family name Kostelanetz as Spanish, even though my father was born in Russia; so that when I'm asked to spell it, say over the telephone, I hear back C-0-S. K-0-S, I repeat, with emphasis on the first letter. C-0-S, I hear again. K-0-S, I must repeat, often for a third time. "K, as in King." There's usually a pause on the other end of the line, because the letter K isn't common in Spanish and I sense Latino listeners think I'm deceiving them. Actually, Latinos aren't wrong in what they hear. What was Kah-stel-ja-netz in Russia, with emphasis on the third syllable, probably came from Castellanos, likewise emphasizing the third syllable, which is to say someone from Castile, whose ancestors left Spain hundreds of years before. Perhaps this accounts for why my parents were married in Sheareth lsrael, the Spanish-Portuguese synagogue on 69th Street in Manhattan, and why my grandfather Kostelanetz chose to be buried in its current cemetery in Cyprus Hills. I always speak of my friends Richard Castellana and Vincent Castellano as "having the same name as mine—just spelled differently."

Perhaps because I descend from a mixed Jewish marriage, so to speak, I've always been aware of the exclusion of Sephardic Jews from histories and generalizations about the American-Jewish experience. Too many of them say nothing about Jews who came to America speaking not Yiddish but archaic Spanish, or Levantine French, as in the case of my grandparents. The word Sephardic sometimes doesn't even appear in these books' indices, which likewise lack Jewish names ending in vowels, to recall an Italian-American friend's advice on quickly identifying Mediterranean monikers. The only Sephardic included in Abraham Chapman's anthology of *Jewish-American Literature* (1974) is the nineteenth-century poet Emma Lazarus. I can't find any Sephardim in Daniel Walden's *On Being Jewish,* an anthology likewise from 1974. Look at the recent *Prairie Schooner Anthology of Contemporary Jewish-American Writing,* and you'll find only one surname ending with a vowel—Harvey Shapiro's—and he's not Sephardic. Of the 75 writers meriting individual entries in Joel Shatsky and Michael Taub's *Contemporary Jewish-American Novelists: A Biocritical Sourcebook* (1997), the only name terminating in a vowel is Max Apple's, which sounds like an abbreviation of a name that isn't Sephardic either. In Steven J. Rubin's *Telling and Remembering: A Century of American Jewish Poetry* (1997), there is Emma Lazarus, a token in more ways than one nowadays, and three Shapiros—Harvey, Karl, and Alan—but no other Sephardim. Need I go on documenting omissions? Maybe such recurring neglect reflects a general Ashkenazi snobbery toward all people, Gentile as well as Jewish, whose names end in vowels.

For many years the only Sephardic name ever included in such American-Jewish literary gatherings was Edouard Roditi, a Surrealist poet who was publicly gay as early as the 1960s. Born in Paris in 1910, Roditi was educated in England before coming to the University of Chicago in the later 1930s and obtaining American citizenship at the time. After World War II, he lived mostly in Paris working as a polylingual simultaneous interpreter. Looking back, I've come to think of him as the token exotic of modern American-Jewish literature, as much for homosexuality and his continental residence as his Sephardic name.

You could say that Sephardic Jews and Mizrahi Jews descending from places to the east of them are a minority's minority to the degree that the majority of the minority doesn't often acknowledge their (or our) existence. It is scarcely surprising that Sephardic Jews had an epithet for the Ashkenazi that I heard as the "lach-lee," which I was warned not to say publicly, apparently because it means "dirty" and was (and perhaps still is) as offensive as "kike" or "spic."

Several years ago, I tried to get support for an extended audio feature about the sound of Judeo-Spanish, or Ladino. My plan was to interview Ladino speakers living in America in English about the differences between their language and the Spanish generally heard here and thus to have them define acoustically as well as conceptually the distinctiveness of Ladino. Having previously composed multitrack audio of and about the sound of certain unique sources (the language of prayer, the Hebrew of the Diaspora, New York City, and so forth), I figured that I would conclude this feature with a piece of audio art about characteristically Ladino articulations. However, this proposal didn't get any support, not even a nibble, perhaps because it epitomizes that kind of avant-garde Jewish art that customarily gets better support in Germany or because few funders here were aware of the existence of Judeo-Spanish or Ladino.

I've come to think of Sephardic Jews as culturally different from Ashkenazi. They are closer to other Mediterranean peoples, such as Italians and Greeks, especially if they came from Greece or, like my mother's parents, from that part of Asia Minor that was culturally Greek before World War I. (Note that I said Asia Minor to locate Smyrna, rather than saying "Turkey," where my grandparents' home city is now called Izmir.) It is indicative that one great modern Sephardic cultural figure, Rosa Eskenazi, was the celebrated singer of Rembetica, also called Rebetica, which is the common name for Greek underground music in the 1920s and 1930s. Born around 1900 in Asia Minor, she went to Greece after World War I, reportedly with an Armenian circus troupe, and she lived there well into her eighties, into the 1980s, even though her most notorious song, first recorded in 1932, was called

"Why I Like Cocaine." Rembetica music was so radical, don't forget, that whenever generals assumed power in Greece, as they did from time to time, beginning in the late 1930s, they banned it.

One book owned by my late friend Diane Tong, a book I never saw, alas, is a Rosa Eskenazi autobiography published around 1970, which I'd like to read in English sometime if only to learn how she survived. The small-print notes to a recent disk of her historic recordings acknowledge her debt to a great Turkish singer named Isak AlGazi, born a few years before her, who was also Jewish, about whom I'd like to know more as well. I can't think of a prominent Ashkenazic musician in America who was comparably declassé. (The B'nai-Brith-oriented institutions of Jewish publicity would have probably discredited him or her.) The closest semblance was the jazzman Mezz Mezzrow, who wrote about his heroin addiction. The only Ashkenazic analogy that comes to mind is the comedian Lenny Bruce, born Leonard Alfred Schneider, who likewise had experience with hard drugs and the law but survived only into his early forties.

One way in which American Sephardic Jews have resembled Greeks, to be frank, is the lesser value they place on advanced education, unlike Edouard Roditi's parents, say, who sent him to Oxford before he came to America. Many American Sephardim grew up in houses devoid of books. In my case, as I recall, there was a bookshelf; but since my mother didn't read books, it never occurred to her to put a lamp next to a chair. I always ask American Sephardim of my generation if their parents supported their going to college. They are far more likely than Ashkenazim to reply that their parents thought high school was enough education and that, once they collected their high school diploma, they should think about establishing some kind of biz. An Italian-American friend tells me that she was discouraged from continuing beyond high school because her father feared his children would become smarter than he and thus undermine his patriarchal authority. I wonder if a similarly defensive motive informed Sephardic fathers and thus whether a Sephardic resistance to book-learning accounts for why Sephardic Jews, who were culturally ahead of Ashkenazi several hundred years ago, fell generally behind in America.

I've discovered informally that Sephardic Jews in America conducted kinds of enterprise unknown to Ashkenazim. In my mother's family, some relatives imported olive oil while others brokered cashew nuts and comparably exotic foods. Their ideal appeared to be self-employment with all the freedoms and responsibilities involved. (Self-employment has been my ideal as well.) The father of the painter Micaela Amato was a wholesaler of Latino herbs found in a Botanica, which is a kind of shop unknown to most Americans, if not most Ashkenazi Jews.

If Sephardic Jews are indeed culturally different, even in America, then Sephardic-American art should be different as well—as different as Rosa Eskenazi's songs are from Al Jolson's, say—or in my case at least half-different. That's a question that Sephardic-American artists, as they (we) recognize a common alternative Jewish heritage, will hopefully explore.

PEARL ABRAHAM

IF ONLY: FINDING AMERICA IN HASIDISM

A recent *Newsweek* article reporting on a field of study called neuro-theology asks whether our brain wiring creates the idea of god, or whether god created our brain wiring.[1] It's similar to the question linguists have been asking about the structure of language: Does language reflect the attributes of our brains because it was designed by us, or do our brains develop in childhood to accommodate linguistic structures?

I suspect the answer, if there is one, is mixed, that a little of both takes place. In my particular case, whether or not I was born with religious wiring, certainly by the time I was in my teens I should have grown into a fervent Hasidic woman, prepared to marry at eighteen, give birth to eight or ten children, marry them off, await dozens of grandchildren and great grandchildren, and consider this existence the happiest on earth.

From every angle, the circumstances of my life pointed me in the direction of a devout religiosity. I didn't follow this path, and the question is why. Why is there no religion in my daily life?

My mother's response to this question would be: *If only*. She believes that I would have remained religious if only the family hadn't moved to America. After years of shrugging my shoulders, I'm beginning to understand that America did have a great deal to do with who I became, but not altogether in the sense my mother has intuited.

A particular episode in my life inspired in me an acute self-awareness. It happened when I was fourteen or fifteen, and Aunt Rachel from Israel was visiting. We were in Brooklyn for the day, waiting in the car for my mother and sister, who had stepped out to purchase something at the local health food store. My father was in the driver's seat, reading from one of his religious books, psalms or mishnah, as was his habit during such stops. Taking my cue from him, I immersed myself in a novel.

Aunt Rachel, who must have been bored, tried to engage me in conversation, which I discouraged. When my mother returned, Rachel informed her that I was a child who ought to be watched, that I was dangerous.

My father was upset that this had been said in front of me, and called it nonsense. I was deeply thrilled because it confirmed for me what I had known all along, though perhaps not so clearly: that I would be someone different, dangerous somehow.

In one of his introductions to *Omens of Millennium*, titled "Prelude: Self Reliance or Mere Gnosticism," Harold Bloom refers to what might be a universal childhood experience, when one feels with certainty that one is not after all the child of one's natural parents. Bloom calls this sensation curious and asks whether it isn't an awakening to the knowledge (Gnosis) of something in the self that's older even than one's parents, "that cannot die because it was never born." He goes on to write of the experience of deep reading in childhood, which provides the "pleasures of excited thought, of a thinking that changed one's outer nature, while opening up an inner identity, a self within the self, previously unknown."[2]

Reconsidering the event from this late present-day perspective, various aspects stand out; for example, my father's awareness that such an announcement is in itself damaging, or empowering (depending on the point of view). More significantly, that it wasn't the mere act of reading that brought forth the criticism (though that later became a subject of debate), but the fact that I had refused to engage in what was decent social behavior, what any Israeli child, Rachel pointed out, understood perfectly. In other words, I was growing into an American. I had placed personal desire above the needs of others, thereby rebelling against the familial institution.

Daniel, in E. L. Doctorow's *The Book of Daniel*, describes this social responsibility, in a sentence I liked enough to memorize: "And all my life I have been running from my family, and I have been intricate in my run, but one way or another, they are what you come upon around the corner and the Lord God who is so anxious for recognition says you must ask how they are, and would they like something to drink, and what is it you can do for them this time."[3]

Recall how much is made of the biblical Abraham's generosity as a host and you'll understand the significance of offering your relatives a drink. In any case, Daniel performs precisely the type of duty from which on that particular day I exempted myself, and Rachel was able to detect, in a way my parents weren't, the impudence in my refusal to respond to her. She also knew that in taking my father's example, I, a daughter (not a son) intended only for a domestic life, had in this one brazen act elevated myself to my father's level. Something else that no one mentioned that day was the disparity of the texts in question: by every rule I'd grown up with, my profane novel should not have been conflated with the holy book my father was reading. Though she might not have articulated it in just this way, Rachel understood something significant about institutions and the individual, namely that their interests run counter to one another, that the self-reliant individual is a threat to family and community, and most certainly to institutionalized religion.

At the time, I was living with my family in a small town near Spring Valley, New York, where Greyhound left off and Red and Tan buses picked up. Kids on their way up to Woodstock roamed the area, hitchhiking to get a mile up or down Route 59, and my father, who was new to driving and knew what it was to need a ride, made a habit of picking up anyone who needed one. At the dinner table he showed us their version of a handshake, the peace sign. To the kids my father must have seemed one of them, at least from a distance, a hippie with a beard. His perpetual slowness—he was never in too much of a hurry to listen to someone's story—must also have been attractive.

The story of the hippies, like all stories my father told, had its didactic turn, i.e., the youth of America are searching for something their parents have neglected; they want more than houses and cars, they're seeking transcendence. We Jews are fortunate, we have the Torah.

I should perhaps explain that for various reasons, not least because of my father's antinomian sensibility, my family settled near, but on the outer edge of Jewish communities, and they weren't Hasidic. There were enough orthodox, reform, and conservative Jews in the town; my teachers at school were members of these communities, which meant that I often felt that I was in enemy territory, until my teens when I developed what one teacher called the proverbial chip on the shoulder.

What actually happened was that I finally understood that American Jews looked down on my family, we who still dressed like the old variety of Eastern European Jews, and spoke the old language, and, though we lived in America, were quite uneducated in American ways. We remained unassimilated, unlike other immigrants to the United States, not because we were living in an isolated Hasidic community (we weren't), but out of conviction. Our distinct way of dressing and speaking made us unintentionally flamboyant and this fact turned certain Jews apoplectic.

At the time, the accepted mode of life among American Jews was to accommodate in their lives both (this is a translation of a Hebrew phrase) *Torah and the ways of the land.* To this end, Yeshiva students attended college at night to study business or a professional trade. Reform and Conservative Jews of America worked at nothing as hard as fitting in, melting into the great melting pot, growing prosperous, thereby proving their worthiness as Americans.

This was the 1970s. I was coming of age, and just comprehending the various messages. The contrast between the American-Jewish disposition toward accommodation and the Hasidic insistence on remaining distinct engaged my teenage sense of right and wrong. Fortified perhaps by the era's leanings against the establishment, I considered the idea of accommodation a dishonesty.

At the same time, a seemingly airborne idea that appealed to me was the great possibility of who and what one can be, in other words, of the tremendous potential of the individual. It didn't seem to matter what family one came from: I as an individual could become anything or anyone, as if I'd sprung up from nowhere, or simply from within, a self-created self.

As it happens, this idea of self-creation isn't distant ideologically from the supreme task of the Hasid: to achieve a measure of divinity. Having grown up charged with this task of personal growth, I was familiar with the dedication necessary to such pursuits. What I didn't know then was how much these ideas resemble those of Emersonian self-reliance and rugged individualism, the foundation of what we might call, after Harold Bloom, the American religion.

I have the sense, not easily proven, that America, unlike other nations, including Israel, was able to provide for Hasidism a place to thrive precisely because it is the one country in the world that shares with the 200-year-old movement the grounding in the idea of the holy individual.

This belief made Jews susceptible to the false messiahs of the seventeenth century, Sabbatai Zevi and Joseph Frank, and later, to the charismatic leaders who became the renowned rebbes and miracle healers of Hasidism. An American variation on a Hasidic leader would be Walt Whitman. And he comes to us in our own image, complete with hat and beard.

In *God and the American Writer*, Alfred Kazin writes that Ralph Waldo Emerson remade Jesus "into an orphic genius like himself." Consider the words of Jesus, which Emerson quoted in his Divinity School Address: "I am divine. Through me, God acts; through me, speaks. Would you see God, see me; or, see thee, when thou also thinkest as I now think."

Kazin explains Emerson's point of view. "In short, any of us can be as commanding a force as Jesus. Any of us, expanding to the full circle of the universe, may yet enjoy the jubilee of sublime emotion that Jesus knew in recognizing God in himself. God dwells in us, too."[4]

That Emerson read and appropriated ideas from Jesus Christ is not news. However the parallels between Emersonian and Hasidic (kabbalistic) teachings, with their shared focus on individual potential, are surprising. Even stranger are the similarities in the historical progression of the old-world ecstatic movement and the new world product of divinity schools, where they began and where they thrive today.

Jesus Christ's relationship with Judaism is easy enough to confirm, since his mentor was James the Just, who is believed to have been a member of the Essenes, a non-normative Judaic mystical community that dates back to 150 B.C.E. Despite rabbinic censorship, strains of Judaic mysticism existed through the First and Second Temple periods, and continued developing in the Diaspora. After the Spanish crusades, Safed became a renowned mystical center. And in the 1600s, Sabbatai Zevi initiated the messianic movement. A hundred years later, Hasidism arrived on the scene.

And where are we today? Just as Transcendentalism lost its ruggedness—the whole cult of the divine self has descended into a therapeutic New Ageism with its vocabularies of the inner child, self-esteem, twelve-step programs, self-help books, and Oprah—so too in parallel development in the Jewish world, there is the radical Jewish revival culture. A recent article in *The New Republic* describes a New Age Passover seder on a beach in Israel, complete with newly conceived rituals, and not many traditional Jewish ones.[5]

It's worth noting here that Hasidism only survived by turning itself into a popular movement, complete with appealing features such as the royal courts in all their ritualized grandness. Along the way, the ascetic lifestyle, which could only attract a small elite, was eliminated. Contemporary Hasidic courts are no longer so grand, nor is the lifestyle so far from mainstream Jewish orthodoxy, which is also why they're more acceptable to established Judaism. So long as Hasidism retained its non-normative character, as long as charismatic individuals, such as Nahman of Breslav, could hold sway over thousands, institutional, rabbinic Judaism felt threatened.

Which brings me back to my experience of the individual within the institution. Oddly enough, early Hasidic sages would not have found my modern project of self-development threatening; if anything, they would have endorsed it. Though I had lost the humility necessary to subordinate myself to the religious institution, I was in a sense pursuing the ecstatic's way. The writing life, I propose, is comparable to the ascetic lifestyle of the early mystics.

Readers of my books, and interviewers, who are only occasionally readers of my books, often ask whether I am religious. My response is necessarily incomplete because, for one thing, the answer isn't entirely straightforward. I say something like: it depends on the point of view. Today's Hasidim wouldn't classify me as a Hasid, nor even as a religious Jew.

That I can't even be classified as a Reform or Conservative Jew, or any form of practicing Jew, troubles some people. One interviewer, I think from Cincinnati, grew furious with me because, as she put it, she and other American Jews were spending money sending their children to Jewish day schools and I seem to be throwing it all away.

The problem: I defied standard expectations that I would develop an affiliation with a more modern Jewish institution, the reform or conservative movement, or even the revivalist and New Age fringes. But I believe the expectations were misplaced.

Having experienced at an early age both the comforts and discomforts of traditional institutions, I was unlikely to join another. Consider what happens to revolutionary movements. Nothing dissipates a revolution faster than institutional acceptance. I seem to have learned—much of this is on a subconscious level—this lesson early, and remain in my adult life suspicious of institutions. And yet, though I have emancipated myself from religion, it's not quite true to say that I am completely without any.

If you believe that the holiest project on earth is to pursue an inner knowledge and to grow maximally as an individual—in kabbalah terminology, as I understand it, this is the ultimate purpose of man—then you would agree that I am religious. Since it isn't an institutionalized religion, but a rather personal one, it doesn't have the usual constraints. What it does have, strangely enough, is a grounding in Emersonian ideas, which is to say that under the influence of American religion, I returned to an earlier Hasidism. You might say that embracing the new world, I became an old world, anti-establishment Hasid.

NOTES

[1] Kenneth L. Woodward, "Faith is More than a Feeling," *Newsweek*, 7 May 2001, 58.

[2] Harold Bloom, *Omens of Millennium* (New York: Riverhead Books, 1996), 13–34.

[3] E. L. Doctorow, *The Book of Daniel* (New York: Signet, 1971).

[4] Alfred Kazin, *God and the American Writer* (New York: Alfred A. Knopf, 1997), 40–56.

[5] Yossi Klein Halevi, "Nitzanim Beach Dispatch: Inner Peace," *The New Republic*, 30 April 2001, 20–21.

JONATHAN BOYARIN

THE LOWER EAST SIDE UNION OF ALL THE SHULS I GO TO

August 2002

Herewith an update on some of the things, including me, you might encounter if you happen to find yourself in a synagogue on the northern part of New York's Lower East Side any given Saturday morning. While these sketches are perhaps not limned in enough detail to be properly called ethnography, they should have their intended effect as a reminder that, yes, there are still people inside.

I. WHAT IS THE "UNION"?

A. The Union Could Be "Real"

My fantasy Union is not to be confused with the actual United Jewish Council of the Lower East Side, known in the neighborhood as the UJC. Suffice it to say, however, that the existence of the UJC in no way obviates the need for my Union. Part of the reason for this, as explained in a bit more detail below, is that the UJC focuses its preservation and advocacy efforts on the neighborhood bordering the Grand Street co-op houses. If there is any center linking the members of my Union, it is more likely Houston Street, several blocks north of Grand. Moreover, unlike the Grand Street area, the blocks on which the members of my Union are located can be described as being not only on the Lower East Side but also in the East Village, Loisaida, Chinatown, even Little India. Likewise, it is fair to say that, to the extent that the UJC projects an institutional vision of its mission, it is to defend and maintain the Jewish community as it presently exists, rather than to imagine how the Jewish character of the neighborhood can most creatively be transformed.[1]

So, even though my Union has no actual existence, I think it would be a good idea. Why not? Why couldn't all the attendees, all the trustees, all the stubborn obsessives keeping their own doors open, realize the shared potential of an organization designed to help see each of these institutions through to the next social form it's going to take? If, instead, those who care about the institutions think of their perpetuation as a zero-sum game, a Lower East Side shul economy in which one Jew more at another institution means one less at mine, all of them will eventually die. On the other hand, if they came to think of the other members of the Union—and, of course, I don't just mean the ones I've almost arbitrarily chosen to describe above but all the other shuls too (Roumanian-American on Rivington Street, Chasam Sopher on Clinton Street) and not just the shuls but also . . . —as other *facets* that could be shined to reflect upon each other a glow that is now, still, all too weak, then maybe we wouldn't have to bury another member for a long, long time.

B. The Union Is Only in My Head

Right now there's no such organization, of course, not even on any paper other than the one you're reading, and unless I get an extraordinary burst of energy or someone else gets the same idea, there won't be such an organization in the near future. Rather, my unconventional—un-Orthodox?—Shabbes morning itinerary is the only thing that brings these different buildings and their congregations together in any regular way. (That my son attends one of the members and my wife another—at neither of which I regularly participate on Shabbes mornings—adds for me further elements of refracted connection.) It's not just that I don't really want to miss any of these places and their people, but also that no one of them, by itself, really satisfies me. (I used to joke that there was one shul where I liked the congregation; one shul where I liked the rabbi; one shul where I liked the ritual; and one shul where I liked the shul. They aren't the four members of the

Union, either, so don't bother trying to guess which is which.) For now, the union is only in my head and on this paper. Those existences are not trivial, because now at least you, too, know that the shuls are not only relics, that they are more than just *lieux de mémoire:* There are people living inside. You can join them if you like.

II. THE MEMBERS

A. Deceased: The Eighth Street Shul, Bnei Moses Jacob Anschei Zawichost v'Zosmer

The synagogue on East Eighth Street between Avenue B and Avenue C was the first Jewish place where I "belonged" in this neighborhood.[2] After years of legal struggles and attempts to maintain religious activities there—all of which deserve to be chronicled, but not here and now and not, in fact, by me (take this whole bit of reportage, if you will, as a program for a graduate practicum in Lower East Side Jewish ethnography)—the building has been sold. It still stands, apparently empty, apparently unrenovated. Bulging brickwork near the top indicates, perhaps, the building's structural weakness. No trace remains of the Hebrew sign that once proclaimed the name of the congregation, but one can still make out the common synagogue inscription that can be translated as: "This is the gate of the Lord; the righteous will pass through it."

I start with Eighth Street not only because one of the proper functions of a society like my titular Union is to commemorate its dead at appropriate times. More prosaically, its absence provides me with a sometimes convenient way to explain that none of the current members described below commands my full or even primary allegiance. It is as if I were to say, "Well, really *my* shul is the Eighth Street Shul—but of course it's gone." This is also why my "union" is not the union of "all my shuls." The difference between that and "all the shuls I go to" does represent a loss. The *loss* is mine, though not exclusively, and it is not a bad thing only.

B. Application Rejected: The Bialystoker Shul

Now here's a bit of real chutzpah on my part. I certainly *do* go to the Bialystoker Shul on Saturday mornings, and it's the most prominent synagogue on the entire Lower East Side. Unlike the other members, it's centrally located for the Orthodox population of the neighborhood—right off Grand Street, in fact on the Bialystoker Place that was in turn named after the shul.

What would draw me, a fetishist of Jewishness at the margins, to such an "establishment" institution? Not the elegant frescoes, since the early 7:00 a.m. minyan I sometimes attend is held downstairs in the relatively plain *bes medrash*—the study hall that, as in several of the other shuls described here, also is where the *kiddush* refreshments are served after services. I started going for family convenience, to be able to participate in Shabbes morning services and then return home for childcare later in the morning. My friend and teacher Yosi Rosenbaum,[3] who first told me about the early minyan, has a different reason for going. When this minyan finishes, around 8:30, he can run upstairs to see his children for a few minutes, then walk a mile or so uptown to the Young Israel of Fifth Avenue at Sixteenth Street, where he is the regular Torah reader. Once Yosi explained to me, "You know, I'm the only one here who attends this early minyan for the original reason. It was created for guys who had to go to work on Saturdays."

Today, the class of Orthodox Jewish men who would admit that they ever went to work on Saturdays is a null set. To the contrary, the early minyan, consistently numbering not-thirty to not-forty, includes among the regulars Rabbi Reuven Feinstein, the son of Reb Moshe Feinstein, who now heads a yeshiva on Staten Island, and Sheldon Silver, the speaker of the New York State Assembly. I wear a black hat when I go there, I look like I fit in, I like the express and yet dignified services, everyone welcomes me; but it's really not my crowd. When I go, I sit a bit apart in the back section reserved for women, and on the rare occasions when a woman actually comes in, I am forced to search awkwardly for an inconspicuous place among the male regulars.

I have already claimed, however, that I don't really "belong" to any of the shuls that do make up the Union, so why isn't the Bialystoker Shul included? For a simple and ultimately selfish reason: I don't think it needs me.

Most of the times I get up early enough to go to the 7:00 a.m. Bialystok minyan, I stay there until it's time for me to go on to the Greek shul. But that itinerary eliminates one of the members entirely, so let's say this week I was lazy or I overslept.

C. Active Members

1. The Mezritsh Shul—Kehillas Edos LeYisroel Anshei Mezeritsh

Now we're closer to the part of the Lower East Side where my family lives—a little bit less marginal than the dead Eighth Street Shul, considerably less central than the comparatively flourishing Bialystoker Shul, on East Sixth Street snugly between First Avenue and Avenue A, across the street from the Village View housing complex, which still has enough Jews to keep the Mezritsh Shul going, and led by Rabbi Pesach Ackerman, who apparently continues to serve the congregation for beans.

Like Eighth Street, and like two of the Union's other three active members, Rabbi Ackerman's shul is what I call a "tenement shul," its long narrow dimensions dictated by the lot on which it was built. Yet here I'm less interested in telling you what you would see if you came in on a weekday than whom you would meet if you came on a Shabbes morning. A couple of former regulars from Eighth Street, now therefore acquaintances of mine for over twenty years, both of whom, however, live across the street in Village View rather than closer to the Eighth Street Shul. Another couple, veterans of the Eighth Street Shul's more recent incarnation, now resident in housing for the elderly on that shul's block. Two Englishmen in their thirties, friends and both musicians; I don't know how they found their way here. Chaim Rosanez and his brother Usher, the *kohanim*. The rabbi's son Sandy, an enthusiastic Yankees fan and no enthusiast of prayer at all, who lives in the shul during that part of each year he doesn't spend in

Israel. Bill Feinerman, a proud and learned Jew nearing ninety, who by his own account was once one of the leaders of the Young Israel of Fifth Avenue (see above) but whose feet won't carry him nearly that far now (remember that one of the defining characteristics of an Orthodox synagogue is that, by necessity, it is a *neighborhood* institution). Mr. Edelstein, also slow on his feet, distinguished (as far as this anthropologist is concerned) by the fact that both of his married daughters brought their husbands to live, permanently, nearby him in the same housing complex, thus offering an example of Jewish patrilocality, from which no generalizations whatever can or need be drawn. Mr. Edelstein's daughters don't come to Mezritsh, though the gravelly voiced candy lady Mrs. Schwartz—also an Eighth Street Shul veteran—comes every week all the way from Avenue C and Eleventh Street. She's sometimes joined in the minuscule women's section by Mrs. Stern, the widow of a former president of the congregation, and by two or three other "ladies," as older women are still called in New York.

I haven't listed all of the Mezritsh regulars. I've come to like and respect the individuals, but they are not so extraordinary. What's special about Mezritsh might accurately be described as the absence of anything terribly special, of any agenda other than assembling a minyan for, and carrying out, the particular service required at a particular date and time. No special spirituality, no great sense of camaraderie; even the regulars don't necessarily get along well. A little joke, a little drink, a kaddish when you need it. A kaddish when you need it: a minyan.

2. The Greek Shul: Anshei Janina (Ioannina)

As I said, if I haven't gone to Bialystok I'm likely to go first to Mezritsh—either simply to join in the prayers for the first part of the service or sometimes as a substitute for the regular Torah reader. If I have gone to Mezritsh, though, I always have to hurry away as soon as the Torah reading is over, because my regular gig as a Torah reader is *chez les grecs,* at the Janina synagogue about eight blocks downtown, on Broome Street just off Allen. Anshei Janina was founded by people from that city in northern Greece, not—as they will insistently clarify—Sephardic Jews, but Romaniote, practitioners of a distinct and ancient Greek Jewish rite who were there long before the Spanish Expulsion and, as their own origin story runs, since the exile attendant on the destruction of the Second Temple. To compare this congregation, in a nutshell, with the others I've mentioned so far: unlike Eighth Street, they're still functioning; unlike Bialystok, there's very little pretension of communal power, and thus community politics appear to remain quite muted; unlike Mezritsh, the members and most, at least, of the participants still share a common origin and a distinctive and wonderful rite.

Janina, too, is a tenement shul, but of the Union's members, it is the only one where women (except those no longer able to climb steps) actually sit together upstairs in the three-sided balcony during the services, rather than in the back or to the side of the same level as the men. Seated around the narrow, U-shaped opening that overlooks the central platform from which the service is conducted and the Torah is read, they are better equipped to share and to oversee the ritual performance than the women at Mezritsh. And these women at Janina—especially the older ones, well versed in the traditional rite—do not hesitate to call down corrections and emendations to the men below as needed.

Generally, however, the women don't bother trying to correct my Torah reading, perhaps because my style is too strange to them. I, a grandchild of Lithuanian and White Russian Jews, clearly don't "belong" at Janina. How I got there is simple. With rare exceptions, services are held at Janina only on Saturday (how can I call it "Shabbes" at a Greek synagogue?) and holiday mornings. Friday nights, therefore, Hy Genee, who has run the services at Janina for years, comes to Mezritsh instead. A few years ago, an elderly member of the Janina congregation who had been their regular Torah reader for many years, chanting faithfully the weekly portion using the Romaniote pronunciations and cantillation, passed away. No younger member of the community lived in the neighborhood and was willing to come every week to take his place. Knowing that I'm able to stumble through the weekly Torah portion in a pinch, Hy recruited me to read at Janina, and I haven't quit myself of the obligation yet. Every week for the last two years or so, therefore, I've helped to keep the Romaniote services going; but, since I haven't acquired the Romaniote pronunciation of the text, I simultaneously contribute to a moment of cultural extinction, the erasure of this ancient tradition.

Actually, though, I'm not the only one at Janina who is not from a Romaniote background. Since there is, evidently, no other non-Ashkenazi congregation in Lower Manhattan, the place has become by default the synagogue of choice for those nearby of Sephardic or Arab Jewish backgrounds. Though the burden falls most often on Hy, any male congregant who is willing is welcome to lead a portion of the services, which therefore sometimes echo Aleppo or Fez more than Janina. For my part, much as I regret the loss of Janina patterns in the Torah reading, I am reduced to getting through the text as accurately as I can in the only cantillation I partly know. Fortunately, while Hy and the other congregants are quite consciously dedicated to keeping the Romaniote tradition alive in North America (and in fact the synagogue is open on Sundays as a museum), there is no obsession with performative purity here.

3. The Community Synagogue

My communal duties for the morning are finished when the Torah reading is over at Janina. Unless I've been to Bialystok for the early minyan, I still haven't personally completed the additional prayers that follow the Torah reading. No matter: of late I haven't the patience to stay on and finish with the congregation at Janina, so I leave—but I don't go home.

I might instead head back up to Sixth Street, this time one block west of Mezritsh, to the imposing and elegant Community Synagogue between First and Second Avenues, across the street from Indian restaurant row. By this time—Janina runs late—the services at Community are almost over, so I rarely enter the lofty main sanctuary of this erstwhile German Lutheran church, where, among other notable features, the seating area is equally divided, lengthwise down the middle, between the men's and women's sections, providing a formal equality that is not matched—not yet?—by any presence of women on the *bima* at the front. If I hurry, though, I arrive in time for the *kiddush,* which, some weeks, includes potato kugel and even a meat *cholent.* Please don't think I go just to eat. Actually, at the Community Synagogue (unlike any of the other members of the Union), even though I don't regularly participate at Shabbes morning services, I *do* belong; I pay annual family membership dues, because at Community they asked me to, and no one else really has. Of course, it doesn't hurt my standing in the Union that my wife, Elissa Sampson, regularly donates money to Mezritsh, to Janina, and to Stanton Street, the last member, described below.

I try to show up at the Community Synagogue—less rigorously Orthodox than Bialystok, less heymish than Mezritsh, less distinctive in its traditions than Janina—which has also somehow become my sixteen-year-old son Jonah's shul, maybe in the way that Eighth Street was once "my" shul. Again, I put in an appearance at the Community when I can because—with its grand and austere sanctuary, a capacious reception room and professional kitchen downstairs, more money than the others, a pressing awareness of the need for a new constituency, and what might be called an elective affinity that's apparently sprung up between myself and the chairman of the board—of all the members of the Union, it's the one where my particular fantasy of a renewed Jewish life, at once "religious" and "cultural," on the Lower East Side can most plausibly be indulged.

4. The Stanton Street Shul (Erstwhile Rabbi Singer's Shul)

After Eighth Street, this is the "shul I used to go to." Like Eighth Street, the Stanton Street Shul once inspired me to more rigorous interrogations of Jewish community and identity, in which I suggested wrongly that the congregation would not survive the loss of its rabbi.[4] And as recently as a year or two ago, it looked like Stanton Street might go the way of the Eighth Street Shul, sold off for non-religious use (at Stanton Street, by a faction with a dubious claim to rightful ownership). To give credit where at least much of the credit is due, my wife, Elissa, in the course of investigating the legal status of the Stanton Street Shul in order to avoid a repetition of the nasty fight over the Eighth Street Shul and of its sad fate, got wind of the purported sale of the Stanton Street Shul in time to rally the congregants and petition the state attorney general, whose approval was required for any such sale.

In the course of the ensuing legal battle—whose results, not entirely conclusive, seem to have left the shul in the hands of the congregants, who intend to maintain a functioning synagogue—a number of young adults started attending regularly. They include married couples in their twenties and thirties, along with single men and women. They seem to get along warmly with the older Yiddish speakers, some of whom came because they were attracted by now-departed Rabbi Singer's generosity, while others (as we learn now) never got along with Rabbi Singer and his family in the first place. The future of the shul now is up to the generation that's younger than the Yiddish speakers and younger than Elissa and myself. I think it is safe to say, though, that Stanton Street is very much not dead.

So if I don't go to Community after Janina, I'm likely to go to Stanton Street. Maybe Elissa, if she's feeling well and isn't too exhausted from work, has made it there and is sitting around the *kiddush* catching up with her friends. In any case, I want to check in, and I somehow want to be counted there, still. I want Benny, the president, well into his eighties, to know I haven't forgotten him. I almost enjoy the piquant novelty of, finally, seeing myself supplanted by younger newcomers, who, far from begging me to participate in their services (and thus necessarily absent myself from one of the other members of the Union), really don't pay much attention to whether I show up at all. And, devotee of fragments of memory that I am, I'm pragmatic enough not to release all claims of identification with an example—even a tentative one—of survival and transformation into the future (Jewish, among many other things) of the Lower East Side.

NOTES

[1]The Lower East Side Conservancy, affiliated with the UJC, has worked for the past several years to fund structural restoration work on the synagogue buildings of the Lower East Side. Without the buildings, of course, my Union would not even exist as fantasy.

[2]See "Waiting for a Jew," in my *Thinking in Jewish* (Chicago: University of Chicago Press, 1996).

[3]See "Voices Around the Text," in my edited volume, *The Ethnography of Reading* (Berkeley: University of California Press, 1993).

[4]"Death and the Minyan," in *Thinking in Jewish* (Chicago: University of Chicago Press, 1996).

MARTHA BANTA

OF WHAT LANGUAGE, PRAY, IS "THE AMERICAN MIND"?

During the first decades of the twentieth century, in an American culture for which sensory evidence seemingly provided concrete data for observation and interpretation (and misinterpretation), the Gentile point of view toward "being Jewish" placed particular weight on view. The Yiddish speech patterns infiltrating the American scene offered two kinds of sensory evidence to the puzzled and sometimes hostile audience of native-born Americans. When set in print, Yiddish was visible to the eye; when spoken, it was detectable to the ear. In addition to what Americans could glean from exposure to this strange language, the look of the bodily forms of the new immigrants also told them what they thought they needed to know. This "look" consisted of a combination of facial features, behavioral gestures, and the outward wrappings of clothing and hairstyles. For many in the States, it was the only way to gain "proof" of the unalterable differences that separated the alien tribes from what "being American" meant to them. The point: however well or poorly this information was processed, it was available to an observer's sense perception—data that signaled that these types were not what the observant eye found familiar and that made it question whether such anomalies could ever be "Americans."

What was involved in becoming "American"? Could the newly arrived undergo shape changes (conceptual and material) from the state of not being to becoming? If possible, by what means? The Gentile perspective allowed two responses. For hardcore Nativists, the alien breed labeled as the Jew would forever remain un-alike. For Progressives, the gaps between differences of sound (speech) and sight (appearance) might be lessened through the Jews' commitment to a series of assimilationist strategies. As for the new immigrants, there appeared to be but two options. Either they would not, or could not, alter their Old World being to fit American models, or they would actively attempt to "pass" as American by exchanging clothing and hairstyles for the New World look, adopting American standards for public behavior, and replacing Yiddish with American modes for speech communication. "Learn English" and unlearn old habits was the ringing message of the *Guide to the United States for the Jewish Immigrant* in 1912. Like admonitions filled its pages, and miracles of metamorphosis were promised.

> English is absolutely indispensable to the workman. . . . Patience and perseverance will enable you to make rapid progress in this strange tongue that seems so difficult. . . . You will be like a dumb man who has suddenly had the gift of speech. You will then be on a level of equality with the native. You will have at your command every advantage that the country offers.

The subtitle for the all-purpose *Guide* (various editions were prepared for distribution to speakers of Italian and Polish, as well as Yiddish) states that this particular version is *A Nearly Literal Translation of the Second Yiddish Edition.* Stop to consider who the intended audience might have been for wake-up calls transferred from the original Yiddish into the English that Jews had yet to master. Yet the point of these magical messages, if comprehended, was clear. Prompted by the admonition "Patience and courage!" the newly arrived were to absorb the sounds and sight of English, but also to discard public acts viewed as crimes in America: spitting, throwing garbage out of upper windows, beating dust from mattresses.

I have drawn you quickly through territory that is familiar to any scholar who works through the immigrant experience during the period of the great waves of entry into the United States. My intention is to lay stress on an area that lies outside the kinds of tangible evidence noted by native-born Americans regarding alien speech patterns, physical appearance, and behavioral acts. My concern is with "the mind," that invisible, largely indefinable entity that forever lay behind the central question of the times: What does it mean to be, or not to be, "American"?

I shall be drawing specific examples from the editorial pages of the original *Life,* an early precursor of the *New Yorker,* which was founded in New York City in 1883. The positionality *Life* brought to any consideration of the kind of alien "minds" with which native-born Americans felt they had to contend by the close of the nineteenth century can be crisply defined: urban; middle- and upper-class; Harvardian; male; Progressivist; "Anglo" in the most literal sense (German, Dutch, French; Scandinavians were not of "our crowd"); "Protestant" (as in Episcopalian—not, heaven forbid, Methodist or Baptist); and "American" (defined as those whose forbears arrived from England and Scotland prior to the signing of the Constitution).

There are several other facts that need to be singled out before dealing with *Life*'s attempt to size up "the Jewish mind" in relation to "the American mind"—first, the devices by which this highly successful comic periodical went about its work of interpreting the American scene; next, a bit of back history regarding the most flagrant occasion when *Life* had to face down accusations of anti-Semitism.

By the nature of the fact that *Life* existed to function as a comic periodical, it projected its satires upon the contemporary scene by means of the pictorial weapons of caricature and cartoon. (It largely ignored making jokes that called on phonetic renditions of dialect—Irish, Jewish, Italian—borrowed from vaudeville practices of the times.) Its art staff relied on centuries-old conventions that read inward character traits by means of standardized iconic types: the pug nose of the Irish, the bent nose of the Sicilian, the hooked nose of the Jew.

On February 6, 1907, in "LIFE and the Jews," the editors printed a full-page explanation of what it meant to be a "humorous journal" working primarily with visual evidence:

> In its impartial fun-making LIFE has found material in every class and race. . . . To LIFE a joke has always been a joke whether its subject was the white man, black man, yellow man or red man. Its humor has dealt with Americans, Irishmen, Germans, Africans, Englishmen. . . . In its satire it has spared neither the rich, the prominent nor the powerful.

Life's editors maintained that the Jew was treated like everyone else in its pages. They expressed wide-eyed astonishment that only the Jew showed "resentment," since you could not picture a Jew without making him Jewish any more than you could picture an Irishman without making him Irish or a Negro without making him black.

In 1905 *Life* was sued for libel by the New York Theatre Syndicate over insinuations by James Metcalfe, the magazine's drama critic, that the Syndicate, out of "typical" Jewish greed, had been complicit in the conditions that had led to the deaths in the notorious Iroquois Theater fire in Chicago. It is important to note that the suit for defamation was based on the cartoon that accompanied Metcalfe's drama column, since its force as a visual insult was considered more libelous than mere words. *Life* won the case yet was embarrassed by the publicity given to its drama critic's rabid anti-Semitism. The magazine's belief in itself as a liberal and enlightened journal had been seriously called into question. In a series of editorials, *Life* tried to distance itself from the prejudices against Jews that it insisted were only held by "the common mind"—that is, not by the uncommon mind *Life* asserted it possessed—a contradiction that posed a dilemma for a periodical whose success lay in its ability to represent what it intuited the American mind to be.

I am about to concentrate on four articles devoted to the nature of "the Jewish mind," written by *Life*'s leading editorialist, one Edward Sandford Martin. As I have stated elsewhere in great detail, I do not like Edward Martin.[1] Still, I find his pronouncements of great value in reflecting the attitudes held by men of his type and generation toward what he himself called "one of the most important and interesting forces in modern life"—the fact of the arrival in the States of dynamic alien forms and concepts represented by the Jewish immigrant population. Before quoting from Martin's editorials, however, I need to bring up two further points. First, behind Martin's efforts to define "the Jewish mind" over against "the American mind" lay the haunting question, "What is an American?" raised in 1782 by Michel Guillaume St. Jean de Crevecoeur's *Letters from an American Farmer.* Behind Martin's arguments also lay Theodore Roosevelt's claim in 1894 that the

English language was the defining factor for the attainment of "true Americanism."

Roosevelt's essay "True Americanism" asserts that all immigrants to the United States must adopt English as their only tongue. Only by this sacred act would the nation's citizens fend off the taints of "hybridity," "hypenation," and "cosmopolitanism" Roosevelt so feared. Dual allegiances were impossible. Those who insisted on clinging to the oral or written traditions of Old World speech would never be able to adapt to the New World present. For Roosevelt, resistance to English blocked any chance at assimilation with the goal of "becoming American." Such hybrids were condemned to an existential impasse wherein they became "nothing at all." This was the fate that awaited a Yekl and a Gitl if not fully transformed into a Jake and a Gertrude. And what was Roosevelt's True American to do with a man who concluded his immigrant narrative by confessing, "I cannot escape from my old self. My past and present do not comport well. David, the poor lad swinging over a Talmud volume at the Preacher's Synagogue, seems to have more in common with my inner identity than David Levinsky, the well-known cloak-manufacturer"? What Roosevelt's "True Americanism" implies is this: to retain one's Yiddish heritage is to remember. To replace Yiddish altogether with English is to forget, thereby erasing one's past—the entirety of one's racial and cultural consciousness. "Erasure" was what many Americans demanded as the mark of true patriotism at times of war. This plays into the fact that the context for Edward Martin's four editorials of 1916 and 1918 on "the Jewish mind" was World War I—a time of fear over the possible disloyalty of recent arrivals in the States who could not—would not—break all ties with the Old World.

Written prior to the entry of the United States into the European conflict in April 1917, the opening sentence of "Four Minds of Uncle Sam," appearing in February of 1916, reflects the urge to classify—held in common by cultural anthropologists, clinical psychologists, and editorialists—and the need to categorize the degrees of "friendship" to the American Way of which the "four minds" were capable.

Martin states that there are four dominant minds in the United States: the Irish, the Jewish, the German, and the Scotch and English. They are all classed, very properly, as

"American," but they are different minds, with different experiences of life behind them, different racial traditions, different religious training, different points of view. Next, the throwaway phrase: "Of course there are other *breeds* of mind in the country—Italian, French, Scandinavian, Negro" (my italics)—a phrase that racializes the concept of "mind" in ways that recall contemporary attempts by W. E. B. Du Bois to define "the Negro consciousness" as somehow both cultural and racial.

In speaking of the different emotions that Americans might hold toward the fearsome events taking place in Europe, Martin comments that if "you are an American of English or Scotch descent," the "background" for your responses "will be English law, literature, religion and history." Martin here sets up a stark contrast between the American mind and the fact that "back of the Jewish mind is Russia or Germany and the Jewish race, religion and history, and back of the German mind is Germany." In making the distinction between the "background" possessed by the "you" of English or Scotch descent and the "background" of the Jew or German, Martin is in agreement with the evolution theory Roosevelt slammed home in "Biological Analogies in History," his Romanes Lecture, delivered at Oxford University in 1910. That is, "the English past" is not really the past; that time is alive in today's America, only more so. That is, the True American's time scheme includes all of English history, whose values were neither realized nor real until they manifested themselves in the New World. That is, those other "minds" of Uncle Sam (Irish, Jewish, German) will always be different in kind since they are bound to an actual past, thus permeated by the tainted habits of the Old World forever unassimilable to America's "present."

In the same editorial of February 1916, Martin declares: "The American will is the resultant of four principal wills of different and more or less antagonistic derivation. Three of them . . . are Teutonic; the other is Semitic." This is the challenge that Martin believes confronts his America: how to harness these four minds/wills to benefit the single cause of true Americanism, when Jews are best suited to "the inter-ethnic, the international age": "Jews are usually faithful to the country they live in, but their chief interest is in Jews, and next to that, in the human race." Martin holds the unsettling notion that Jews are "probably the best internationalists," but not necessarily the best Americans.

By June 1918, the twin facts that America was at war and that Russia's world had been overturned by revolution loomed large over Martin's editorial "The Jewish Mind in These States." Martin focuses all his attention upon the Jewish mind, singling out what are for him its most distinctive qualities: "It is the most destructive mind in the world, the most grasping and unabashed, one of the ablest, one of the most aspiring, and, in its own view, the most concerned for human welfare." Martin applauds the contributions of men like Bernard Baruch but worries about "the I.W.W. Jews, the revolutionary Russian Jews," who use the destructive powers of the Jewish mind to rend society rather than to knit it together.

The following month brought a reprise to Martin's June editorial. "'The Jewish Mind in These States'—an Answer" opens with a long letter sent to *Life* by "a distinguished New York lawyer" who voiced strong objections to Martin's association of the Jewish mind with Bolshevism, to his use of "the threadbare phrase of the Prussian anti-Semitic and the Russian pogromist," and to his assertion that the Jewish mind is not devoted to "the preservation of American institutions and of liberty." Martin responds with the oddest kind of logic, by arguing that since the Jewish mind "gave us our religion" (Christianity), that mind should be honored for making possible the destructiveness of "the words of Christ," which overturned "the whole fabric of society" for the common good.

Martin, however, sensed he could not leave his attempts to analyze the nature of the Jewish mind in such a muddle. In August 1918, he leads off his final editorial, "More About the Jewish Mind," with the rhetorical question, "Is it censure or compliment to call the Jewish mind destructive?" He answers himself by saying, "Nobody thinks less of gunpowder for being destructive" when its use is needed to destroy what is "proper to be destroyed." He praises Louis Brandeis and Felix Warburg as reformers who have put the force of their "Jewish mind" to the task to "clear away, or make passage through, an existing structure." He concludes: "What is the most destructive thing in sight? Mustard gas? The German General Staff?

No; Liberty!" In all this, Martin picked up on the argument *Life* had offered on other occasions, particularly during its "socialist" period in the early 1910s, when Art Young and others on the magazine's art staff attacked the corporate greed of Wall Street's WASPS and when the editors praised Jack London and Emma Goldman for their efforts to eradicate the ills of the status quo. It would seem that Martin was willing, for the moment, to credit the Jewish mind for the corrective disdain it expressed toward "the existing order and its operators" and for the concern that mind felt for all the peoples of the world, in lieu of limiting itself to the needs of any single nation.

What have we here in these four editorials? The fumbles of Martin's "American mind" as it ricochets wildly about in an attempt to define that alien entity the Jewish mind, which could not be seen via speech, yet existed as a force with real consequences in the world. If Martin was done in by his struggles over the Jewish mind, was he any more successful at pinning down the American mind or in defining the work it had to do on the American scene?

I turn away from Edward Martin toward a piece by Henry James entitled "Democracy and Theodore Roosevelt"—his review of Roosevelt's *American Ideals,* the 1898 collection of essays that included "True Americanism." As I quote from (and paraphrase in part) key passages from James's review, be alert to the significance of the fact that James uses the word "consciousness" rather than "mind"; to the weight he gives to the need for consciousness "to think"; and to the crucial distinctions he makes between Roosevelt's notion of "the American mind" as a stable set of monolithic, unalterable preconceptions and his own belief in the denationalized "consciousness" as a thing of "process," "development," "absorption," and "adaptability" to ever-changing and diverse conditions.

> Mr. Theodore Roosevelt appears to propose . . . to tighten the screws of the national consciousness as they have never been tightened before. . . . [His notion of patriotism is] a very fierce affair [though it is] not the practice, but the theory that is violent [even though it must deal with a world that is given to] multiplying contact and communication, to reducing separation and distance, to promoting, in short, an

> inter-penetration that would have been the wonder of our fathers. . . . [To Roosevelt, it] is "purely as an American," he consistently reminds us, that each of us must live and breathe. Breathing, indeed, is a trifle; it is purely as Americans we must think. . . . To say that a man thinks as an American is to say that he expresses his thought, in whatever field, as one.

James states his objections with cutting sarcasm. To describe the way an American thought shall be expressed is surely a formidable feat, he notes. Mr. Roosevelt, he says, makes very free with the "American" name, but it is after all not a symbol revealed once and for all in some Book of Mormon dug up under a tree. In opposition to Roosevelt, James views "the national type [as] the result, not of what we take from it, but of what we give to it, not of impoverishment, but of our enrichment of it." He concludes with the warning that—unless the national consciousness foregoes the "impoverishment" that comes from a fixed state and unless we devote ourselves to "making" that consciousness by working "as hard as we can"—we will be left with "stupidity" as "the great danger to avoid."

I am hardly one to overlook James's highly complicated and controversial responses to the speech patterns he found strange to his ear during his return visit to the States in 1904–1906. In *The American Scene* James had much to reflect upon regarding the "alien" sounds reverberating throughout New York's streets. He was both anxious and excited over the new speech that had poured into the city of his boyhood: anxious because excited by the creative energy transmitted by the performances in the Yiddish theater he attended and excited because anxious over what such destructive energy portended in the future for people of "his kind."

Compare James's mix of fascination and dread to his reaction to the disgusting sounds he heard from the lips of the native-born Americans he met on this same trip—reactions he voiced in lectures and wrote down for publication in "The Question of Our Speech" (1905), "The Speech of American Women" (1906), and *The American Scene* (1907). About those sounds and that vocabulary James felt high anxiety but none of the excitement aroused by his encounters with Yiddish on the Lower East Side. To James, the all too "American" speech of traveling salesmen and young girls on the loose signified intellectual monotony, lack of emotional nuance, staleness of consciousness, and the "stupidity" that was the "great danger" Americans must try to avoid. This was the speech that trapped "the American mind" within a form of "true Americanism" that erased memory and annihilated the cosmopolitanism of complex consciousness that defies containment by a preordained national destiny.

I draw the following admonitions from these examples. No living language can sanction the forgetfulness of a complex linguistic past, as urged by Theodore Roosevelt, by John R. Dos Passos's 1903 *The Anglo-Saxon Century and the Uniformity of the English-Speaking People,* or by Pat Buchanan's politics of elimination. The American experience has to be "yiddish"—made up of fertile acts of language and consciousness taking place within heterogeneous communities, whereby the remembered past joins with the active present and the multilayered future.

NOTE

1Banta, *Barbaric Intercourse: Caricature and the Culture of Conduct 1841–1936* (Chicago: University of Chicago Press, 2003).

STEPHEN GREENBLATT

A EULOGY

On the occasion of the first anniversary of my mother's death

Today's Torah portion—Leviticus 1:1 to 5:26 and Isaiah 43:21 to 44:23—represents something of a challenge for a modern Jew. It is not only that it describes in exceedingly unpleasant, graphic detail the aspect of ancient Hebrew worship that is most difficult for us to understand and to sympathize with—the sacrificial cult of the ancient Temple—it also seems to insist on precisely those elements in the cult that are the furthest from our sensibility. God likes the sweet savor of burned animal flesh, we are repeatedly told, and he will accept only male animals without blemishes. Burnt offerings can include birds, as well as beasts; priests should pinch off the heads of the birds, cleave them but not divide them completely in half, tear off the feathers from the wings. In all of these cases, God particularly wants Aaron's sons always to be careful to sprinkle the blood liberally around the altar. In peace offerings, as distinct from burnt offerings, God has a peculiar interest in the fat that covers the innards and the kidneys; on the other hand, he does not want the skin of sacrificed bullocks or their dung. There is a certain grotesque ethnographic interest to all of this, but our ancestors begin to seem more like Aztecs or Trobriand Islanders than like the children of Israel.

We are good, of course, at making moral sense out of the ancient codes—that is, after all, what our tradition has trained us to do. So we can focus on the guilt that the sacrificial rituals were meant to address and rectify. We modern Jews are after all supposed to be experts in guilt. But quite apart from the strangeness of killing animals in order to atone for guilt, the passage from Leviticus insists upon forms of guilt that we tend to reject: pollution incurred unconsciously, inadvertently, unintentionally. For most of us, this is not properly guilt at all, since there was no willed transgression, but the passage treats certain unintentional acts as if they were the full moral equivalent of deliberate choices.

In the cheders of old, I am told, Leviticus was the first book taught to children. It seems surprising—one would expect that study would begin with Genesis. But perhaps there was canniness, rather than perversity or indifference, at work: it is children who are more likely to feel guilty at acts that they did not mean to commit. Adults learn to distinguish between the accidental and the intentional—and hence they are more likely to be troubled by Leviticus.

We turn then with the expectation of relief to the Haftorah, for it is there that we are accustomed to find our moral and spiritual bearings. And the expectation is intensified by the fact that the selection is from Isaiah, usually the most ethically alert as well as eloquent of the prophets. But today's passage is, if anything, more troubling than the verses from Leviticus. Isaiah here seems willfully to misunderstand the religious practices of other peoples, practices he condemns as idolatry. He is witheringly scornful of people who cut down a tree, burn half of it for firewood and then carve the other half into a statue that they irrationally worship. But we know perfectly well—and, more to the point, Isaiah must have known perfectly well—that this is not an adequate account of the function of statues in religious practice, no more accurate in describing the cult of Baal than it would be in describing the practice of Buddhism or Christianity. Isaiah sounds uncomfortably to our ears like a member of the Taliban, whose conjoined destruction of "idols" and sacrificial offerings of animals bring them uncomfortably close to today's readings.

All of this is to say that Judaism is not a fixed and settled affair, but a religion that has constantly interrogated itself and grown and changed. And this in turn enables me to say that the Judaism of my beloved mother, may she rest in peace, bore very little relation to the subject of today's passages. Hers was not a religion of guilt and propitiation. She gave little or no thought to what would smell sweet in the nostrils of an angry God. She was no breaker of idols. She kept a kosher house, observed the holidays, lit the Shabbas candles, loved to come to Temple Emanuel to sing and to pray and to say Kaddish for her parents and siblings and to feel part of the Jewish community. But there was very little theology. When I was an adolescent, I was baffled and even nettled by this almost complete absence of speculation about the nature of God, or the existence of the afterlife, or the paradoxes of spiritual existence in a secular world. But I have come to think of my mother's quiet, simple practice of Judaism as one of the sweet strengths of her life. There were other strengths: her modesty, her sense of decency and propriety, her extraordinary alertness to the feelings of others, and her intense, unwavering, deep and virtually all-consuming love for her family. None of these qualities is enjoined in today's verses from Leviticus, but I am quite convinced that they, more than the fat of animals, are a sweet savor in the nostrils of God.

GREGORY ORFALEA

VALLEY BOYS

I am an American writer with Arab roots; Daniel Pearl was an American writer with Jewish roots. We both grew up in the San Fernando Valley section of Los Angeles. Knowing that one fact tells me something about him.

Dan Pearl lived in Encino and went to Birmingham High School at Victory and Balboa; I lived next door in Tarzana and went to Crespi Carmelite High School at Ventura and White Oak, less than a mile away. I did not know him, but I know him.

I know that because he grew up in Encino he loved oak trees, not the pin oaks of the East that stand straight and tall and have little, sharp leaves, but what we call—we, being Daniel and I—live oaks, trees that sport a gnarly, sprawling set of branches that smell of Italian pasta, many so low to the ground that a boy can haul himself up into and perch in them on a summer day, and eat a banana or drink an Orange Julius purchased on "the boulevard" (Ventura Boulevard, the street of our youth).

The reason Encino is Encino is because there are oaks; Encino means "oak" in Spanish, and oaks are symbols of things which do not die. I'm not sure of the exact location of Daniel Pearl's family home, but I'll bet on many a day he drove his bicycle past the huge live oak no one—not even California suburbanites—would remove from the middle of the street on Louise Avenue as it flows into the hills. And he would have touched it with his hand as he passed, maybe right where I touched it when I passed as a boy, happy to know it was thriving in spite of all the tawdriness around us. He would have continued to do this as a teenager with his first car, squeezing by the Old Oak of Encino, a hand out the window on its flank, knowing how rarely people let things live that deserve to live.

(After a long fight to save it, the Old Oak was finally felled two years ago due to disease. But the commemorating stump remains, impeding traffic with its memory.)

I know Daniel Pearl because I went to his school's famous dances. My school, being a Catholic boys' school, did not have famous dances. My school had only terrifying dances, ones where the mothers lined you up on either side of the library and demanded that you dance with the jacketed girl far across the room against the Geography stacks.

But Daniel's Birmingham High School had a reputation for getting the great bands of L.A. to perform live. Could this be where he got his love of music, his facility with several musical instruments? Birmingham drew such bands as the Seeds, the Doors in their infancy, the Nitty Gritty Dirt Band ("Buy for me the rain, my darlin', buy for me the rain"). Birmingham also had something we never had: girls that looked like girls, in fact, looked better than girls, looked like women. They wore spangled mini-skirts and we Crespi boys would pay our lucre at the door and spend hours working up the nerve to ask one of these dark angels to do the Mashed Potato or the Surfer Stomp.

I know, or surmise, that Daniel, like me, had his heart broken in the Valley as teenagers have their hearts broken in valleys everywhere, but never so much as in this Valley with its long boulevards of endless shops that faced each other like a phalanx of longing in the implacable sun. It was not a place for someone with a brain. Or a particularly deep heart.

But it had its secret orange grove—Bothwell's below the hill on the Tarzana–Woodland Hills border—and Daniel and I furtively scouted it. Daniel and I stole oranges, because that was one of the secret pleasures of a place overrun with oranges, as the whole Valley once was before it was overrun by highways and malls. He put his hand over the barbed wire or took the low-hanging fruit that was trying to escape from captivity as he wheeled by on his bicycle.

I rode my bike to Encino every day to school. Daniel too knew those back alleys because they helped us imagine a world where people didn't just sleep and commute to a far-off basin to work. We dreamed of journeys to places like India or France. At the same time we paid respect where respect was due, for example to the pies at Dupar's or to Dead End Beach.

I am sure Daniel loved the seashore. There was nothing like driving there on a Saturday over Malibu Canyon, inhaling all the sage and rosemary, your hands out the window, your voice wailing about "Dirty Water" (Boston) or some guy named Louie, until you saw, in the dip of hills, that blue egg of the ocean.

It pulled you elsewhere, you who had a desire to know, to understand, and to love those unlike you, even those who did not like you. You knew you had a gift for language. You married late, if you were Daniel or Greg, because you had been in thrall to the language and finding others where they ticked. But you were so grateful you did finally arrive and find the right Other. And you were on your knees to the Almighty who for some reason made Jew and Arab, Encino and Tarzana, America and Pakistan, love and hate, emptiness and longing, for that boy coming your way with your gift, I mean, life.

I did not know Daniel Pearl but I know him. And I know the people who killed him did not know him. Those who did this horrible thing do not know oranges or oaks, Encino or Tarzana; they do not know what America is or can be. They identified Daniel by one word only. Daniel never identified anyone with one word. Even that word they got wrong. Because Daniel was an Arab, a wandering Arab, and I am a skeptical Jew. I do not believe that God is the province of any one people, any one faith; any faith or people who kill in His name are allied with death and not life, not oaks and oranges, not olive and fig trees or grazing land or Kashmir or anywhere but darkness.

I was raised where Daniel Pearl was raised. I am very proud of him. I only wish I had raised my voice sooner, traveled to their hideout in south Asia, offered myself up as an American with an Arab skin and said, "Take me and examine me. Is my blood different from Daniel Pearl's? If so, execute me. If not, look at this genuinely human being, and fall on your knees."

BONNIE FRIEDMAN

MY JEWISH PERVERSION

Who were these men and women staring up at me, I wondered. We eyed each other across three feet of linoleum.

Plump curls fell from blonde manes before me. Shoulders like police barricades spanned the seats. Kindness glowed in many of the Iowan eyes that tracked my path from window to door, from door to window, although in the last row, kicked back on the hind legs of his chair, sat a boy with a pocked face, clicking his pen over and over as if to say, "Shut up, shut up, shut up . . ."

I paced before them in the blue polyester dress I'd worn to my sister's wedding, for most of them their first Jew, their first New Yorker. My black hair was cropped in a wedge. My fingers dug in my pockets. And my eyes found refuge in the green-and-white linoleum that reminded me of the frontpapers of books, which reminded me of my topic: literature. How to guide these students? How to draw them into the passageways dusky with carbon, where prose itself jangled a spooky music, a shamanistic incantation?

"Teach them *Garp*," advised the head of the department.

Garp? *Garp*? But surely they could read that on their own! I came equipped with *Light in August, Hamlet,* and "Prufrock," none of which I understood, but all of which my intelligence grazed like some imperious aunt's mink hat perched high on a shelf. Such plushness when you swept your fingers through it! Such glory, although the thing slid back, withdrawing just as you grasped it.

Teach what I understood? How, even? What was there to say? I wanted to coax my students to the marvelous place where everything was almost out of reach and the value of a thing was proportional to how high you had to stretch. Blue sparks leapt from your fingers if you made contact with the strange fur, and in the flare of a sentence you saw for an instant your own secret face—

But no. The students shook their heads. They hated to reread. It was just the same words, now congealed on the paper. They sighed. They cracked their fingers. As the days passed, more and more of them clicked their pens.

An army of pens, pistons. The withering lawn out the window held their attention more than the words on the page. When they turned to me it was with a wan gaze—as if their eyes were sprayed with furniture polish, I felt! As if a waxy buildup had formed behind which they blithely lived in their prefurnished homes, watching what was on TV, visiting their grandparents and great-grandparents, planning their weddings—or so it seemed to me. "Again?" they said. "Again?" when I asked them to reread. "'Like a patient etherised upon a table.' Okay?"

"Not okay!" I banged the desk. "Is this any way to describe a sunset? And *how* is this a love song? Would you behave like this if you wanted love?"

"Tsk, tsk," said someone in the back.

My cheeks prickled with shame. I'd overreacted. But then I saw a girl spray perfume discreetly. Tsk.

Oh, to rattle them! To goad them! To stick the spur of this sentence into them and make them rear! But no, they already had. Dozens of students hung back on their chairs, a cavalry of frozen horses. Then a young woman let the front legs of her chair slam down.

"Professor Friedman," she said, "this is ridiculous. We're ready to move on. To make some progress."

"Progress?"

"Look, we've GOT it. He's a young man who acts like he's really, really old, like a person with his pants all rolled up because he's shrunken, and he's scared to eat fresh fruit. Okay? We're ready for *Hamlet*."

She sat.

The boy in the back clapped. "This is bullshit," he muttered.

I nodded. But I didn't understand, I didn't understand. They were the hat poised high on the shelf and I had no idea how to reach them. How sedate they seemed to me! How laconic! I wanted to flummox them, to set bugs crawling under their skin. Because bugs must already be crawling, although they didn't acknowledge it. To be alive was to have odd creatures under your skin, flicks and movements wakening you at unknown hours, urges twitching you as you talked to your family, as you laughed with your friends, as you turned the blank pages of next year's calendar.

I wanted to acquaint them with their own bugs but they seemed to have none. And when I asked them to look more closely at the words on the page before them, the familiarity of those words obscured their unfamiliarity. What was the matter with them that they got bored so fast?

"They're caged and don't know it," I muttered to myself as I slogged home. The chants of cheerleaders carried over the fields, shish boom bah! And a girl, floating like a wisp of dandelion, rose over the birch trees and touched her toes.

Well, I was a poor teacher. Of course my students resented it. I rushed in two minutes after class started, clutching a cup of chalky gray coffee and staring at the lesson plan on which I'd broken down the agenda in units of two to fifteen minutes. All the paraphernalia of handing out mimeographs, taking attendance, reviewing the date of the next test—exasperated and delighted me. I longed to be teaching. Teaching terrified me.

Some of my students had trouble reading. When asked to read aloud, some of my students struggled, each word an archipelago of syllables. Others read in a hasty monotone, the sentences blurring together, meaning dispensed with at the outset. And there I stood in my blue party dress recalling the gold corridor in which I'd often sat in the afternoon, locked out of my Bronx apartment, keys lost, and each cabbage-medallion actually a round lock to be twisted this way and that until it sprang open and one was on a ship voyaging far away, to Melville's Polynesia or Tennessee Williams's New Orleans. How to break the swoon down into pedagogical units? "All of teaching is learning how to ask good questions," a man from the South had explained. He was holding a book on question-asking. I'd thought: Questions, how simple! Yet where were the questions that would swing my own students open? They sat in rows before me, and I saw cabbages, cabbages, and not their own far horizons.

"One way to accomplish some original thinking," I told my

students, "in fact, the only way to accomplish some original thinking that ever works for me—is to examine a thing closely."

It was the best advice I could give. I'd discovered that books got more interesting the more you looked at them. Their DNA fascinated, their particular structure, all their strands and rhythms. But at this level most especially I lost my students. "You're beating a dead horse!" they explained. I glanced at the horse. Its eyes gleamed with life! The very fleas on the horse leapt with excitement! "Why do you think it's dead?" I asked.

"Because it is!" they groaned.

Oh. "And when did it die?"

"During the second class when we talked about it."

The it in question was *Light in August*.

"And what was your favorite part?"

"When the girl tracks down the man who got her pregnant!"

"And what did you hate the most?"

"Hightower, and his stupid crazy sermons, and the scene where the boy is being whipped by that man for not knowing the catechism well enough—"

"Did you really hate that or did you just hate the way it made you feel?"

"Hated it! Hated it because it was mean and boring."

Said another: "There was a sentence I liked. It was about going into a diner and sitting at the counter and having a dime and buying a slice of pie. Coconut pie."

"I liked it, too," I said, because I had.

The student shrugged.

"Anyone else?" I asked. "Anyone else want to say their favorite part?"

"The end," said the boy with the clicking ballpoint.

"What happened at the end?"

"I threw the book on the floor and went out."

I smiled. "And what did you do when you went out?"

"It's private," he said.

I nodded.

"We're done with this book," I said. "We're ready for *Hamlet*."

Some of the students clapped, and some picked up their pens to write down the assignment, and some looked thoughtful.

"What does the title mean?" asked a student. "*Light in August?*"

I looked around, question marks in my eyes. And for the first time that semester we had a good discussion.

Iowa taught me how parochial I was. That I exaggerated differences. Naturally there were intellectuals and intelligent people among the Iowans I met. Yet I considered them exceptions. I explained them away in my head. And even though I was now having successes in my teaching—excited conversations, real examinations of the books based on the questions the students were most curious about—I went around feeling more peculiar by the moment.

In some essential way, I believed, I was different from the Iowans and this one trait made all the difference and seemed to display itself everywhere. The cicadas in the trees creaked like a thousand alarm clocks. An invisible sap dangled from the trees. At night it was so dark you felt unmoored from the earth. I was used to the city, where a milky haze floated over everyone, and at two a.m. you could read in bed by the glow from the street. Here I felt like an immigrant.

My landlords, Pat and Pic, collected the rent by hand on the first of each month. At Christmas they left at each of their tenants' doors a gift-wrapped shoebox heavy with chocolate-covered pretzels, homemade cookies, and candy canes. "Oh, that's *different*," they said of anything unorthodox, signaling with an embarrassed shake of the head that they didn't intend to think about it an instant further.

"How many bridesmaids will there be?" Pic asked, smiling. I was getting married, and my wedding was three months away.

"Oh, uh. Two."

"Ah, so. And the dresses! What color are they?" She leaned toward me, her cornflower-blue eyes wide.

"I'm not sure yet."

Confusion crossed her face. She murmured, "You better decide, soon. It takes time to sew them or order them. Unless you want something off the rack."

I blushed, recalling that I'd told my girlfriends to wear whatever they wanted as long as it was pastel.

"And where will the ceremony be?" she asked.

At a big synagogue in Queens.

"And the music?"

But already she seemed wilted.

How explain that the ability to focus on bridesmaids' dresses was beyond me? I'd never achieve the femininity her daughters took for granted. On the one hand, this femininity seemed superfluous, like the bit of hard-boiled egg that surges through the crack in the shell and forms a ruffle. On the other, it seemed crucial, an aspect of being a real girl in America.

"Goodbye!" I said, slowly closing the door behind Pic. "Goodbye!"

I sat in my chair. Pulled the blinds. Tugged the chain on the kitchen lamp. The warmth of the 100-watt bulb lay against my cheek like a hand. I dragged a book toward me and found my place.

Yet how strange I felt! Iowa was making me odd. Day by day I felt more and more like a harlequin creature, composed of books, the heels of my Wallabies splitting into a curling sheaf of cardboard, my entire mind a Tinker-toy of sentences. But weren't sentences the most real thing there was? Before I'd found them I was a miasma, hoisting myself up on a nursery chair, setting my several eyes upon the faces of my brothers, my busy mother, gazing down from my high chair (I seemed suspended against the ceiling) to a population of people I could not reach. Sentences let me reach them. My bones were sentences, my eyes were sentences.

The roar of a football game came softly through the shut glass. Hurrah!

How carefree the players seemed! But what in the world gave their lives significance? The answer was everywhere, of course, yet I couldn't see it (especially with the blinds shut). It was everywhere, but made no sense. I was so used to my pleasure in books that nothing existed that wasn't printed. Books had invented me.

And if one has one's métier, I thought, isn't that enough? Everything else in life had the suggestiveness of that feminine ruffle—like a fairy voice singing in the grass, come hither! As if one were being coaxed to lie down in the dew and gaze into dripping prisms, to catch the flicks of indigo and violet, all of the earth a kaleidoscope burnt away in an hour. You got up with a headache from the sun, the droplets of color evaporated. The life of the senses, I thought. It left no trace. It entranced you and left you empty. In fact, I didn't feel alive or even *real* unless I was reading or studying. I'd been born to study, it seemed, and study is what I did. It was as if I'd been wound up and pointed in a direction. I just went.

What wound me up was the Bronx. The Jews there inhabited lines of prose lit by the candelabra of the *shin* and the pole lamp of the *vuv*, hallways promising that if one went far enough along their tweezering length, one could at last clasp the idea that glowed like G-d. G-d was hidden in the crannies of that involuted alphabet and its jigsaw commentaries. If one studied long enough, studied bent under the Light-O-Lier lamp, studied crouched before the space heater, studied until the whole city was asleep and one's own body had stiffened into a spiral letter, G-d Himself would appear.

In the meantime, he sent His seraphs in the form of smaller ideas. These were "aha" moments, alchemical instants when it became obvious that life itself was merely metaphor, all the streets under my window simply cardboard platforms meant to fold up and fold up again in a Chinese purse, a verbal packet. It was a Murphy bed of a world. Really what existed was the blaze in the head, the moment when prose rasped against the gritty carbon strip of the earth and a fire showed truths that could only be glimpsed in that instant, ephemeral as the faces of family lit by a birthday cake. Make a wish and they vanish. Reality was what you managed to see while an idea kindled.

How many girlhood nights did I collapse into my bed feeling that my mind had almost transformed into that candelabra *shin*! How many times did I make a grab for something in the last instant of wakefulness after hours of studying, studying, during which it seemed that something Eternal and True rumbled toward my field of vision, a coach pulled by a white stallion! Sleep overcame me as I touched a sweaty mane.

The same foolishness in college, the same foolishness in Iowa. Since the Jews I grew up with revered the intellectual, all intellectuals seemed Jews and all nonintellectuals gentiles. My best friends, Sally and Priscilla, were honorary

Jews. All writers were Jews. All psychiatrists. It was the same way all cats are female.

And in the great, thriving world of Iowa, the Jew in me came to feel hunched, bent in and katty-corner to herself. I stood in front of the bakery and gazed at rows of yellow cakes festooned with tiny plastic footballs. I squirted milk into my coffee at the Hamburg Inn with a white plastic ketchup bottle. I wrinkled my nose at the smell of bacon yet wanted to reach out a tentative hand, and close my fingers—and taste.

For I'd come to believe that in that first bite of bacon, a revelation would occur. An epiphany! I'd be a little like the pastel girls with their buttercream yellow hair. I'd understand what they did, with their strawberry-scented lip-gloss. Many of them wanted careers, children, houses. They dared to eat a peach. They did not transfix themselves with mermaid songs. They did not drown when their alarm clocks rang. What was it I wanted them to teach me? My question ticked inside me. If I could taste bacon, I thought, I'd be alive inside time.

The delectable scent coiled under my neighbor's door on Sunday morning. It glazed the air at the Hamburg Inn. I would know the truth of life if I once ate bacon, I half-believed. But it was verboten, and so I substituted phosphorescent fantasy for the taste of it on my tongue.

It was all about us and them, my story. Whatever was us was synonymous: Eastern, neurotic, bookish, jumpy, punny, abstract, psychoanalytic, Jewish. One trait could be substituted for the other. They were all the same in my head—

This was tribalism. What was unfamiliar came to feel incomprehensible. What was novel became exotic and taboo. I brought the shtetl with me, its narrow corridors, its guarded ways—not knowing that the Bronx *could* be a shtetl. It hid its shtetl habits under a guise of cosmopolitanism.

But all shtetls share these traits: an exaggeration of dissimilarities, and a tendency to find the dissimilar where similarity actually exists. In America, only Arabs and Israelis say "Israh-el" and not Is-real. I feel a stab of affinity whenever I hear a Palestinian say that country's name. "You have stolen our food!" said a Middle Eastern woman to me in Iowa. "Babaganoush is not yours! Tahini is not yours! Falafel is not yours!"

I recalled my sister having returned from living in Israel with a beautiful emerald Bedouin dress for me. Now Anita chopped up purple cabbage into a big bowl. She added sliced tomatoes, red onion, grated carrots, cucumber, and feta cheese. She toasted pita bread. She had lived in Tel Aviv and had come back with impeccable Hebrew, stories of an Arab boyfriend, and of the kibbutz that kept a pig. Would she believe that babaganoush was not hers? She loved it, it was hers.

I carried my shtetl all over the U.S.—only slowly recognizing its timid ways and fearful judgments. The ultimate shtetl for me was the book. How much safer to tread ink corridors! To explore cities that always consisted of the exact same words! I'd wanted to plunge deep enough into a novel to discover an imperishable truth. A truth! I wanted to come back from my studies holding something so shiningly true that it arrested time. Then my mother would quit aging. My father would not lose any more verve. Isn't this why they'd set me on my path? G-d was in literature, I believed, and so turned my back on the world.

And then the world made less and less sense, with its leaping cheerleaders and yellow sugar cakes and the melting prisms of its pleasures—all of which seemed evidence that it couldn't possibly yield anything as true as what might be found in a book. The great flaw of the world—that it is forever changing—seemed fixed by literature. It felt safer to have insiders and outsiders. It felt safer to have believers and infidels. It felt safer to tell myself that those who chose a different way just didn't understand. I made a temple of books. I became a strange idolater. Until it became clear that the thing I worshipped was not a way into life but into death, and that the great flaw of the world is also its path to wisdom—everything changes—and that the paper visor I wore, the knight's mask chiseling the air before me in the shape of a book . . . kept me blind.

My black-and-white thinking left out a thousand shades. At last I no longer needed the reassurance of the narrow shtetl corridors. They began to dissolve like pasteboard in the rain. On Montague Street in Brooklyn, the Palestinian man who leads the movement to boycott the *New York Post* due to its pro-Israeli news coverage calls out to me a warm, sincere hello.

"How are you? It's nice to see you," he says. He used to sell me my pet food until I started boycotting him. Now I smile back, startled. My face sags into its own smile.

"It's nice to see you, too," I say. For there he is before me, not a picture in the paper, not a quote in a magazine. He has five children and has run his shop for well over a decade. He smiles a warm, human smile that burrows under my skin like an infection. Easier to keep my categories intact. The world is both sunnier and chillier without them. And without my paper shtetl, my small secret privileged club, I am more ordinary, just a girl on the pavement, chlorine in her hair, chatting with her neighbors, noticing with a worried eye the Norway maple that always goes straight from green to brown, never flooding itself with red, orange, yellow like the sugar maple, its beloved cousin.

JOHN LIMON

DON RICKLES AND DEATH

I am in Oxford, Mississippi, to address the Yoknapatawpha Society. It is the middle of July, boiling, inescapably the South. My host, who like several of the top Faulknerians at the conference seems to know every last utterance of the great man, is taking me out to a catfish dinner. I have assumed that he is a Southerner.

He is talking to me about my book on standup comedy; he wonders why I did not go deeper into the history of Jewish humor, starting in the Bible. I am happy to concede my historical limits, though his estimation of the humor of the Old Testament is higher than mine. Then, somehow, perhaps as another question about what I omitted, the comedian Don Rickles comes up. My host has never gotten over something Rickles once said to Johnny Carson on *The Tonight Show*. I cannot, here, reproduce exactly what he quotes Rickles as saying, except for the last four words. Something like this: "Johnny, you're a big man on television. You've got the big ratings. What's your competition? A nature show on PBS—'The Zebras are Dead!'"

By the time my host gets to the title of the nominal documentary, I know what he is about to say. I almost recite the words, "The Zebras are Dead," on top of his. I hold back to allow him his sudden glory. But I still have the urge to demonstrate my clairvoyance. So I bring this out: "I can tell you the moment, give or take a year, that you saw that: 1966."

"No," he replies to my chagrin, placing the memory, against the timeline of his romantic or connubial life, at a much later date. But I know that Rickles had to have spoken the memorable words around 1966, because I had experienced, at the time, watching the show, a thoroughly convulsed reaction to them myself; and when, a few days later, I went to my friend's house to work on our satirical junior high magazine, which lasted from around 1964 to around 1966, I plagiarized the phrase, imposing it upon a humor piece who knows how. And my friends, hearing it, also fell into an astonished hysteria.

Rickles made his first *Tonight Show* appearance in 1965. He had to have uttered these words around 1966. My host—I work this out in his presence—must have caught the show on a "Best of Carson" rerun. I am disappointed not to have mystified him by announcing with almost magical precision when he had seen a minute fragment of comedy that he had believed to be his own eccentric memory, part of his own peculiar sensibility, for a third of a century.

It finally reaches consciousness that my host is Jewish.

* * *

Most of the time, I do not register at a glance who is Jewish and who is not. I hardly know that I am a Jew, and when it comes to me, it appears as just another bothersome oddity, like the sound of my voice. When I heard the most famous canard of the *Protocols of the Elders of Zion*, that Jews drink the blood of gentile children for Passover, my first thought was that, at last, I was in possession of a historical truth, for I had never quaffed gentile blood on any holiday. My second thought, however, was that even in this egregious case, I couldn't be sure, because nobody ever tells me anything.

And yet—Don Rickles knows everybody's ethnicity at once, it's the essence of his act, and I respond to Rickles. Furthermore, I seem to think that I glimpse (it's just that attenuated) something in Rickles. I can't begin to plumb what it is that I recognize. My family never passed through Rickles's New York; we are repressed, law-abiding, mainly conformist, a different kind of Jew altogether. There are, so far as I can tell, no vulgar, angry, loud-mouthed relatives. We aren't exceptionally funny. My name is pronounced Lyman, and once the wife of the headmaster of my Harvard dorm, Mrs. F. Skiddy Von Stade, wondered if I was a "Boston Lyman." It is just possible that she was serious.

Yet "The Zebras are Dead" immediately called to me, interpellated me, with a kind of rudeness that seemed mysteriously identifying. The humor, of course, like all adult humor, inclines two ways. You might be predisposed to think that the single purpose of the joke is aggression; the ostensible point is the insult to Carson, whose show not only is at an hour (this is 1966) when only PBS is competitive, but airs so late that PBS is competing with its least enticing offerings. The "deadness" of the zebras signals that PBS is not even countering with its most attractive nature shows; and conceivably the antagonism to Carson comes out clandestinely in the word itself. Yet the phrase also bows in the direction of Freud's childish humor: the pleasure is necessarily but not sufficiently based on our sense of the silliness of zebras and the word "zebra." (There is a diminished humorous effect if the dead animal is a bird or lion.) For the four words to sound funny to you, your brain has to be spun into an oscillation between "zebra" and "dead" that keeps you from presuming where you'll land, on the reprehensible side of a taboo or in innocent nonsense. Tom Stoppard got the same effect from his Shakespearean title, *Rosencrantz and Guildenstern are Dead*.

In his great play, Stoppard makes us inhabit the reality that though we may walk fore or aft, our ship sails in the direction of our death. But to put that as a joke is a form of naughtiness that is entirely atemporal, or regressive. I'll acknowledge death, but only at an outing to the zoo. I'll contemplate dying, but only by infantilizing. If that's the essence of Jewish humor, or of Rickles himself, puerile assassin, I can recognize it, or it can recognize me.

* * *

Don Rickles began his *Spritzing* career just after the Second World War, but he was too rough for the nation until the late 1950s, when Frank Sinatra took him up, and then passed him along to Dean Martin; it was on the *Dean Martin Show* "roasts" that Rickles (the only performer on those tribute-insult shows who can still be watched without grimacing) became a prime-time figure. The Rat Pack had Joey Bishop along for Jewish laughs, but when they showed up at Rickles's performances in Los Angeles or Las Vegas, Rickles could not shy away from jokes about Bishop's feminine subservience to the macho Italian crowd. The Rat Pack wanted to come off as gangster gentility, aristocratic sluggers, but they loved Rickles because he had no refinement at all. He allowed them, because it was entirely verbal, to brawl.

Then Johnny Carson took up Rickles, and something much greater happened. I have written elsewhere about the *Tonight Show* chiasmus: the hick, though in New York, is the host; the New Yorker in New York is the guest. The New Yorker, on the couch, is suburbanized in the city, but by a Midwesterner (Paar, Carson, Cavett, Letterman) who could not stay away from New York verbal assault. Out would come Rickles, and the band would play bullfight music, though it was unclear who was to become the matador, who the bull. Carson would, for the sake of the joke, go Midwestern bland, and Rickles would tear him up phrase by phrase. But every so often, Carson would turn the tables, scoring off Rickles, and Rickles would laugh his hard, dirty laugh (his rictus stretching outward so hard it turned his head distinctly pear-shaped), which either signified ecstasy or pain. One night, Carson insisted that Rickles actually play the host and Carson the guest. They circled the desk. Rickles, in Johnny's seat, began, "So, Johnny," and Carson was instantly all over him: "'So, Johnny'! A brilliant start! That's quite an opener! 'So, Johnny'! They pay you millions a year for lines like that."

I loved those upheavals. I was identifying with Johnny Carson, descendant, so I heard, of Kit Carson, scout.

* * *

As a kid, my favorite Red Sox ballplayer was Carl Yastrzemski; I began a scrapbook of clippings when he was still in the minors. It must have been in the winter of 1967–1968 that I saw him on TV on a variety show—he had been American League Most Valuable Player in 1967, which used to mean that you could wind up in a comedy skit. In my memory, the cast consists of Yastrzemski, a black athlete, and Rickles. Rickles, between two stiffs, is allowed to run amok. He says something funny. Yastrzemski claps his hands and says, "beautiful!" Rickles turns to the audience, goes bug-eyed, and yells: "Where does it say the Polish kid says, 'beautiful'?" Yastrzemski doubles over in laughter.

I had noticed, of course, that the black athlete was black, but it never occurred to me that Yastrzemski was Polish. If you had asked me, I suppose I would have guessed Russian. All I can remember thinking about his background was the paradox that a Boston player came from Long Island.

I identified with Yastrzemski as a ballplayer in Boston—I was a Boston Limon—just as I identified with Carson and his couch from the couch of my suburban den. There was nothing except talent that dictated that they should be themselves where they were as opposed to me, where I was. Yet I can reverse face and goblet on these Gestalt tableaux and see Rickles in the foreground and Carson and Yastrzemski in the background; Carson and Yastrzemski are the planets and Rickles is the star; Yastrzemski and Carson are ornaments on the string of my memories of Rickles. If this is possible, it is either a trick of retrospect or a new development.

* * *

It struck me once as worth pronouncing that growing up was the great humiliation. I did not mean growing old; I meant reaching adulthood. And I did not mean that there was anything particularly discreditable about what in particular I was; I meant that it was a humiliation not to be everything. Adulthood seemed to me the shutting down of every potential but one or, at most, a few. How could you face your parents?

I felt this humiliation acutely, but it was near-sighted to universalize it. When in history was it possible to imagine that one might become a WASP talk show host or a Polish baseball player indifferently? On the other hand was Don Rickles, insisting that everybody was one thing only: a Nebraskan, a Polish kid, a Jew. The pull of Don Rickles is the attraction of shutting down possibilities, so you can be sure that you will always be what you always have been. The attraction is comic, which is to say that it is both to perpetual infancy and perpetual rottenness. "Whatever became of the moment," asks Rosencrantz of Guildenstern, "when we first knew about death?" Shouldn't we remember the trauma? The last word of the silliest sentence is "dead."

A Gathering of Poems

ROBERT PINSKY

THE MATERIAL

The moon-stirred volume of ocean sighed
Coconut tanning-oil and frozen custard.

Birch horses and dragons rode the merry-go-round.

A splinter of the herringbone cedar boardwalk
Might be teased from your finger with a steel
Needle purged of germs by a match's flame.

When the sliver was pulled out they held it
Up to your eyes, with bits of your flesh or blood
Stuck to it. Some doctors believe it helps
To see your tumor or gallbladder floating in a jar.

If Nana sewed a button on my shirt while I
Was wearing it, she made me chew a bit
Of the same cotton thread to keep the stitches
From piercing the precious tissues of my heart.

On the Day of Atonement she sat upstairs.

The shul was within sound of the ocean.

Across the street, Our Lady Star of the Sea
With the rumored mutable crackers and wine
Somewhere in its dark. Froth of Communion dresses.

Three round medallions filled the rainbow arc
Of our shul's jewel-colored Palladian
Window three stories tall, with three images:

The eight-branched lamp, the double tablets of law,
The Star of David—Study, Obedience and Pride?
Or blessedness at Home, in Heaven and the World?

Inscrutable as the narcotic English translation my eye
Sometimes swam to from the phonetic surf of Hebrew.

Meaning was in uncomprehended urgent syllables
The cantor sobbed, or implicit in the building's eight
Small gilded minarets, the terra-cotta pilasters
And three high double doors—in the velvet and silver fittings
Of the Torah you were supposed to kiss by kissing
Your talis's fringe and pressing the fringe to the scroll.

It flirted and hid itself in names, Sol Tepper,
Manny Horn, Isador Moss. Iossel, the ever-smiling "simple"
Concentration-camp survivor they treated like a child—
Grinning, but his dark round eyes like pictures
Of the starved, the mutilated, orphans deprived of touch.

The same men called to the bima to pray by secret
Desert-names: Reuven ben Nachman, Moshe ben Yakov,
Yisrael ben Avraham, in wingtip shoes and neckties.

And with Nana upstairs Sophie Gorcey, Molly Joffe,
Suzy Diamond looking down from the balcony.

Nylon stockings, hats, double-breasted suits.
Prescribed times to rise or sit or when people recently
Bereaved were supposed to leave the building
Or remain, or enter again through the three doors
Framed by four Ionic columns.

The church the synagogue the boardwalk all razed,
Merry-go-round carted off—temporary as gestures,
Icons expendable, less enduring than names.

Made things like garments. Means. Conduits,
Like the dark vaulted cylindrical tunnel that ran
Under Ocean Avenue between the pool at Chelsea Baths
And the beach, where people descended from the bright

Stucco pavilions into the dark round mouth
And then padded out onto the beach broiling in the sun:

Dim passageway from one blinding glare
Into a greater one, walkway invisible under the traffic,
Black damp mouth of the real, leading
From incomprehensible brightness to brightness.

JACQUELINE OSHEROW

ECCENTRIC FRACTALS (ISAIAH, MATH AND SNOW)

A swift, thick snow, its whiteness so complete
I think I'm in Isaiah's fulfilled promise;
Remember? *For behold I create*

New heavens and a new earth—but he's precise,
And these are, after all, the same old heavens,
The same old earth, even an old disguise:

White sheets across chairs, table, beds, divans . . .
The universe in linens . . . so why am I
Stuck in a geometric proof without the givens?

For example: which is earth and which is sky?
And what—precisely—*does* Isaiah mean?
It's not as if we'll have the chance to try,

Even superficially, to fathom this version—
The earth alone, much less what's beyond. . . .
We haven't got sufficient information.

But I'd love to watch the heavens and earth abscond
(I see them arm in arm, like that illustration
Of Mother Goose's fleeing dish and spoon.) Planned

Obsolescence? Or just a brief vacation?
And where would we be? Would our feet touch ground
Or some wholly other substance? Ocean not ocean?

Air not air? What would carry sound?
Unless Isaiah's speaking of our own perception,
How the earth and heavens always come around,

Eventually, to our own lines of vision,
Which means, I guess, it's just ourselves we see. . . .
Can we never let anything objective in?

I suspect—too late—there's unexpected beauty
In a wholly different kind of orientation;
I was trying to help my daughter with geometry

And there it was: the perfect explanation
Of the world the way it is: *similarity*—
Fractals, tiny bursts of correlation

In everything: a vein, a leaf, a tree. . . .
We just have to find the right way in. . . .
Which is where that austere branch of poetry—

Algebra—might offer some instruction:
At once precise and full of mystery
With its abiding metaphor—*x* or *n*—

A universe of absolute affinity
But variable—that's us, the variable—
Though there are fixed anomalies, like *pi*,

That master poet who can simply eyeball
A flawless circle every single time.
What a slob she is, utterly unmanageable,

Always something out of place, never a modicum
Of self-restraint or order; endless excess,
But those circles of hers—each one sublime. . . .

She's my role model! Maybe I'm not hopeless!
Maybe there's even the minutest chance
That my own array of bafflement and mess

Could actually get *out upon circumference.*
The closest I've come is this white on white—
If only I could conjure up some eloquence

I haven't borrowed, some perfect insight:
Something to which *x* and *n* have access:
x being *pi*'s airtight final digit,

n, the way a whirlwind begets ice.
Or call *x* the ratio of life to art,
And *n* what muses, left alone, discuss.

x is that open problem, my husband's heart.
(What axiom applies? Will it ever show?)
Okay, it isn't poetry, but it's a start,

Since *x* and *n* are what I need to know;
x is a black hole's extreme interior,
n is what's underlying all this snow,

Itself an intimation of the white frontier
x milliseconds past the speed of light
Where *x* and *n*, as thought and sound, cohere.

x is ambiguous; *x* is concrete;
x is the chanting underneath each rhyme.
On the other hand, *x* makes rhymes obsolete.

Do I really mean that? What a shame!
Isn't *x* any bull's-eye you can fling?
The absolute and infinite delirium

Of whatever captures *n* and makes it sing?
Isaiah, for example, listen to him.
Unless you think that talking to God is cheating. . . .

I say: whatever sharpens your aim. . . .
Think of those gorgeous circles of Isaiah's—
How, led by him, even the humblest item

Can navigate a host of unguessed likenesses,
Then relocate itself, wholly transformed.
You don't believe me? I have witnesses:

The heavens and earth (the old ones), strong-armed
To listen and give ear in his very first line.
I'm sure—prophecy's persuasive—they conformed. . . .

And then he betrayed them with his long-term plan
To do away with them. Were they bad listeners?
They can't have been as inattentive as I've been—

Snow—I chant it yearly—is a refuge for sinners
In Isaiah—chapter one, verse seventeen—
I'm just one of his scarlet petitioners

Inspired by this blizzard to come clean. . . .
Come, let us reason together . . . he implores us,
His voice solicitous suddenly, so serene

I almost think he hates being censorious
And regrets what he's just made us undergo. . . .
That's when we get the unforgettable, glorious

Business about scarlet sins and snow.
I don't know about you, but I'm persuaded;
Who says you can't divide a number by zero?

The most exquisite truths are all occluded
Like the heavens and earth in all this snow,
Each ornate, six-sided speck encoded

With everything I've ever wanted to know,
A fractal of a fractal of a fractal
Of that primary, still burning, fleck of snow

Touched to Isaiah's lips by that angel.
Isaiah had only seen snow from a distance
And so mistook it for a burning coal. . . .

I've been let in on this truth by chance—
Just now, this blizzard. See? My lips still burn
From a random flake that tried to make an entrance. . . .

Was a seraph here with tongs? Will he return?
I will put my words in your mouth. . . . How did I miss this?
Too much writing, too little reading. When will I learn?

That I may plant the heavens—is that a promise?—
And lay the foundations of the earth . . . words
In *our* mouths, this time. Not like Genesis. . . .

But there's a catch: we have to beat our swords
Into ploughshares first. Feed the hungry.
And oversee all kinds of farfetched concords:

Leopard/lamb, wolf/calf, asp/baby.
Do what you like, but I won't hold my breath.
Is it blasphemy to deem Isaiah's prophecy,

At times, almost as slippery as my math?
I, too, meant to be precise, to equal something,
But I had to give my x and n some breadth

If they were going to have a chance to sing. . . .
Isaiah, too, seems familiar with this problem.
Of course, he had a real gift for believing,

Not to mention a coherent social program,
But, still, he's mostly after what's abstruse:
Inaccessibility's compulsive beauty. Come,

Let's reason together. What do we have to lose?
Who says we can't impersonate this snow?
Quick, before it all starts to diffuse:

Multiply x by n. Divide by zero.
Make the universe an offer it can't refuse.
Then read Isaiah aloud. Pretend it's true.

Think *waters of salvation*. Think *watchman's voice*.
Think *as one whom his mother comforts I'll comfort you. . . .*
Your heart will rejoice, your bones will flourish like the grass. . . .
Behold I'll make the earth and heavens new. . . .

CHANA BLOCH

THE NEW WORLD

My uncle killed a man and was proud of it.
Some guy with a knife came at him in Flatbush
and he knocked the fucker to the ground.
The sidewalk finished the job.

By then he'd survived two wives and
a triple bypass. He carried the plastic tubing in his pocket
and would show it to you, to anyone.
He'd unbutton his shirt right there on the street
to show off the scar.

In the old country, his father was killed by a Cossack.
Some drunk came after the old man with an ax
and his sister Anna tried to staunch the wound
with a hunk of dry bread.

That's the old country for you:
they ate with their hands, went hungry to bed,
slept in their stink. When pain knocked
they hurried to the door.

Now he was a good-looker in a pin-striped suit
and spiffy shoes. No sense living
in the Dark Ages, he would say with a wink.
Oh the endless drive to Brooklyn when I was a child,
his snorting and laughing at the door:
I'm gonna take a bite of your little behind.

CHANA BLOCH

"AND THE DARKNESS HE CALLED NIGHT"

I was trying to keep things neat and shiny.
I had two sets of dishes, for love
and for hate. I kept them in separate cupboards.
Eat love and hate at the same meal
and you'll get punished.

The rabbis taught us the mathematics
of keeping separate. They divined
the micro-moment when day flips over into night:
when the third star presents itself in the sky.
They drew a line through that point like a longitude.
You must navigate the evening blessing
with precision, not one star too soon.
But night comes on slowly.
It takes all day.

When I couldn't love what I needed to,
it was shame that punished me. Was it visible,
the disgrace? Was it spreading?

I know a woman whose father was killed in a car crash.
She hated him. Oh how she hated him.
When the police called, she drove to the ditch
where his wrecked Chevy waited for the tow-truck.
The body was gone. On the dashboard, broken glasses
and a notebook splotched with his blood.
Without knowing why she was crying,
she tore out his stain on the blue-ruled paper
and took it in her mouth.

GRACE SCHULMAN

KOL NIDREI: SEPTEMBER 2001

All vows are cancelled now,
all words undone like chains
that snap, their lockets smashed.
All sentences cut short,

main clauses powerless
to govern their dependents
or lead the voice in prayer.
All syllables annulled.

Verbs lag. All images
envisioned by blind eyes.
All pencilled lines erased
that trembling hands composed.

My court, a grove at sundown:
Sunrays pour through stiff branches,
unearthly yet of earth;
stump of a fallen oak

whose mate once flourished green
and now looms red and yellow
like towers burst into flame.
No ark with scrolls, no benches,

no prayer-shawls, holy books
or ram's-horn. Only trees
stand witness in this silence
and autumn's humid air

blurs a bark's crevices.
As this cloud turns to vapor,
all forms circle in smoke,
all promises unravel,

all pages torn to shreds
and blown to drift in wind
whose words cannot reveal
the truth of what I've seen.

DANIEL MARK EPSTEIN

THE MESSENGER

"The movements of faith must constantly be made
by virtue of the absurd. . . ."—Kierkegaard

Neither cherubim nor seraphim
Could bear the order. God Himself
Spoke those dire words to Abraham,
To take his only son into Moriah,
Three days from home. All that way
On foot and assback, he had to brood
Over the strange commands of Elohim.
So they traveled, father and son (the wood
To roast the lambkin stretched a saddlebag),
And two grown men for comfort or defense.
He was much too old, the boy too young
For such a journey, far from Beer-sheba;
The rocks hid brutal thieves and murderers
Moved by voices mortal and profane.

All this I saw as I hovered near the earth.
God told him to stab the child to death,
Then burn him on the altar, such and such
A mountain, He said, and His word was law.
Spying the crest God promised, he would not
Let his young friends travel the last mile
With him, but said: "Wait here with the ass
While I take the lad to worship yonder."
Loading the firewood upon his son,
He took torch in one hand, knife in the other;
And as they went the child thought it a game
They played. What a joy to be with father,

Alone at last! Though now his father seemed
A little lost and troubled. "I see the fire,"
The boy said. "Here is wood for sacrifice.
This must be the place. Where is the lamb?"
"God will provide," he replied. So He would.
The boy I think still thought this was a game
As father laid him down upon the sticks
And tied him there—except for the odd light
In those faithful eyes, and suddenly the knife.

All this I watched, and here I drew the line.
I am no special angel. Of the nine
Choirs I dwell farthest below the seat
Of the Most High and those Councillors
Who take their glory straight from God,
Or powers who rule stars and wind and rain.
Little more than a muse am I, more kin
To Helicon's fair nine than the Lord's Thrones.
I whisper truth and guard the innocents.
Knowing the Lord had more then on His mind
Than one graybeard gone mad with piety,
I took it upon myself to countermand
Words spoken in a fit of jealousy
Of human love (He is a jealous God!).
Quick as a thought I flew to the man's side
And told him lay down his weapon, do
No harm to the child. "Put down the knife
Before he dies of fright or you of grief.
We see you would do anything God says
(Or think He said, for how can you be sure?)
And I am only an angel. Please believe
This word in your ear is equal to the Word
You heard or think you heard three days ago.
And look," I sang, "behind you toils a ram
Caught in a thicket, just as you are bound
In the wilderness of Moriah and your mind—
Between the past and present, death and life.
Give God the beast, old man; embrace your son."

RICK HILLES

YOM HASHOAH IN FLORIDA

(In remembrance of the Holocaust, observed in the Hebrew calendar on the anniversary of the Warsaw Ghetto Uprising)

Here, the trees pay their respects, mourn openly,
        wear dreadlocks of hanging Spanish moss
sun bleached ash-blue and swaying; in seawind
        they become prayer shawls
salted with dust, grief threads of every kind
        of human hair, some washed ashore
in mollusk shells, some rescued from mass graves,
        appearing now as storm-torn curtains,
silver-blue and smoke-stained, as tattered
        boas flapper-thrown from bygone

Mardi Gras, sweat-ruined scarves and handkerchiefs
        hanging like empty hives of dried lilac
& wisteria. Squinting and sweaty in the midday heat
        I can almost believe they shine for the
unlikely blessing on Tadzik, my Ohio pediatrician,
        who emerged from a Warsaw Ghetto
bomb-flooded cellar & walked out drenched
        into the clutches of laughing armed SS
and lived. The Gestapo, in laughing, forgot
        to shoot Tadzik and the nurses—Bela,

Sabinka. His fiancée, Fredzia. Her brother, Henio.
        Maybe if I stare at them I will see that
these trees wear the torn clothes of the vanquished
        like medals: Bela's torn blouse, her
skirt and underthings ruined at Umschlagplatz

by Gestapo who pulled her by those prized
blonde streaming curls into another room . . .
. . . and, later, on the train ride
to Treblinka, when Bela kissed Fredzia & said
"Help me" and her hostaged

friends lifted her up together, up, like a child,
up to the window without glass
—the train's pistons pumping furiously now—
her wish to fly finally fulfilled
when she pushed herself from the cattle car,
as Pinek had instructed her,
and how in leaping she became a paper moth,
before the rush of bullets pinned her
to the sky above the sun-scorched earth;
if I look hard enough, I will see

these heaps of Spanish moss are the spun
legacy of Henio Grin, the strewn yarn
of his lost story, for which there are still
not words enough. Not for Henio,
who was sixteen and would not live to see
another time. He was the first one
off the train at Maidanek, winning the prisoner
race easily—by two whole lengths—
to the gated building beyond a field of dust,
turning around an instant to cheer on

his slower friends, certain his track-star speed
would save him, though it would not.
Only Tadzik, who stumbled, was saved
when the SS egging them on held out
a white-gloved hand to block Tadzik's last-place
finish to the death showers, an act both
merciful and arbitrary. My doctor was shoved
aside, and the Gestapo said: "You
idiot" and "Don't be afraid, your death won't
amount to one flash of lightning

in the night sky." And what if the trees in Florida,
covered as they are with Hawaiian

leis and luau dancers' skirts & struck piñatas
        whose treasures kids made off with
long ago, are also a kind of code still waiting
        to be cracked, saved ticker tape & streamers,
fanfare for homecoming parades that won't happen
        till everyone comes home. Or they are
the nests of promises, each strand thrown
        by a spouse whose marriage vows

extend beyond the grave; the mosses certainly are
        woven of Bela's braids, and countless others,
which now smell forever of summer & brush
        fires near everglades. For each specter circling
the earth, and all who still believe blue Shoah smoke
        shall block *our* way to Paradise, the trees
observe this breach, the break in covenant. Listen.
        How gently they rattle their worry beads
for us on a day that begins in Hebrew at sunset.
        When the first three night stars are visible.

LAURENCE GOLDSTEIN

THE CELEBRITY

To tell this story I have to start close-up:
the odor of schmaltz, the acrid tang of herring,
the obscene tint of gefilte fish—some affect
of tribal communion in the City of Angels.

Then add backstory: the day's gut-wrenching
last-minute win by the Rams: Bob Waterfield's
slow dance in the pocket—pump once, twice–and
a mile-long pass to Elroy "Crazylegs" Hirsch.

After the touchdown, the celebratory
late-afternoon ethnic feast, downtown,
"and then we'll pay a call on Aunt Esther,
poor woman, the last Jew in Boyle Heights."

So far this is standard-issue urban memory,
spot of postwar time for the nine-year-old
relishing the soon-to-be-served wonder of it all,
like Wordsworth's boy at the lakeshore, waiting

for hooted echoes from the ghostly woods.
spreading sour cream on my latkes,
savoring the Yiddishkeit, more pungent
than the plain English of West Side assimilation.

Here's what makes this story different, deep.
My father wraps my hand in his, leans,
whispers feelingly, "Look at that man behind you,
corner booth, in the grey suit and blue tie."

I catch the conspiratorial tone, drop
my napkin, bend down, fire a glance
at this simian heavy-browed object of more than
my scrutiny, none of which he acknowledges.

"That's Mickey Cohen," my mother hisses,
less awestruck and quick to add an epithet,
"the vicious gangster, he's killed plenty."
So I look again, but never catch his eye.

Crazylegs was my favorite athlete; I piously
hoarded his cards, clipped his portraits from *Sport,*
lined up for his far from classic movie bio.
In reverie I still recreate his eccentric moves

galloping down one sideline, Tom Fears
down another, and gathering the peanut-sized
ball to his white jersey with stupefying grace;
everyone in the stands would rise and shout him

into the end zone ten yards ahead of any tackler.
He was one kind of California idol,
faster and more nimble, a flash of spirit
wrapped in a body any boy would die for.

You see I'm being evasive. You know enough
about narrative to keep your eye on the cameo,
the significant fact sitting there in the deli
arching an eye at the eavesdropping staff

while his kreplach cools and thrilled
customers nudge spouses and kids like myself:
look, they say, how brazenly crime's
famous agents live among us, nothing

like New York, but here too Murder Incorporated
has a franchise, a Jewish pantheon
to house the psychotics of our very own
chosen family, the FBI's most wanted

here on our prosperous frontier. They got Bugsy,
they'll get Mickey soon enough, so feast your eyes,
Larry, for some day you'll be sitting in a deli,
searching for some way to impress your friends,

and you'll say, "This place reminds me, I've got
a story of the 50s . . ." And we guarantee, as long
as you speak about this Prince of Israel, you'll be
the center of attention, the voice of your city.

RODGER KAMENETZ

THE LOWER CASE JEW

T. S. Eliot appears before the rabbinical court in Jewish heaven.

The Prosecutor:

T. S., I got to tell you the *emes*
—Bleistein here, pardon the cigar—
remember me, *palms turned out*
Chicago Semite Viennese?
Like I'm some kind of ape?
You didn't like my baggy pants—
now I'm here to take your measure—

To prosecute is *drek,* but I got assigned.
You think God don't have a sense of humor?
It's punishment for you, but also me.
I have to read these stinking lines
you wrote about the Jews. Exhibit A:

The jew squats on the windowsill, the owner
Spawned in some estaminet in Antwerp—

Squats—what's the matter?
Did you owe your landlord rent?
And spawned—like shrimp in a tank—
or in some dank cabaret after hours
two Jew toads humping on a table?
And what about that lower case j ?
You must have hated us
to break the rules of grammar,
most bank clerkly of Englishmen.

Still I got to admire your style,
the classy way you built those lines.
The sounds kick back and forth:
"jew" and "spawned," "owner" and "Antwerp," "squats"!
You've got a delicate ear.
The w sounds kiss word to word
before they stick in the craw.
But the lower case "jew"
that spawned them all, that I don't forgive.
You were a poet, T. S.,
you shoulda known better,
a guardian of the tongue.
That lower case j was
a country club sign:
No dogs or Jews allowed—
to keep us out of the poem
or make us stoop to enter.

Now here comes Exhibit B:
Rachel née Rabinovitch
Tears at the grapes with murderous paws;
Me I'm an ape, okay.
Look what you did to poor Rachel.
A raccoon you made her—
that gorgeous girl with the dark eyes—
she's dead now fifty years. . . .

I remember you liked to watch
her and the one in the Spanish cape.
You peeked in through the barroom door
in your bank clerk suit buttoned up tight
clutching your umbrella handle.

Premature dirty old man,
did you dream Rabinovitch,
a rabbi's daughter,
would softly claw your grapes?

If only you weren't so scared.
If only you had known her.
What a world of wonder she hid.

You were drawn by what was under,
and you were afraid too—
undersea, under skirts,
the secret under-name,
for the secret underneath
where you thought you might drown:

I should have been a pair of ragged claws
Scuttling across the floors of silent seas.

Pardon the dime store Freud
from a Chicago Viennese,
but about yourself you didn't feel so good
so you took it out on me
and Rachel and Sir Ferdinand Klein.
Was he the only phony—
you fake English from Saint Louie, Missouri?

Because you were ashamed
that you liked to sniff around
dirty bars, back alleys, looking
for rolled up condoms on the ground
testimony of summer nights.
Hey, everyone's got a hobby.
Sweet and dirty, high and low,
Shakespeare and Dante in your ear,
slime in your eye, a stink in your nose.
You liked to mix it up.

London and Jerusalem,
you called them *unreal cities.*
Maybe what made those cities unreal
was you never saw the people in them,
just toads, raccoons, apes—and rats.

For rats you had a special feel.

A rat crept softly through the vegetation
Dragging its slimy belly on the bank

Rats feet over broken glass,

And here's Exhibit C:

On the Rialto once,
The rats are underneath the piles.
The jew is underneath the lot.

And that time in Venice
a Jew got between you and a painting
what did you see when you looked in his face?

A lustreless protrusive eye
Stares from the protozoic slime
At a perspective of Canaletto,

Protrusive eye? Protozoic slime? Canaletto?
You should plant your head like a potato
and grow your eyes under ground!

Instead of rats,
you could have had *rachmonis,*
the love a mother feels in her belly,
rachmonis, rachmonis—
you could have felt for people
like what you felt for rats.

I rest my case.

Defense:

Sir Ferdinand, here for the defense.
What Bleistein's done is most unfair.
Excerpts, scraps, bits and pieces,
not the whole art, not the song. . . .

Let's admit there's much that's ugly
in the fragments he's presented.
The world is also quite imperfect.
Do we then condemn creators?

Besides, what harm's done in the end?
They're only words in a poem,

and poetry makes nothing happen:
a few bad moments for a Jew
in English class; black people too
and women have to take far worse.
If we must comb each crumb of hate
from every line of verse,
there would be little left to read.

Without aversion there is no passion.
Without abomination there is no law.
Surely that's clear to a Jew.

Judge, addressing Eliot:

I wonder, do you think that so?
Does language do no harm?
Does music have no power?
When Hitler wrote his crude poems
on the walls of the heart,
like you he made a metaphor.
Jews were pests—
and Zyklon B a pesticide.
To bad men, bad poetry
gives marching orders.

Eliot:

But what, as Bleistein said, rach . . . rach . . .
Mercy, he meant.
Surely you can't blame me
for what the Nazis did?
I wrote those lines before the war.
It was a different time.
My copyright expires soon,
punishment enough.
I'll be in public domain.

Judge, to Eliot:

All the worse. You never once apologized,
retracted, or removed those lines.
You published them up to the end.

Eliot:

But I won a Nobel Prize. Surely—

Judge:

—there are plenty of them in hell.

Come, stand before the golden scale
holding your book—Gerontion
Sweeney Among the Nightingales
and Bleistein with Cigar.

Here in the light, one particle of hate
weighs more than a lifetime of poems.

Your defense is your indictment.
Your judgment, your readership.
You will be loved most passionately
by those who cannot see themselves:
phonies, snobs, deluded social climbers,
pseudo-English fake professors
in bow ties and tweed, anachronisms,
wine snobs, false Christians who preach
but cannot feel the pain of others:
hypocrite readers, your sisters, your brothers.

Now in the name. . . .

Bleistein (interrupting):

Excuse me your honor—we Jews have a sign
when we want to speak—we interrupt.

Judge:

What is your objection?

Bleistein:

Condemned to his readers? That's too soft by half.
What punishment is that? They'll love him to death.
They'll excuse him in public and in private they'll laugh.

Judge:

What more do you suggest?

Bleistein:

If it please the court—purgatory.

Judge:

That's fine, but it's Catholic for Catholics
and Jewish for Jews . . . he's neither.

Bleistein:

I propose you send him
to Hyam Plutzik's grandson's bar mitzvah.
For the Jews it will seem all afternoon.
For him, a hundred years:

He'll hora with Rachel née Rabinovitch
and kazatzki with Allen Ginsberg
who will give him wet sloppy kisses
(it's okay, he's a little *meshuganeh*)
while his landlord, from that Antwerp night club
leads the klezmer orchestra.

Put him at table 16 with that comedian Myron Cohen.
He'll torture him with jokes.
A million setups in English,
a million punch lines in Yiddish.
Then when he's hungry—for that delicate English palate,
matzo ball soup with shmalz on top, gallon after gallon
and a thousand miles of dishes shaking glaucous jelly,
each with a *shtikel* gefilte fish stamped with a capital J.

Eliot (groaning):

O, I am bound to a bagel of fire. . . .

Judge:

Silence. As the accused seems unrepentant,
we'll take Bleistein's suggestion to heart.

(Turning to Eliot:)

And now in the name of the letter J
which every eye can see—
J that stands for Jehovah,
Jesus but also for Jew,
that little j you left behind
now stands for justice—too.

Bleistein (aside):

Poets—you should be careful the words you choose.
Remember, there are no lower case Jews.

Essays, Stories, Histories

SARA BLAIR

JEWISH AMERICA THROUGH THE LENS

What is the relation of Jewish-Americans, or that elusive set of identifications marked out by Jewishness, to art in America? No field of art production has so begged, and begged for, the question as photography. Itself a notoriously mixed genre—part science, part ethnography, fighting from the outset for life as a form of legitimate art; as conducive to the glossy fashion spread and the muckraking montage as to the modes of celebrity, surveillance, and reportage—photography emerged by the mid–twentieth century as America's preeminent visual form, rivaled only by the moving pictures of Hollywood as an archive for the nation's self-imagination. Within its annals, scholars have long remarked but rarely probed a surprising fact: an astonishing majority of its most influential, indeed defining, practitioners have been Jews. Alfred Stieglitz, Man Ray, André Kertész, Robert and Cornell Capa, Germaine Krull, Paul Strand, Weegee, Brassaï, Lisette Model, Ben Shahn, Helen Levitt, Margaret Bourke-White, Aaron Siskind, Robert Frank, Lee Friedlander, Garry Winogrand, Diane Arbus, Richard Avedon, Joel-Peter Witkin, Nan Goldin, Annie Leibovitz, to name but a few; photographers of Jewish descent have defined the work of picturing America to itself in such preponderance that any history of photography without them is virtually unthinkable. And this is true, it turns out, not only of image-makers, but of key inventors (to whom we owe, among other things, precision and soft-focus lenses, Kodachrome, and the instant gratification of Polaroid), collectors, curators, historians, critics, and even sponsoring institutions.

So what is the connection between people of the book, enjoined by Mosaic law to abjure the graven image, and the storied life of the photograph in America? Only in the last decade, at safe enough remove from troubling claims about Jews and the decadence of modern images, and in the context of broader scholarly exploration of ethnic identity and aesthetics, has the question been broached. In 1996, photographer George Gilbert (né Gelbert in 1922) self-published an unprecedented study, *The Illustrated Worldwide Who's Who of Jews in Photography*, whose 500+ entries catalogue the contributions of Jews (however defined) to the history of the form. The volume exposes all the obvious problems with the who's-who enterprise, itself a genre favored by marginal communities seeking affirmation of their cultural citizenship: it remains untroubled by distinctions between Judiasm and Jewishness, or modes of affiliation; it stops well short of making connections between Jewish history or experience and photographic practices or styles; and it leaves unexplored the question of photography as individual vs. collective (or ethnic, or communal) response to the pleasures and terrors of modernity.

But Gilbert's volume has broken ground for others to explore, and they have done so with gathering alacrity. Historian of photography A. D. Coleman uses the *Who's Who* as point of entry into a meditation on the structural analogy between the work of the camera—essentially, in his Benjaminian reading, that of witnessing and remembering—and the organizing imperative of Jewish religion and culture alike. Jehovah's prohibition against images, Coleman suggests, was intended to force the tribes of Israel to sustain an internalized image of God in the form of ever-watchful conscience (a reading that owes as much to another epochal Jew, Sigmund Freud, as to anything in Tanach).[1] In the wake of centuries of displacements, pogroms, exiles, and specifically the Holocaust, the originary injunction to bear witness takes on a new kind of ethical meaning; it is no accident, Coleman suggests, that "in Hebrew the words for *history* and *I remember*" are one and the same. For the children of this history, the camera becomes a witnessing eye, the instrument through which, paradoxically, the defining imperative of the tribe can be honored and obeyed.

Coleman's keynotes—memory, witnessing, displacement—were echoed to insistent effect in a 2002 show at the Jewish Museum in New York, entitled "New York: Capital of Photography." Exploiting the synecdoche between America's first city and Jewishness as a motley array of cultural codes, guest curator Max Kozloff—himself a celebrated photo editor, photographer, and art historian—gathered a trove of more than a hundred images spanning the last century by photographers both Jewish and not. Kozloff's aims are multiple. Most obviously, he offers a genealogy of photography in the U.S. privileging the mode of the "active witness," so as to counter trends in a post-modernist art world dominated by canons of illusion and visual manipulation. Honing in on New York, and on the preoccupation it generated among photographers of very different temperaments with the place of the human figure (and human being) within the cityscape of unrestrained industrial capitalism, Kozloff foregrounds the generic ambitions of photography as a mode of cultural critique—and implies a structural centrality for Jewish experience to that project.

Thus, Kozloff argues, classic instantiations of modernist fascination with the city—Paul Strand's iconic image of telescoped human figures, dwarfed by their knife-like shadows, posed against the epic proscenium of Wall Street (1915); Alfred Stieglitz's ur-pictorialist *The City of Ambition* (1910), dominated by architectural forms made starkly massive against the atmospheric play of light, water, and trailing clouds of smoke—owe their affective logic to the photographers' exilic cosmopolitanism. Likewise, the socially conscious codes of the New York Photo League (the prominent leftist arts coalition of the thirties, committed to documenting the material conditions under which ordinary Americans struggled to get by) evolved out of the photographers' shared experiences of immigrant culture, the Lower East Side, and the deforming effects of assimilation. Even the formalist icons of photographic high modernism—Margaret Bourke-White's vertiginous shot of Sergei Eisenstein being shaved with a straight razor on her terrace, high above the magisterial cathedrals of commerce and pleasure (1930); Lisette Model's storied series of images of café and bar storefronts, imaging their human subjects in the multiple refractions and reflections through which they see themselves and come to be seen (Fig. 1)—even these, Kozloff implies, reflect a culturally inflected sense of alienation and displacement that ultimately breaks formalism's key illusion: that of the camera's containment of disorder via the visual structures it finds and creates.

A mordant attraction to the urban condition of essential loneliness, and the anomie generated by technology, power, and speed, is hardly surprising in a generation of Jewish practitioners working through their own histories of exile in the context of the imminent, then accomplished, destruction of their ancestry in Europe. For Kozloff, their highly particular condition of "outsiderness" becomes intrinsic to the photographic way of looking in and at America. So the alternatively stark, intimate, dynamic, and evasive images of the deracinated postwar masters—Arthur Fellig (aka Weegee), Arbus, Model—attest. Weegee's shot of a weekend crowd at Coney Island (1942; Fig. 2), a startlingly dense image encompassing a crushing mass of bodies, each rendered with uncanny focus and particularity, brings to bear the raw insouciance of his mug work and scene-of-the-crime shots (*Bodies Taken from Burning Building*, c. 1940; *Their First Murder,* 1936) on the *Life*-style project of imaging the leisure worlds of postwar America. It is Weegee who thus literalizes Walter Benjamin's aperçu that every photograph is the scene of a crime. Here, his living subjects, eerily distinct yet de-individualized, offer themselves up to the camera with an eagerness that borders on the freakish, if not the menacing. Increasingly, Kozloff suggests, as the norms and conventions of postwar U.S. culture harden into the cheery platitudes and Cold Warriorship of the Eisenhower era, images made by Ted Croner, Louis Faurer, Sid Grossman, and Saul Leiter (Fig. 3) insist on the photographer's mission as outsider, on the felt sense of cultural, ethnic, and social alterity as the grounds for photographic vision. Training their cameras on the broken promises and unfinished business of American democracy, they produce aching, provocative images of individuals in the interstices, on the margins, within the shadows, of the ever more monolithic city.

Well served as both scholarship and pleasure are by Kozloff's claims, his ways of linking Jewishness with photographic history in the U.S. create as many questions as they answer. Most obviously, the exhibition begins to lose ground, or edge, as it nears the present day; the rubric of "active witnessing" simply can't account for the highly mediated responses to present-day America of contemporary photographers (whether Jewish or otherwise other), who respond as powerfully to art-world Zeitgeists as to the history of their medium. Sylvia Plachy's soft-focus color images of the emptied sites of the post-industrial city—e.g., *Meat Market* (1997)—glow with suggestion, but their logic is that of a studied interiority, the cityscape serving as an objective correlative for the artist's own oneiric disposition. In images by Ralph Gibson and Jeff Mermelstein, the raw eccentricity so courted by the past masters of marginality is prettified or made amusingly quaint, as in Mermelstein's Cibachrome print of a tiny Chihuahua perched aggressively atop a sidewalk pile of copies of the *New York Times* (Untitled, 1993). In a selection from Gibson's *Gotham Chronicles* series, we encounter a luminescent pair of blue shoes, shot against a turquoise wall adorned with a styrofoam cut-out of a human figure, all stripped of identifying context (Untitled, 1999). Neither menacing nor empathetic, the shot seems curiously unaware of its own antecedents—most obviously, Walker Evans's iconic image of a sharecropper's workboots—and thus cut off from the visceral, genuinely social, power of alterity.

The problem isn't that these photographers are more or less Jewish than their precedessors. Rather, the set of conditions, experiences, and identities to which "Jewish" refers is no longer the same. If, as Kozloff claims in an interview, Jewish photographers contribute something distinctive to photographic practice in America because they are "mov[ing] through territory they can't quite say they've claimed," the exhibition ultimately fails to register the ways in which both the territory and the nature of Jewish-American purchases on it alter—subtly, radically, structurally—during the decades in question. The category of "outsider," so intrinsic to photographic practice on both sides of the Jew/Gentile divide, surely takes on new resonances and references for Jewish-Americans, and Americans at large, in the wake of HUAC and the Army-McCarthy hearings (viz., Roy Cohn gloating over the death by electric chair of Ethel Rosenberg), the advent of hippie culture and feminism (pace Jerry Rubin and Gloria Steinem), the rebirth of Wall Street in the form of junk bond free-for-alls and insider trading (after Ivan Boesky and Michael Milken), the various Middle East crises, embargos, and intifadas, with the pressures they exert on Jewishness on the domestic front. Given this kaleidoscopic history, any unitary understanding of Jewish-inflected outsidership must be insufficient to the charged, complex circuits of self-understanding, the funhouse effect via which "American" and "Jew" reflect, interpenetrate, and mediate one another.

So what happens to marginality as a Jewish and/or photographic inheritance, a stylistic point of social departure? A case in point among classic practitioners is the controversial Diane Arbus (1923–1971). Daughter of a wealthy Jewish family, the Nemerovs—her father owned the thriving Fifth Avenue department store, Russeks; her brother Howard would become Poet Laureate of the U.S.—Arbus began her career making advertising images. In the mid-fifties she began studying under Model, at the same time choosing to "dissent" (as the critics have it) from fashion aesthetics and focus on what would become her signature subject: freaks. Infamous for the terrible accuracy of her images of asylum inmates, cross-dressers, carnival touts, baleful children, and mongoloids, all of whom display their desires for her camera with abandon, Arbus positions the viewer oppressively close to, and disturbingly distant from, their vulnerability. Critics have had mixed responses to her project—they note "the bad taste needed . . . to carry out her most chilling effects" and the "delicate superiority" her subjects endow on us as we "admire ourselves for respecting them";[2] no one seems to have understood it as a response to the psychic pressures of assimilated Jewish life.[3] Yet Arbus's embrace of freaks as—in her curious phrase—"aristocrats," individuals who have "already passed their test in life" by virtue of the embodiment of "trauma," smacks of "dissent" not merely from mid-century representational styles but from the codes of high bourgeois Jewishness at mid-century.[4]

Indeed, Arbus's most durable images (judging not only by exhibition catalogues but by the content of current personal websites) feature a variety of subjects variously coded as Jews. The iconic *Identical Twins, Roselle, N.J.* (1967) makes affective capital not just of the girls' generic sameness, but of their phenotypical and sartorial adherence to what registers as the physiognomy, the look, of Jewish striving in the age of Aquarius. *A Jewish Giant at Home with His Parents in the Bronx, N.Y.* (1970) features the professional giant Eddie

Carmel, whose head nearly grazes the ceiling of the family's generic lower-middle-class living room as he towers over his visibly bewildered parents. The image draws the energies of freakishness not only—perhaps not even primarily—from the spectacle of the giant; it is the absurdity of these wanting Jews, these little people, and the desires writ so palpably in their pretensions to belonging, that powers the dynamic of the image. Likewise, *King and Queen of a Senior Citizens Dance* (1970), whose elderly subjects (originally identified by Arbus as Yetta Granaf and Charles Fahrer) are rendered pathetic in the solemnity with which they allow themselves to be swathed in the accouterments—flimsy enormous robes, oversized crowns, rhinestone scepters—of a fantasy that ill befits them. Throughout Arbus's oeuvre, Jewishness serves less as a vector for the photographer's alterity than as itself a kind of stigmata, a source of freakishness the troubled camera deploys as a weapon and mode of escape.[5] What Arbus seeks, it might be argued, is not simply the vantage point of outsidership, but a decisive rejection of the bourgeois vulgarity—that is, the confidence in America—that characterized a family read as archetypal Nixon-era Jews (cf. Philip Roth's 1969 novel, *Portnoy's Complaint*).

The freak and heroin chics of photographers like Arbus and Nan Goldin, then, may owe their power not to alterity as an ethnic lineage so much as to alienation from success stories and assimilation narratives, to tribal rage or embarrassment, to an equation (however self-conscious) of Jewishness with insurgent conservatism no less than decadence and strident dissent. A similarly complex relation to Jewishness galvanizes the controversial aesthetic of Richard Avedon (b. 1923). Avedon began his career as a fashion photographer shooting achingly mimetic portraits, on location in the haunts of the Jewish West Side, of his sister, cousin, and mother in the house style of *Harper's Bazaar*. The retrospective fascination of these images has much to do with the ways in which he wills their dark, Ashkenazic faces and beloved forms into the postures of WASP style; it is here, we might say, that the signature ambiance of Avedon's storied shots of supermodels Suzy Parker, Dorian Leigh, and Elise Daniels—what one critic has called "the new look of meaningful angst"—is created.[6] Throughout his career, certain of Avedon's favored subjects allow him thus to flirt with the theatricality, the mystery, not of fashion or even celebrity but of Jewishness, an identity at once legible and invisible, inherited and created extemporaneously, genetic and existential. This kind of canniness underlies the 1946 images that are said to mark Avedon's epiphany about the possibilities of white-background portraiture, that hallmark device so conducive to generating menace and anomie. One day an elderly female Western Union messenger arrived at Avedon's studio to deliver a telegram and agreed to pose for him. The resulting images masterfully exploit the tension between photographic glamour and the subject's ethnically inflected look: men's shoes, bangle bracelets, shapeless garments, all suggesting a distinctive old-worldliness, a theatricality oddly genuine in its conjunction of alterity and innocence.[7] Here as throughout the body of Avedon's work, alterity is a richly varied resource: a will to photographic power and a mode of its refusal, a condition accessed by the photographer's Jewishness and a means of evading or transforming the meaning of that very tradition.[8]

All of which leaves us even farther from the prospect of defining a distinctly Jewish contribution to American image-making—to the good of nuanced thinking both about photographic history and the social experience of American Jews. For example, closer attention to image-making among first-generation Jewish-Americans offers complex object lessons in the perils of reading between "native" and immigrant experiences of American modernity. The Farm Security Administration images of Ben Shahn (1898–1969), particularly those shot in the rural South, have long been celebrated for their nuanced responses to U.S. racial history; less attention has been trained on the body of work he generated in response to his native grounds, the Lower East Side. In one particularly haunting image (*Untitled, Lower East Side, 1936*; Fig. 4), Shahn meditates on the structural paradoxes of an immigrant life experienced in tension with its received iconography. Arrested in front of the storefront of a kosher butcher, his three subjects suggest not only alternative modes of Jewish-American identity but competing aesthetics aligned with them. The figure to the viewer's right, partially cropped, eyes shadowed beneath the bill of his workman's cap, suggests the mute stolidity of the ethnographic subject à la Jacob Riis, denied the power of a returning gaze. The figure to the left, reduced to his jaunty white hat, becomes a mere compositional element, the embodiment of an instrumental modernity embraced by photographic modernism (cf. Berenice Abbott) and the alright-nik (cf. Abraham Cahan's David Levinsky) alike. Mediating both is the slight out-of-focus figure of the young woman: dreamy, evocative, intensely privatized. Neither ethnographic certitude nor the ordering powers of formalism alone can do justice to her; exceeding them, she generates the felt requirements for an alternative way of seeing. Grounding this effect is the camera's confrontation with the storefront, into whose interior we are unable to see and whose Yiddish emblazoning—a mark of hybridity, or mordant commentary?—reads "*kosher tshicken ma[rket]*." Who, in fact, is reflecting, reflecting on, whom? To what degree does Jewish immigrant experience, far from shtetlesque or merely imitative, already refract American modernity in ways that remain invisible to native, English-speaking, Americans?

Shahn's work on the East Side makes such questions about cultural transaction central to photographic looking; he bequeaths street photographers a visual language for calibrating the ambiguous relation to its subjects of the photographer: participant-observer, elegist, witness, thief. Among the many image-makers who follow in his wake, few so consistently thematize that ambiguity as Ryan Weideman. Born in 1941 to immigrant parents on the Lower East Side, self-taught like many of the premier photographers of the disproportionately Jewish and immigrant Photo League, Weideman belongs to a larger cohort of image-makers for whom documentary conventions are both provocative and suspect. Literalizing the problem of the photographer's place and role in the act of image-making, Weideman has produced a body of work sited in the taxi he drives to support himself, shooting actual passengers (and, most often, himself) with an improbably hand-held camera. The resulting double portraits eschew any pretense of disinterested looking. Inseparable from an economic transaction, admitting the photographer's dependence on vagaries of time, chance, and circumstance, they tap the vein of theatricality inherent to street photography yet insist on its mutuality, its life as an exchange between image-maker and subject. In one shot, a Latina woman thrusts her elbow insouciantly through the cab's opened partition as she gazes out the window; her reverie is unbreachable by the shutter's click that captures Weideman in full frontality, eager to connect. Another image, conversely, shows a middle-aged man leaning toward the camera with a hopeful smile and a hat smacking of Boca Raton; countering his openness is the massed figure of Weideman in the foreground, eyebrows arched, dark homburg swooped monitorily low. A latter-day rebuke to Walker Evans's infamous subway portraits—Evans used a hidden camera on subway trains without his subjects' knowledge or consent, reducing them to case studies in urban alienation and despair—Weideman's portraits record not just the theater of urban anonymity and self-staging, but the complexity of the photographer's desires, and their active role in the photographic event.

That Weideman's work relates this dynamic of contact and withdrawal to Jewish alterity is clarified in *Self Portrait with Passenger Allen Ginsberg* (1990; Fig. 5). Taking advantage of a chance encounter with the ur-figure of Jewish/American outsidership, author of the Beat anthems "Kaddish" and "Howl," Weideman's image stages a kind of midrash on the contending claims of photography and poetry as America's exemplary democratic form. From the rear of the cab, Ginsberg proffers a fresh bit of verse, penned on a curling ribbon of unclaimed cab receipts; his Whitmanesque effusion celebrates the encounter between "New York taxi-dermist, . . . Ryan Weideman" and "A Passenger Allen Ginsberg." But the shot recording this confident gesture constitutes a rebuttal to it, twinning its subjects only to distinguish them. Weideman counters Ginsberg's posture of expansiveness with a piercing intensity; against the parataxis of Ginsberg's verse he proffers the photographic fact of instantaneity. What is at stake here is no less than democratic representation itself, after documentary and Whitman alike. Incontrovertibly restive, variegated, aleatory, should it frame and contain multitudes, or submit itself to them? The thrust of the image is to make the Whitmanian project contingent on an alterity relocated on the terrain of Jewishness. But there, the shot implies, it has become a form of cultural capital, a commodity (literally, the price of Ginsberg's ticket), and even a mode of shtick. How, in the end, do claims for distinction and belonging move us; who, after all, is driving the vehicle?

If Weideman makes serendipity—in essence, the found Jew—serve an exploration of Jewishness as an aesthetic resource, the documentary work of Mary Ellen Mark takes the gesture another step. Born in 1940, Mark has been widely hailed as a photographer who tempers the dystopic vision of Arbus, Frank, and William Klein with genuine interest in the hard-fought identities of her marginal, alienated, and subcultural subjects; her best-known work features the Damm family in L.A. (its addict parents living in their dilapidated Ford), teenage runaways in Seattle, and female asylum inmates in Oregon. Mark has never identified herself as a Jewish photographer, although some of her earliest work centers on the Jewish-inflected communities of burlesque comedians and marriage brokers on 42nd Street; it was her growing reputation as a photojournalist that led to an assignment shooting the ballroom and retirement communities—not exclusively but preponderantly Jewish—of Miami. The resulting photographs are remarkable in two ways. First, they employ color, a strategy whose radical departure from the aesthetics of the witnessing tradition can hardly be overestimated. (Mark's notable subsequent work in color has been her visual record of such "exotic" subjects as brothels in Bombay and circus performers in Vietnam; its use in the playgrounds of Jewish retirement may signal her desire to exoticize a culture to which she remains uncomfortably close.) Second, they tap a vein of ambiguity with respect to their subjects—do they read as Jewish, and how? what kinds of cultural and social boundaries do they respect, inhabit, cross?—that intensifies their own productive ambiguity.

In this work, Jewishness notably becomes a matter of interplay between received ideas and the complexities of lived experience. One shot features an elderly man in a wheelchair, turned away from the camera (and apparently from life) as his tired caregiver, a black woman in nurse's whites, gazes out of the frame toward the sea. In another, we confront an elderly lodge member standing with proprietary pride beside a massive display of flags, ornaments, and paraphernalia featuring the Star of David and the American flag, in lurid colors and luxuriant combinations. Serape-draped mariachis serenade dozing retirees on the beach; men lounge poolside, their heads draped in towels, keffiyeh-style, their prominent noses daubed with zinc oxide; a couple sporting his-and-hers leisure wear shows off the property for which they presumably fled the old enclaves of Brooklyn and the Bronx. Throughout these images, Jewishness is both marked and invisible, present and imagined; it is by turns vestigial, stylistic, and evasive, the vanishing-point where Mark's purchase on what she calls "voyeurism" as a photographic practice meets the self-imagination of her subjects (Untitled, 1979; Fig. 6).

Here, we can see, we have left behind the premise—or rather the understanding of Jewishness—that governs both Kozloff's show and key responses to it. (What is at stake is hardly the biologism embraced by *New York Times* critic Richard B. Woodward, who worries about the number of photographers in Kozloff's catalogue who are "only half-Jewish," and argues that a "more profitable line of inquiry" might be made by focusing on "the history of photography as"—surprise—"a technology and a business."[9]) For whether Jews or Judaism remain the explicit subject of the camera's gaze—as they do in Leonard Freed's work among Hasidic communities, "The Dance of the Pious"; in the rabbinically trained Saul Leiter's early work; in the nuanced shots of modern Orthodox communities by London-born, L.A.-based documentarian Bernard Mendoza (see p. 277)—the one-to-one correspondence between Jewishness and marginality has been ruptured. In Weideman's images as in Marks's, we feel the play of gazes between subjects and modes of witnessing or looking variously assimilated under the rubric of "Jew." Indeed, identifying an embrace of marginality as the most salient characteristic of photography (Jewish-American or otherwise) discounts some of the most powerful social gestures accomplished through the medium. It is not only a will to photographic power that is served by the fashion work of an Avedon, a Louise Dahl-Wolfe, an Irving Penn. Likewise, in the field of abstraction, self-invention as American moderns by Jewish émigrés has been the order of the day. Man Ray (né Emmanuel Radnitsky, 1890–1976) essentially founded street photography's most powerful alternative—the lineage that emphasized formal experimentation and the manipulation of images for aesthetic effect—when he began collecting and publishing images from

Eugène Atget's documentary project on vanishing Paris. Manipulating image sequencing, narrative possibilities, and context, Man Ray appropriated the work of his classic predecessor in something like the way Jewish-American intellectuals of the next generation—Lionel Trilling, Philip Rahv, Alfred Kazin—would rewrite the oeuvre of Henry James. (It was with similar logic, it can be argued, that the Jewish and immigrant makers of canonical street photography responded to the work of non-Jewish predecessors like Walker Evans and Lewis Hine.) To the extent that Jewishness equated with shared experiences of immigration, the extraordinarily tight social networks of the Lower East Side, left culture, and the tenement form, the founding cohort of street photographers can fairly be said to have created a unified and distinctive photographic vision. But that understanding of Jewishness, while compelling and ready to hand, ill serves the complexity of Jewish Americans' shifting relations to the tradition they are said consciously or unconsciously to exemplify. However prominent or preponderant among U.S. photographers, those of Jewish descent define and respond to their relations to image-making, and thus their purchases on witnessing, with a far greater range of affects than the outsider model implies.

What, for example, of the significant cohort of Jewish-American photographers who—following on Avedon and Arbus—make capital of long-standing associations of Jews and Jewishness with theatricality, excess, artifice, and the stage? The most powerful vector of assimilation and self-representation for Jewish immigrants in the New World was the Yiddish theater, out of whose traditions and institutional forms grew, as recent scholarship reminds us, American avant-garde theater, Hollywood, and Broadway alike. For Kozloff, a narrow version of theatricality is central to the tradition of witnessing: the transient and serendipitous eventfulness of the momentary encounters, the glimpsed possibilities, that make up the life of the urban street. But another kind of theatricality enters into the picture. In the work of photographers like Les Krims and Joel-Peter Witkin—the latter infamous for his lush stagings of such perverse tableaux as *Shoe Fucker and Woman Who Believes She's Becoming a Camera* (1998) and *A Day in the Country* (1998), a shot of a woman about to be penetrated by the fantastically engorged penis of a horse—exploration of desire and stress on cultural links between theatricality, deviance, and Jewishness go hand in hand.[10]

That the shock effects of such work are predicated on a popular iconography of Jewishness is foregrounded in the Gen-X images of Charlie White (b. 1972). A recent graduate of New York's School of Visual Arts, White works out of the cultural matrix of Pasadena, California; his images map the rapidly shifting territories of belonging, ethnicity, assimilation, and alienation we otherwise know as SoCal, the Valley, and greater L.A. In his most extensive series to date, *Understanding Joshua* (1995–2000), White photographs his tellingly named puppet-cum-alien, a "living, breathing" avatar of "insecurity," in staged scenarios of abjection, class (or rather ethnic) hatred, and longing (Fig. 7). That "Joshua's" not-quite-fantasy world is sharply "divided between blondes and brunettes," the former inhabiting "a superior world of cleanliness, beauty, and organization," suggests the continuing power of ethnic iconography in the very site where it is most powerfully produced and disseminated.[11] Yet White's work deftly eschews the obvious frisson of the Woody Allenesque schlemiel. More visceral and unpleasant, his images revel in the obscenity of a male self-loathing openly coded as Jewish yet more broadly, more representatively, American.

Very different modes of theatricality or image staging, and of play with fantasies implicating Jewishness at their core, inform the work of David Levinthal (b. 1949). A native of San Francisco, Levinthal began his career as a landscape photographer after the ur-goyish landscapists Ansel Adams and Edward Weston, but abandoned that mode for the studio. His first published project, *Hitler Moves East* (1977), was a collaboration with Yale classmate Garry Trudeau including photographs of re-enactments of Hitler's Eastern campaign staged with four-inch toy soldiers. Levinthal has since produced Polaroid, often large-format shots of toys composed in elaborate dioramas featuring everything from Barbies and Wild West figurines to noir-styled tableaux (which might well be read as an ironic commentary on the photographic tradition of alterity privileged by Kozloff); recently, *XXX* (2000) shows lifelike dolls in fetish wear striking industrial-strength S/M postures. Some key oppositions run throughout this body of work. Always beginning with actual artifacts (in the case of

"Blackface," for example, tiny turn-of-the-century figurines of Uncle Tom, Eliza, and Simon Legree), Levinthal's images insist on the persistence and depth of the fantasies these objects bespeak. He keeps us oscillating, uncannily, between a monumentality achieved via extreme close-up and the scale of the miniature; glossy and color-saturated, his images make a certain beauty instrumental to our encounter with scenes of abjection, trauma, and violence.

That Nazis and Holocaust material find their way into Levinthal's work hardly qualifies them as Jewish in any coherent sense. Rather, Levinthal suggests how deeply national mythologies, no less than private desires, are sustained through the manipulation of images and icons. Further, he notes, the historical materials of the Holocaust, not unlike those of blackface minstrelsy, have become intrinsic to America's self-imagination.[12] Like cops and robbers or cowboys and Indians, the ur-drama of Axis vs. Allies offers itself up to baby-boom America's definitively Manichean imagination. But the results are hardly (to use the obvious phrase) black and white. With what or whom does the user of these toy stand-ins, or the viewer of these photographs, identify? What do we make of the initial sensation they inevitably afford, that of coming home to beloved childhood objects, to popular visual conventions, to cultural icons? Nowhere are these questions more pressing than in Levinthal's *Mein Kampf* (1998), a series of evocative yet ambiguous re-stagings of Holocaust history for a U.S. audience. In one image, the viewer is invited to delight in the detailed articulation of a model railroad car, complete with a tiny figure gazing from the platform into the shadowed interior of the car. That this image also references an *Aktion*, a historical step in the work of the Final Solution, is a fact we experience as eerily extrinsic to the pleasures of recognition. In another shot, the scarlet blur of a fringed Reich banner held aloft by two toy soldiers in silhouette, shadowed against a soft-focus backdrop of monumental columns, is thrillingly theatrical, affording all the pleasures of the wax museum and Ripley's Believe-It-Or-Not in one (Fig. 8). Analogously, Levinthal's images render their Jewish "subjects" troublingly beautiful, wracked yet eerily human. Throughout, these Holocaust tableaux are staged with an ambiguity that challenges America's confident mythologizing.

Playing with history, they also suggest how fully it exceeds our grasp.[13]

Like the toy objects in Levinthal's photographs, then, Jewishness itself as an aesthetic or cultural resource at the start of the twenty-first century has become more than a bit unfocused. But the fact that non-Jewish photographers, or those who can only be tentatively identified as Jews, might produce these kinds of images is precisely the point. No longer meaningful as the originating social experience of the first and second photographic generations, the Jewishness that drives, impels, informs, or troubles photographic production is too various and complex to take unitary form. At the same time, the originary ethnic matrix—immigrant status, cross-cultural moorings, generational affiliations, ethos of witnessing—that defined early street photography has itself become intrinsic to the history and generative energies of the medium. If Jewish photographers became self-styled alienated Americans by appropriating the techniques of non-Jewish masters, their visual strategies and self-presentation—variously marked or coded as Jewish—make themselves available to later practitioners for the same kind of love and theft. Kozloff's "Jewish eye" is thus presumably available for adoption (or implantation?) by photographers at large, particularly those questioning what it means to witness, to work across borders or boundaries, to make images in an increasingly media-saturated and globally commodified world. Like it or not, all photography in the vein of documentary—and of street work, and of fashion, and of photomontage, and of social consciousness—partakes in, references, talks back to the sensibility of the masters.

Exemplary is the recent work of photographer and installation artist Zoe Leonard (b. 1961). Often identified with gay and lesbian activism through her projects with ACT UP and radical feminist networks, Leonard has remained silent on the subject of her ethnic affiliation; her best-known images include portraits of contemporary performance artist/bearded lady Jennifer Miller and shots of women's vaginas mounted alongside reproductions of canonical Western paintings.[14] But lately she has begun a series of color photographs (again, the hint of exoticism) of storefronts in minority and working-class neighborhoods in New York. That project only apparently departs from earlier works coded as politicized, deviant, or queer. In getting back to basics—the iconic storefront work of Atget, Evans, Shahn—Leonard is also revisiting the cultural project of street photographers like Siskind, Levitt, Arnold Eagle, Walter Rosenblum, and Sol Libsohn, whose purchase on the vanishing folkways and economic struggles of black Harlem was predicated on their collective connections with earlier, Jewish Harlem and with the tenement form. Stripped of visual ornament, Leonard's shots of shuttered family businesses and failing neighborhood shops—*Shoes, 425, Mandel Tobacco* (Fig. 9)—reference not only a historical past, in which Jewish experience was visibly marked on the urban landscape, but a photographic one; thus the unwitting continuity between Shahn's image and the evocative *Mister Chicken* (Fig. 10). Her images read ultimately not as elegies to lost community so much as a testimony to the photographer's attempt to codify her own relation to an archive of Jewish—or maybe "Jewish"—witnessing.

Nowhere is the felt fact of this Jewish trace within photography—that medium obsessed with its own status as a trace, what Susan Sontag calls "something stenciled off the real, like a footprint or a death mask"—more marked than in the work of Pedro Meyer.[15] Born in 1935 to German parents who had fled the Nazis for Spain, Meyer moved with his family to Mexico at the age of two after the expulsion of Spanish Jews under Franco. Although he started his career as a documentary purist, producing "straight" black and white images of Mexican oil workers, Nicaraguan guerilla camps, Israel after the 1967 war, he began experimenting during the 1980s with the possibilities of digital camera work and has never looked back. For Meyer, the shift from the image as a metallic imprint to a computer-generated dot grid is liberating rather than distorting; it frees the photographer and viewer alike from the illusion of unmediated representation, of singular truth to experience. He thus views his composite, enhanced, and collaged images as powerfully documentary, in the sense that they record with even greater fidelity the lived act of witnessing: "To the silver halides or dyes," he argues, "I can now add my own memory."[16]

The most extensive record of this digital work to date is the aptly titled *Truths & Fictions*, first published as a CD-ROM catalogue in 1995. Subtitled *A Journey from Documentary to Digital Photography*, the project is also the record of Meyer's literal journey on a Guggenheim grant—15,000 miles of road tripping—documenting America as northern neighbor, image factory, world power, and dream world. Critics have canonized these images as an updated version of Robert Frank's iconic study, *The Americans* (1959). But Meyer's descriptions make it clear that he intends to counter Frank's anomic vision—the masterful evocation by the knowing outsider of a people frozen in postures of angst and despair—with a more complex understanding of the encounter between the camera and its subjects. For Meyer, America can no longer be viewed from any stable and unitary outside; it has "become a mosaic of different cultures," necessitating a more nuanced positioning of the photographer in relation to a heterogeneous landscape.

That act of location turns out to be crucially linked not merely with the new technologies of memory but with Jewishness itself as an ur-form of cross-cultural engagement (rather than alterity tout court). Indeed, in the reception of Meyer's work, the fact of his anomalous Jewishness—perched between Ashkenazic and Sephardic sites of generation; put in conversation with a Mexican, and indigenous mestizo, cultural heritage he has self-consciously adopted—is inseparable from his embrace of post-documentary witnessing.[17] An influential critic sympathetic to his work thus sums up Meyer's general reception: "why has an author, who for more than twenty years belonged to the cult of straight photography, suddenly converted to an opposite religion?"[18] But Meyer has decisively not "converted"; the "hybridization" that defines the new visual imaginary in a digital world is both symptomatic and synecdochic of the Jewishness that serves him as an aesthetic resource. If the lush, textured images that ensue from Meyer's work in the lab and on the screen raise questions about their own status or ontology, they also predicate the "new" documentary consciousness on a syncretism to which Jewish-inflected experiences of mobility and continuity alike are key.

To be sure, the syncretism Meyer's images create and insist on is quite catholic—and often mestizo Catholic—in content. The Statue of Liberty's torch arm is welded onto a residential street, where a passerby appears to muse on the visitation. The plaster statuette of a Spanish conquistador looms over a rocky rural landscape as an ancient Mixtec woman, gnarled fingers to her mouth, gazes from painfully weathered eyes at the camera. The dramatic shot of a ruined temple, into which a colonial residence has been inserted, is presided over by a Oaxacan deity; at the center of this sacred space protrudes a human arm, holding aloft like a sacrament a glowing orange basketball (Fig. 11). Throughout Meyer's work, devils tempt, saints float, the dead walk; the magical realism we associate with Latin and Latino Americas abounds. But what unifies this body of work is an argument for the fact and possibilities of bracing cultural encounter, of the vibrant and strangely beautiful spaces created as subjects carry their memories and spiritual experience across time zones, temporality, and other psychic boundaries. The grounds of that argument is not Jewishness per se, but the fact of some imprint thereof, writ as a commitment to the frictions and surprises of multiply migratory, multiply embedded histories. If Kozloff's masters of urban anomie are never at home, Meyer's composite subjects carry a home within, in the form of a capacity for memory not degraded but enhanced by its dislocation.

Meyer's most charged images are thus not the obviously narrative, or easily ironic, shots of American vs. Mexican stand-off, but those that render the terrain of cross-cultural encounter dreamlike, palpable, uncanny. Emblematic of his attempt to create a new kind of visual experience is *Moses and Wonder Woman, Teposcolula Oaxaca* (1991/93; Fig. 12). Here, two figures pose for the camera in the center of a muddy flowing stream—Red Sea, Rio Grande—whose steep slopes are lined with leafy trees. A woman in a purple flowered dress, holding a plastic cup, sports a cheap mask of the comic book heroine; her male companion, dressed in a serape and traditional straw hat and carrying an earthen water flask, gazes at us from behind an oversized and garish mask—the Moses of the title—striking for its chalk-white color and plaintive expression. Tapping the iconography of crossing, conflating the Promised Land narratives of Jewish-Americans and Chicanos, Meyer suggests how richly palimpsestic, and how mutually informing, are the fantasies of overlapping diasporas. There is no simply originary mythic ground, no obvious vector of assimilation. The masks and identities donned as these subjects move across borders and checkpoints, and within fantasies, bespeak real histories of loss and conflict, but they also hold out the possibility of a transformative synthesis by which collective memory might be heightened and more profoundly engaged.

It is, Meyer boldly suggests, photography itself that creates such synthesis, at once aesthetic and social, rather than the luck of found truth or the so-called decisive moment. In a twenty-first-century America that feels increasingly virtual, media-driven, rhizomic, and implicated, photography's power resides not in the incessant production of images, whose fidelity to experience we have learned to distrust, but in its generation of what Meyer calls "the memory of images": an archive of witnessed moments that repay our continuing scrutiny with their provocation to confront what it means to put ourselves in history. To that archive, Jewishness has been crucial—but in no singular form, and with no unitary, readily traceable effect. The body of photographs that comprise an American history is, and is not, the purchase of American Jews on the culture they were transforming as they framed it. What that archive does exemplify is the mutually mediating effects of "American" and "Jew" over the course of a fraught and storied epoch. Like the lost subjects to which images bear witness, neither could, or ever will, remain quite the same.[19]

NOTES

Thanks to Anthony Allen, David Levinthal, Bruce Silverstein, Charlie White, and Pedro Meyer, and to Sean Ulmer, University Curator of the University of Michigan Museum of Art.

1A. D. Coleman, "No Pictures: Some Thoughts on Jews in Photography," in *C: The Speed of Light* (New York: Image/World Syndication Services, 1997), 2; http://www.nearbycafe.com/adc/adcmenu/readings/jews.html. I am indebted at large to Coleman's encyclopedic accounting. In mounting this argument, Coleman elaborates on the popular jeremiad of Neil Postman, *Amusing Ourselves to Death: Public Discourse in the Age of Show Business* (New York: Viking Press, 1986).

2Max Kozloff, "The Uncanny Portrait: Sander, Arbus, Samaras," in *Photography and Fascination* (Danbury, New Hampshire: Addison House, 1978), 163; Amy Goldin, cited in Kozloff, "Uncanny Portrait," 160.

3Compare here Susan Sontag's exemplary reading in the indispensable *On Photography:* "Arbus's work is reactive—reactive against gentility, against what is approved. It was her way of saying fuck *Vogue,* fuck fashion, fuck what's pretty." *On Photography* (New York: Farrar, Straus and Giroux, 1970), 44. To this list might easily be added "Jewishness," or rather the striving WASP-identified Jewishness Arbus conflated with fashion as her own family's enterprise. In the wake of Patricia Bosworth's highly controversial and unauthorized *Diane Arbus: A Biography* (New York: Avon, 1984), which speculates freely on Arbus's sexual and erotic relations with her freak subjects, attempts to link Arbus's private life with her images have been discredited. This may account for the absence of speculation about Jewishness itself, historically linked with perversion, eccentricity, and deviant sexuality, as an informing element of Arbus's work. An incisive reading of her attempts to shift a cultural understanding of "the relationship between deviance and normality" that nonetheless leaves the issue of Jewishness unexplored is given by Rachel Adams, "Freak Photography," in *Sideshow U.S.A.: Freaks and the American Cultural Imagination* (Chicago: University of Chicago Press, 2001), 112–37; for Adams, Arbus's reference to Jewishness in "Jewish Giant" "amplifies the photograph's ambiguity" rather than generating its distance or anomie (247, fn 29).

[4]Diane Arbus, *Diane Arbus: An Aperture Monograph* (Millerton, New York: Aperture, 1972).

[5]Other suggestive images in this regard are *A Widow in Her Bedroom, N.Y.C.* (1963), *A Family on Their Lawn One Sunday in Westchester, N.Y.* (1968), *A Jewish Couple Dancing, N.Y.C.* (1963), *Transvestite at a Drag Ball, N.Y.C.* (1970), and *Woman on a Park Bench on a Sunny Day, N.Y.C.* (1969); all are included in the canonical monograph *Diane Arbus*.

[6]Adam Gopnick, "The Light Writer," in *Richard Avedon, Evidence 1944–1994,* ed. Mary Shanahan (New York: Random House, 1994), 111.

[7]These early images, along with Avedon's first white-background portraits, are available in *Evidence*, 122–23, 125–26, 128.

[8]Nor did Avedon neglect the possibilities of play with codes of Jewishness from behind the camera. Among his most storied images—one that irrevocably altered received notions of the contract between photographers and their subjects—was his 1957 portrait of a distinctly haggard and abject Duke and Duchess of Windsor, giving themselves up to the camera with startling intimacy. Having arrived late to their sitting, Avedon improvised a story about his taxi hitting a dog; it had the desired effect on his subjects, he noted, "because they loved dogs a lot more than they did Jews." Avedon, cited in Michael Kimmelman, "Images that Burn into the Mind," *New York Times*, Arts, September 27, 2002, 1:1.

[9]Richard Woodward, "Behind a Century of Photos, Was There a Jewish Eye?" *New York Times*, Arts and Leisure, July 7, 2002, 2:1, 30.

[10]On Witkin's identifications with Jewishness as the primal source of his "true pervert" sensibility (in spite of the Catholic inflection of his imagery), see Cintra Wilson, "Joel-Peter Witkin," *salon.com*, May 9, 2000; http://archive.salon.com/people/bc/2000/05/09/witkin/.

[11]"Interview," "Charlie White: Photographer," *TheArtBiz.com;* http://www.theartbiz.com/peerarchive.asp?WHICH=7.

[12]Conjointly with the Kozloff show, the Jewish Museum in New York mounted an exhibit curated by Norman L. Kleeblatt entitled "Mirroring Evil: Nazi Imagery/Recent Art"; the exhibit was designed to explore the uses made of Holocaust artifacts, images, and icons in the work of thirteen Jewish and non-Jewish artists working mainly in Europe. Levinthal's work was not included here, presumably because it so centrally concerns the texture of American fantasies and elaborations of U.S. national myths. The full range of images can be found in the exhibition catalogue, *Mirroring Evil: Nazi Imagery/Recent Art*, ed. Norman L. Kleeblatt (New Brunswick: Rutgers University Press, 2002).

[13]In the Detroit Institute of Arts exhibition of *Hitler Moves East* (1991),

Levinthal included not only his photographic re-enactments of the movements of the German army but the playsets that were his actual subjects—the soft plastic figures, props, and tin backgrounds manufactured for the pleasure of American children by such immigrant Jewish entrepreneurs as Louis Marx and Company. That strategy seems designed to gesture toward the actual social history that produced the encounters on which Levinthal riffs—i.e., those of American children with toy models of Nazi and Russian armies contrived by displaced Jews.

[14]Evidence of the terms of Leonard's reception as queer and activist artist is amply provided in "Zoe Leonard Interviewed by Anna Blume," in *Secession: Zoe Leonard 23.7–14.9, 1997* (Vienna: Wiener Secession 1997), 8–23. For a project description that exemplarily conflates social activism against gentrification, a feeling for the beauty of vanishing cultures and urban landscapes, and the "connectedness" of such ethnically "migratory" neighborhoods as Harlem and the Lower East Side—both sites of Jewish photographic and social intervention—see Leonard, "Out of Time," *October* 100 (Spring 2002), 88–97.

[15]Sontag, *On Photography*, 153.

[16]"Expanding Memory: An Interview with Pedro Meyer," *Truths & Fictions* (New York: Aperture, 1995), 108.

[17]Meyer's work will inevitably recall, both in content and use of folk objects and color, the popular visual form of retablo painting. That his aim is the redirection of photographic, rather than folk or more specifically Mexican or Chicano folk, conventions becomes more apparent when his digitalized images are viewed in contrast to his own earlier work. For a helpful contextual discussion of retablo and its relation to the social contexts of criollo, mestizo, and border identity, see Jorge Durand and Douglas S. Massey, "The Origins of Votive Painting," in *Miracles on the Border: Retablos of Mexican Migrants to the United States* (Tucson: University of Arizona Press, 1995), 5–22.

[18]Joan Fontcuberta, "Pedro Meyer: Truths, Fictions, and Reasonable Doubts," trans. Dalia Rabinovich, in *Truths & Fictions,* 10.

[19]Meyer, "I Photograph to Remember" (Produced by Thomas Luehson), 1991; http://www.zonezero.com/exposiciones/fotografos/fotografio/pag1.html.

JEWISH AMERICA THROUGH THE LENS

A PORTFOLIO

Fig. 1. Lisette Model, *Reflection, New York*, c. 1939–1945
© Lisette Model Foundation
Courtesy Galerie Baudoin Lebon, Paris

Fig. 2. Weegee (Arthur Fellig), *Coney Island at Noon, Saturday, July 5, 1942*

Collection of the International Center of Photography

Fig. 3. Saul Leiter, *Barbershop 75 cents,* c. 1950s,
© Saul Leiter
Courtesy Howard Greenberg Gallery, New York

Fig. 4. Ben Shahn, *Untitled (Lower East Side, New York City),* 1936
Courtesy President and Fellows of Harvard College

Fig. 5. Ryan Weideman, *Self-Portrait with Passenger Allen Ginsberg,* 1990
Courtesy Bruce Silverstein Gallery, New York

Fig. 6. Mary Ellen Mark, *Untitled (Miami Beach, Florida)*, 1977
Courtesy Mary Ellen Mark

Fig. 7. Charlie White, *Cocktail Party,* from *Understanding Joshua*, 1995
Courtesy Andrea Rosen Gallery, New York

Fig. 8. David Levinthal, from *Mein Kampf,* 1993/94
Twin Palms Publisher, 1996
Courtesy David Levinthal

Fig. 9. Zoe Leonard, *Mandel Tobacco*, 1999/2001
Courtesy Paula Cooper Gallery, New York

Fig. 10. Zoe Leonard, *Mister Chicken*, 1998/2000
Courtesy Paula Cooper Gallery, New York

Fig. 11. Pedro Meyer, *Religious Syncretism, Santiago Nu Yoo, Oaxaca,* 1990/93
Courtesy Pedro Meyer

Fig. 12. Pedro Meyer, *Moses and Wonder Woman, Teposcolula Oaxaca,* 1991/93
Courtesy Pedro Meyer

ALISA SOLOMON

INTIFADA DIPTYCH

1. Withdrawing from Lebanon

It's in the *Lebanon Star*—an English-language daily published in Beirut—that I first read about the suicide bombing of a Tel Aviv discotheque on June 1, 2001 that kills twenty-one Israelis, almost all of them teenagers. I study the paper, drinking thick, sweet coffee in a cafe overlooking the glinting Mediterranean in a northern coastal city of Lebanon called Tripoli, where I have come to cover a two-week workshop the Living Theater is conducting with some forty theater students from the University of Beirut. I imagine the site of the attack—the Dolphinarium—whose own Mediterranean shore I sat gazing at exactly a year earlier.

I had been in Tel Aviv for an academic theater conference in June 2000—my only trip of half a dozen to Israel so far when I haven't been on assignment as a journalist. So, for a change, I was not racing from the Negev to the Galilee, finding my way around the West Bank and Gaza Strip, nor turning every conversation with a friend, relative, shopkeeper, waiter, peace activist or cabdriver into a pesky interview. I marveled—guiltily, of course—at how relaxed I felt, at how much I could actually enjoy the place. Having been to Israel previously to cover crises—the first Intifada in 1988, the Gulf War in '91, the period after the Rabin assassination in '95—I had always arrived at Ben Gurion in one unshakable way like the American Zionist I was raised to be: with a mission. Never mind that my politics had long swerved away from the milk-and-honey homilies of Hebrew School (in part, precisely because I had visited the territories and seen the occupation in all its demoralizing and destructive detail); I had absorbed well the principle that I was to go to Israel not for fun or careerism (if that's what academic conferences represent), but out of a sense of duty.

But there I was, in a sparkling spring, enjoying grilled fish by the sea, arguing aesthetics till all hours in friends' apartments, even going to the beach. I had harbored few illusions about the Oslo accords. I had been at Manger Square on *erev*-Christmas in 1995, when IDF troops were redeploying from Bethlehem, the red-and-green pennants festooning the plaza doing both national and yuletide duty. Amid the celebrations, a young man named Khaled told me: "It's impossible not to be excited here. Usually Christmas means curfews and Israeli soldiers keeping us away. It's never been like this before that we could come out and sing and dance in our own city. But that doesn't mean the Oslo agreement is good. The problem of refugees isn't even mentioned. The Israelis still control our roads and electricity and water. Tonight feels like freedom, but tomorrow the people will be stopped at a roadblock and wake up." A joke going around the West Bank at the time held that Palestinians had made a special deal with Japanese automakers to produce special cars for the checkpoint-laden roads: no fourth gear. I knew very well that land expropriation and settlement building had accelerated since '93, especially under Ehud Barak. Still, June 2000 was a hopeful, largely trouble-free time. My partner and I asked a friend to take us for a day's drive through the Golan, figuring it might be our only chance to see the Banyas waterfalls or eat kanafe in Majdal Shams without a Syrian visa.

For the first time I'd felt in Israel the mood I had been well-trained to expect there: the promise of new possibility. And, though more guarded, such eagerness was palpable in Palestine, too. Take my little scholarly precinct, for example: an actor we met, a Palestinian citizen of Israel, invited us to the opening of a play about the experiences of the 1948 refugees, which he was starring in at a new theater in Ramallah; the production as well as the new facility and all its vibrant activity, he beamed, was evidence of the ever-growing vitality of inquiry and creativity in Palestine. Just a few weeks before we arrived, a Tel Aviv friend, a Jewish director, had staged a project with Jews and Palestinians that used testimonies from court cases and journalistic reports, presented by actors as well as actually aggrieved people, as a model truth and reconciliation commission. Both endeavors, because of their footing on frank recognition of the past, looked hopefully, and not naively, toward the future.

Most heartening, right before our arrival that spring, Israel withdrew from southern Lebanon after eighteen years, with wide public support spearheaded by an anti-war group called the Four Mothers. At around the same time, the Israeli courts ruled that a lesbian couple could jointly adopt a child. *Ha'aretz* celebrated the forward-looking spirit occasioned by both developments with a charming cartoon: A child tells an IDF soldier, "I have two mommies." The soldier replies, "So what? I have four." How beautiful it was that June, a cool constant breeze softening the sun's harsh edge.

Now, in June 2001, the same sea breeze is wafting over me in Tripoli, Lebanon. But the climate has changed radically.

The Lebanese have just finished celebrating the anniversary of Israel's withdrawal from their territory, but the Palestinians have had no such cause for rejoicing. It's been eleven months since the Camp David talks collapsed, nine since Ariel Sharon strode to Haram al Sharif/Temple Mount backed by a huge police force to boast that a Jew has the right to go anywhere in Jerusalem he wants, four since escalating violence swept him into office (though not on the landslide the American media reported. Sharon won votes from some 35 percent of the electorate; so many Israelis either submitted blank ballots—"none of the above"—or declined to vote that the old warrior was elected with *fewer* votes than Netanyahu had garnered when he'd *lost* to Barak in the prior election.) Despite the heady feeling of the previous summer, the collapse of the "peace process" could not have been a surprise to anyone who had noticed the continued construction of Jewish-only bypass roads chopping the West Bank up into disconnected cantons, the relentless rise of yet more settlements, the persistent Israeli control of the movement of water, capital, labor, and plain folks. As Jeff Halper, the Israeli anthropologist who heads the Committee Against House Demolitions there puts it, prisoners might be granted 95 percent of a penitentiary's grounds—cells, mess hall, recreation area—but as long as someone else determines where they can go and when, they are not free, independent, autonomous, self-determining. Only the prevailing myth that "Barak made the most generous offer and the Palestinians answered with violence because they just don't want peace" could cloud the fact that the Aqsa Intifada was an effort to resist an occupation that wasn't going away. The myth prevailed all the same, egged on by a massive Israeli PR campaign in the U.S.—and, no less, by the rise in Palestinian extremists' attacks on civilians inside the green line.

Ruchama Marton, president of Israel's Physicians for Human Rights, says that for Israeli Jews, history always begins with the latest trauma. Thus Palestinian violence is detached from context, never recognized as being a reaction—as well as prod—to any assassinations or bombings or house demolitions or civilian casualties Israel might have inflicted. The Dolphinarium bombing—disgusting, deplorable, indefensible, do I need to say?—is quickly pointed to as "proof" of preternatural Palestinian Jew-hatred, of Palestinian insistence on "pushing Jews into the sea," of justification for any collective punishment by the IDF. And collective punishment does come, swiftly and mercilessly. Israel's military commander for the West Bank tells the Israeli press in the summer of 2001 that strangling the Palestinian economy, bulldozing houses, and restricting people's movement *produces* rather than *prevents* suicide bombers. (And a year later, defense minister Benjamin Ben-Eliezer makes the same assertion about the IDF incursions said to root out terrorism: ". . . the operations themselves become a hothouse that produces more and more new suicide bombers. The military actions kindle the frustration, hatred, and despair and are the incubator for the terror to come." Since June 2001, the spiral has tightened and gathered speed, sucking ever more innocent people into the vortex of violence).

Urging people to swim out of the relentless undertow of vengeance has been a central aim of the Living Theater since its establishment in 1948. In Lebanon in 2001, the lefty, international, boho, anarchist-pacifist, experimental theater company founded by rootless cosmopolitans is trying to create a show with several dozen diverse Lebanese students who are just old enough to have real memories of their fifteen-year civil war, which claimed nearly 200,000 lives and displaced two-thirds of the population of four million. Here, the news of the Dolphinarium bombing becomes a flashpoint for exposing the wide rifts in perception not only between the American/European artists and the Arab college kids, but within the Living Theater (LT) and among the students themselves. The crash of reactions splinters something in me as well.

That very day the LT holds an emergency meeting in response to bad news they've just had from their trip organizer, Habiba. In addition to presenting their anti-death penalty play *Not in My Name* in Tripoli, the group plans to perform in Khiam—the site of the former notorious prison where fighters against Israeli occupation, as well as their relatives, neighbors, and many other innocent bystanders, were detained and tortured, mostly by troops in the South Lebanese Army, Israel's proxy militia. Word has just come that the work must be approved by censors from Hizbullah, the militant Shi'ite faction that controls southern Lebanon and the museum/memorial that Khiam has become.

A gray-haired, gray-suited apparatchik of Hizbullah turns up in Tripoli to have an advance look at the script. Though skeptical, he's held off somewhat when he's told that there isn't one—the LT is using the method of collective creation to develop a piece with the students, and the workshops are only a couple of days old. But his demand riles up some members of the LT.

The two Germans in the company in particular object to having to be declared kosher by "terrorists." One of them holds up the day's front page story about the disco bombing from the *Herald Tribune*—and a German film crew making a documentary about the LT that happens to be along on the trip zooms in on the tears streaming down her face and the photo of the carnage in the paper. No matter that Lebanon's Hizbullah had nothing to do with the bombing at the Dolphinarium. Such instantaneous terro-porn graphs all attacks on Israel—violence against civilians, assaults on occupying soldiers (Hizbullah's primary target), even verbal critique—onto a continuum whose endpoint is Jewish extermination, and then collapses it all into a single undifferentiated mass, unavailable for analysis.

The Jews in the company—artistic directors Judith Malina and Hanon Reznikov—are the ones to point out that the LT has frequently performed under despicable governments, precisely to bring their defiant message to regimes where it's seldom heard.

"We went to Milosevic's Belgrade. And we went there to object to the violence, the same as here. I'll go and say 'peace' anywhere," Malina asserts. Another actor responds, "As a German I just don't want to be linked to a regime that wants to destroy the Jewish state."

Replies Malina: "Was it okay to be linked to a regime that destroys Bosnian Muslims? What's the difference?"

Jewish history, of course, though no one says so, least of all the Germans. I'm both touched and disturbed by their reaction, knowing too well how the casting of Jews as eternal, innocent victims first of all, conflates Jew and Israeli (or, more precisely, the Jewish People and the Israeli State), and second, constructs us as incapable of committing atrocity except, perhaps, in the justifiable case of self-defense. While Nazis and their enablers may have fantasized about Jewish control of media, finance, and eventually the entire world, no Jewish army ever invaded Berlin. Hizbullah came into existence precisely to resist the Israeli military incursion.

Not that Hizbullah doesn't give me the creeps, but more because they are fundamentalists than because they hate Israel, which stands to reason, even if I object to their tactics. In telling us about the censor's demands, Habiba has also mentioned that the Jews among us—one of the LT actors in addition to Reznikov, Malina, and myself—might not be allowed into the south; the rest of the LT would have to take the students there while we would wait behind (or maybe go east to tour the spectacular ruins of Baalbek, I'm already thinking.) But a policy of no-Jews-allowed turns out to be Habiba's paranoid invention—the gray apparatchik never mentioned it. Still, the day of discussion around this possibility stirs my own formidable queer/Jewish panic, and it bubbles up like yeast from its always fermenting place in my breast as I contemplate entering Hizbullah territory with my American passport, butch haircut, and a name that might as well be a neon implant in my forehead, flashing "*yahoud, yahoud.*" Before the falseness of the policy is exposed, Habiba recommends some strategies: Can any of us pass for Russian or something? *Reznikov* doesn't necessarily ring Hebrew in Arab ears, she tells us. Even more cheerfully, she assures us that *Malina* sounds Italian, or maybe Spanish. Besides, we can all assert that we reject Zionism and if Hizbullah isn't satisfied in my case, they can go to the *Village Voice* website and read my stories that expose the occupation.

I am not relieved. In fact, I become indignant. In my years of anti-occupation and anti-racist activism in New York, I have always bristled when I have sensed that I was being embraced as an Acceptable Jew and now, in Lebanon, I feel the shiver under my skin that tells me that a primal nerve has been hit. I refuse to submit to a test that would determine whether I could step "beyond" my Jewishness and acquire honorary status as an ordinary human being. And though it's not that long ago that my mother—a Hebrew school principal, no less—was mortified to hear me say that I am not a Zionist, I cannot say, especially not in a command performance for this audience, and certainly not without a long disquisition on what we mean by the terms, that I am an anti-Zionist.

A different anger—at myself for feeling flattered and vaguely pleased—flushes my cheeks when Sasseen, one of the students in the workshop with whom I have been enjoying lengthy political and theatrical discussions, tells me, "I'm proud you are the first Jew I have met. I hope when I meet my first Israeli, I will also not be disappointed." Like the other students in the workshop, he's impressively well-read, urbane, trilingual. All of them are politically aware and interested—and they are amused that an American college teacher would find such student engagement astounding. But at twenty-two, Sasseen seems more driven than the others to dive into some direct means of making the world right. Like me, he's obsessed with what's happening in Israel and Palestine; like me, he's marginalized in his community—Maronite Christians—because he supports Palestinian freedom. He asks me to send him some books about Zionism when I get back home—they are not for sale in Lebanon—and he shows me a scrap of an Israeli soccer magazine that he has taken as a souvenir from an abandoned IDF post. (His friends, he says, preferred to collect bullet shells and other military detritus.) He is astonished to learn that Hebrew, too, runs from right to left.

Sasseen also tells me, that day after the Dolphinarium bombing, "I hope I am not shocking you, but I was delighted when I heard the news." Moral arguments can't dampen his vicarious craving for retribution. "It's not even one for one," he reasons, "but one for a hundred." And tactical arguments fare worse. "It's revolutionary violence that drove Israel out of Lebanon. What else do the Palestinians have?"

Little surprise that a few days later, he's one of the dozen students who don't show up for rehearsals. They have decided, they explain in an evening meeting when they read us their hastily drafted manifesto, that they cannot participate in *Not in My Name* because it advocates pacifism and they do not want to be misunderstood as not having supported the resistance to the occupation. Though the Khiam play is not yet finished, they fear that the LT's thorough opposition to violence will seep out no matter what they create collectively, and especially in Khiam they don't want to be perceived as rejecting Hizbullah's victory. These students leave the project, expressing friendship and respect for the LT, but rejecting their ideology as utopian and naive—and debating the point vociferously with the majority of the students who stay. There might be room for dreams of nonviolence in the privileged West, the defectors say, but in the face of occupation, such fantasies are death.

So it's a smaller group that finally makes the trip south. The drive takes several hours, racing perilously along the coast into Beirut, then winding through severe hills. Greenish from a distance, they're all scruff and scorched scrabble up close, the almond orchards that once shaded the earth long decimated in bombing raids. Portraits of resistance fighters flap from lampposts along the roads with exhortatory slogans (alongside others that urge, visit this cafe, buy that skin cream). The faces are young, always male, the portraits medieval in their use of light and upcast eyes: saintly. Small versions can be purchased in the Khiam museum—posters, keychains, stickers. I retreat from my impulse to buy what I can only regard as Hizbullah kitsch: the horror of the site won't let me make a joke even of these tchotchkes.

I can hardly stand to be at Khiam. It isn't that the small cement cells are punier or harsher than other prisons I've seen. Or that the guard tower looming over the grounds still seems threatening. Or even that a guide displays torture devices with expert narration. The "death to Israel" slogans scrawled all over the place sicken me—because it is unavoidably obvious why they are there. *We did this.* Shame and sorrow sweep through me like nausea. Many times over the last fifteen years I have listened to Palestinians in the West Bank and Gaza describe in harrowing detail the abuses and humiliations they'd suffered at Israel's hands. I'd reacted with sorrow, of course, but never with shame, for I'd never felt that Israel acted on my behalf or represented me—how could it, given my wholeheartedly diasporic posture? On the rocky pathways of Khiam distance fails. I am ambushed by the inescapability of my bound-up Jewish fate.

As for many progressive Jews of my generation, it was Israel's invasion of Lebanon in 1982 that first punctured my romance with our putative homeland. I hadn't yet visited, but my brother moved to a kibbutz as a teenager in the mid-70s and stayed, on and off, half-a-dozen years. Years earlier, a first cousin had made aliyah, married a sabra, and was raising a family in Ber Sheva. More distant cousins had arrived directly from smoldering Europe.

Despite my years in Hebrew school and in the Zionist youth movement Habonim, I was not burning to make the summer roots-trip that so many of my suburban cohorts made (in part, because even then I had an inchoate sense that my roots, though violently dug up, were in Vilna and Krakow), but as I come from a long line of Hebrew educators, talk of the wonder of Israel, along with debate over the perpetual crisis of Jewish continuity, dominated dinner-table discourse in our liberal Midwestern home. I accepted that somehow Israel belonged to me, and I to it, the way I might acknowledge that I had relatives, say, in Argentina whom I'd never met: attached, alluring, yet an abstraction.

But my unperturbed sense of Jewishness came from other places: holidays, rituals, Marx Brothers movies, my grandmother's recipes, the harangues of the Prophets, the Gershwin *Preludes* my sister practiced endlessly, Wise Men of Chelm stories, Shabbas, table-thumping debate. As I began to get politically engaged as an undergraduate in Ann Arbor in the mid-70s, Israel seldom came into the picture. Stirrings of pro-Palestinian activism on campus, and the infamous Zionism=Racism resolution passed by the UN in 1975, made me nervous, just as Sadat's visit to Jerusalem in 1977 gave me a thrill, but none of it gripped or unsettled me.

The massacres at Sabra and Shatila did—for all the same reasons the war in Lebanon was the first to divide Jewish Israeli citizens and to spark a refusal movement among reservists and a mass peace movement there. And this split, in turn, created an opening for dissent within Jewish America's unqualified support for Israel, which had coalesced during the 1967 war. Now, twenty years later, in the heat of the Aqsa Intifada, the Jewish establishment in the U.S. has, with haste and hostility, reassembled the old consensus. Like George Bush *fils*, they are drawing lines: You are with us or against us.

Outraged by Israel's siege of Beirut, the great civil rights and anti-death penalty activist Henry Schwarzschild, who had fled Germany shortly after his post-Kristallnacht closet bar mitzvah, wrote a provocative and passionate editorial in *The Nation* in 1982. "The price of a Jewish state is, to me, Jewishly unacceptable," he charged, "and the existence of this (or any similar) Jewish ethnic-religious nation-state is a Jewish—i.e., a human and moral—disaster and violates every remaining value for which Judaism and Jews might exist in history."

I came across this editorial only years later, after I had come to know Henry (*olevasholem*) as a mentor in the fledgling years of the New York grassroots group, Jews for Racial and Economic Justice. Though the Lebanon war shifted my paradigms, there's no particular moment when I stopped being an American Zionist (which I qualify to mark a distinction from Israeli patriotism and nineteenth-century European Zionism, both quite different creatures). I didn't experience a sudden epiphany, a brutal rupture, or a political conversion that has propelled me to evangelize. It's been, rather, a gradual grinding down, the sad wasting away of idealism and hope and faith that justice was being served. This dissolution has paralleled, of course, the emptying out of the very term "Zionist"—except, perhaps, in its very American meaning: not just the religion of American Jews, but a wellspring of that invigorating admixture of Jewish power and vulnerability. But this erosion has not in the slightest eaten away at my sense of, or even pleasure in, being Jewish. That is no doubt why I have come to think that Henry could be right. And to yearn for his own prophetic harangues in these perilous times.

2. Selling Our Birthright

In preparing for my trip to Lebanon, I had read some histories of the civil war as well as some personal accounts of the siege of Beirut. Mahmoud Darwish's motif of morning coffee in *Memory for Forgetfulness: August, Beirut, 1982*—the systematic search for water, the careful method of moving the pot on and off the fire, his assessments of people based on the scent of the coffee they make, his stubborn insistence on the normality of the daily ritual—still rushes into my imagination any morning I wake to the aroma of java brewing. Darwish writes with a terrible beauty of the relentless attacks: "The sky hugs the earth with a smoky embrace. It hangs down, heavy with molten lead, a dark gray whose nothingness can only be penetrated by the orange leaked from jets whose silver flashes to a blazing whiteness. Graceful airplanes, slender, riding securely the furrowed air." And he reflects on exile, the poet's responsibility to the resistance, the function—and distortions—of collective memory.

In *Beirut Fragments: A War Memoir*, Jean Said Makdishi also recounts the ravages of the civil war and of the Israeli invasion, chronicling the narrowing of physical movement and imagination wrought by the violence, as well as the war's corruption of language. Both works are elegiac, reflective, literary, and thus easy to enter, lovely to read despite their dreadful tales.

Now, in 2002, one more June later, from the breezeless heat of still-wounded New York, I read a less mediated genre of memoir: the blurted chronicles of trauma that arrive by e-mail every day from Nablus, Jenin, Ramallah, sometimes forwarded by Israeli peace activists in Tel Aviv, Haifa, Jerusalem. Unlike the measured prose of Darwish or Makdishi, pleading for us to remember a disaster in danger of being forgotten before being understood or redressed, the missives that pour into my inbox, some dozen each day, are raw appeals for simple recognition, a detailed and desperate sort of electronic graffiti: We are here.

We are here, where our living rooms are trashed by IDF

soldiers—bookshelves heaved to the floor, drawers dumped out, family portraits smashed. Where women give birth and patients die at checkpoints because soldiers won't let them continue on to a hospital. Where children are shot on their way to the store, and crops rot on the vines because farmers cannot go out to harvest.

These testimonies share space in my inbox with the panicky postings of relatives and friends in Israel, explaining how they have rerouted their daily patterns to avoid public squares or crowded markets, stopped going to cafes or to the theater, can hardly bear to send their kids off to soccer practice.

I check my e-mail each morning to find Jewish terror and Palestinian horror meeting in a virtual chorus of discordant despair. Often I break down at the computer.

I go religiously to the *Ha'aretz* website. And I keep up my subscriptions to the *Jerusalem Report* and the *Forward* and god-knows-how-many left-Israeli newsletters and bulletins. And I scan the websites of Palestinian NGOs. In part, I have fallen for the Internet-induced illusion that staring into a screen is a means of engagement; in part I am like a neurotic who can't interrupt a pattern of masochistic relationships.

As I have never acceded to the now hegemonic principle that all Jewish identity must emanate from an Israeli center, why can't I proclaim my Bundist affiliations, curl up with a volume of Rokhl Korn or Michael Chabon, blare the Klezmatics on my Walkperson, and learn to look away from Zion?

Not simply because Israel claims to speak in my name and on my behalf, an assertion that carries as much weight with me as, say, Bush's promise to protect my security by running roughshod over the Constitution. Nor because my visits to Israel—not hitting just the UJA high points, but also the development towns that never developed, the unrecognized Palestinian-Israeli villages, the foreign worker neighborhoods, the gay bars—have made the place too concrete to function as a free-floating metaphor for my Jewish self-invention.

More important, Palestinians have become concrete—specific, individual, diverse—because, quite simply, I have talked to some, visited their homes, shared meals. What ought to be a most unremarkable fact contains a fundamental rebuke to American Zionism, which requires that Palestinians be a fantasy: an unaccountably enraged population fueled by anti-Semitic passions. Such absolutes are required because to "love Israel" as an American Zionist is not at all the same sort of experience as to love, say, Italy.

One can have a fulfilling, even mature, romance with Italy—and who doesn't?—without ever being asked to declare her position on Berlusconi (much less on the history of Mussolini) because loving Italy has to do with art, food, landscape, opera—features that endure and define the culture even if there's a corporate despot in office, or a fascist resurgence in the north. Denounce Berlusconi, rail against the anti-immigrant secessionists in the Veneto, complain about the motorini or the cat-calling men: your affections are not compromised.

In contrast, I am crazy about the architecture of the Hebrew language (though I speak it execrably), the light in Jerusalem, the hills of Haifa, the cafe culture of Tel Aviv. But that's not what is being asked of me when I'm expected to declare my devotion to Israel. On the contrary, it's the state qua state that is supposed to make me swoon, even if there's an accused war criminal in office or a fundamentalist movement colonizing the West Bank with full governmental support. Denounce, rail, complain: you're a self-hating Jew.

Arrested adolescent adoration means, of course, that the love-object must be idealized. American Zionism grants the favor—along with millions of dollars in annual donations—as a down-payment for some imagined future when another anti-Semitic calamity would require the Jewish state to take us in. Despite our success in America, Jewish fear persists—the *pintele yid* in its twisted essence; harboring such fear may be the only way some Americans remain Jewish. And it leaves no psychic room for recognizing a terrible contradiction: that Israel is not making Jews safe. With its vast military might and American backing, there is little chance that Israel's existence as a state can be threatened; individual Israelis, however, are acutely endangered by the current hostilities. But to sustain the just-in-case availability of Israel as a refuge, American Zionism cannot allow that Israel might share any responsibility for the brutal conflict. The violence must be entirely the fault of the Palestinians.

The deep seepage of the doctrine of demonization into Jewish American Zionism roared notoriously to the surface at the pro-Israel rally in Washington in April 2002, when hawkish Paul Wolfowitz got viciously booed by the crowd for daring to mention—along with asserting his unqualified support for Israel—that Palestinians have suffered, too. No Jewish leader reprimanded the protesters from the stage.

I saw the syndrome reveal itself more insidiously when I spoke on a panel a few weeks later at a conference for Jewish college-student reporters on the theme of covering Israel. I offered a few anecdotes, trying to explain how I position myself as an alternative journalist (lacking the infrastructure, access, and cash of mass media's local bureaus) to look for the stories that the mainstream media neglect. During the first Intifada, I told them, I wanted to move away from the daily clash stories and try to get at how the uprising was lived day to day by Palestinians and Israelis, so chose to build a collage of profiles. I described, too, how in my most recent trip—most of August 2001, just two months after my visit to Lebanon—I decided to do one of my three stories about the ongoing occupation, a situation largely lost on American readers, and so went to Gaza and the West Bank to interview farmers whose crops had been uprooted by the IDF, villagers whose water was repeatedly turned off by nearby Jewish settlers, and so on.

Their responses astonished me. Not all, but many of the students who spoke up went on the attack: if I have interviewed Palestinians who say they have been victims of human rights violations, have I interviewed the relatives of Israelis killed in suicide bombings? I tried to explain that although I have talked to such families, they are covered extensively in the mass media—which I can't compete with in any case—and that I'm trying to strike a balance on a larger scale. In principle, they took issue with my willingness to give voice to Palestinian experience, but they were polite, congratulating me on my courage: how dangerous they imagined it must have been for me to sit with a Palestinian in her kitchen in Ramallah, or to hang out in a family's living room in a Gaza refugee camp. I appealed to their duty as journalists, insisting that they must at least be willing to hear a narrative, and accept it as the teller's own, even if they don't agree with it. But they had been well counseled precisely in how not to hear any Palestinian narrative. They rebutted me by stressing that as Jewish journalists, their first obligation is to report on Israeli experience, and by asserting (like Ehud Barak not long before) that Palestinians lie by nature, and thus are unworthy sources for their stories.

Mainstream Jewish-American organizations have made a priority of shoring up such self-righteous Zionism among college kids. Hillel sent hundreds to Israel to "improve their Israel advocacy skills" this spring, and AIPAC has hundreds of college affiliates. The organizational response to the rise of pro-Palestine activism on campuses—as any number of panicky op-eds in Jewish papers around the country have baldly stated—has been to defend: not to provide a place where Jewish students of all perspectives and with many questions might be exposed to a range of views (even if it were only a range of Israeli views), learn something, grapple toward their own conclusions, and maybe even engage in genuine dialogue with their apparent activist foes. Rather, the institutions have moved in to indoctrinate. And to circle the wagons. At many universities, a Jewish kid with misgivings about the occupation has nowhere to be Jewish on campus. I fear that she might just stop being Jewish.

Increasingly, the self-proclaimed guardians of the Jewish-American future are constructing Jewish identity on the negation of another people and the wrong that has been done to them in the name of Jewish survival: their land was taken, their homes destroyed, their lives constrained, their dreams deferred. Jewish life has no moral future if we do not own up to these incontrovertible facts. Whether Palestinians really want a state in all of historic Palestine is not the point. Negotiations and fixed borders and security arrangements presided over by one of the world's most powerful armies can guarantee that even if Palestinians will it, it will remain only a dream.

Acknowledging Jewish responsibility for the dispossession of Palestinians in 1948 does not have to mean the dismantlement of Israel, as the state's supporters always fear whenever the Palestinian catastrophe is even mentioned. But we cannot persist in building Jewish identity around the hollow core of disavowed knowledge. It's just plain wrong. And also, ultimately, very bad for the Jews.

The lengths to which American Zionist leaders will go to sustain the foundational lie is staggering, imperiling the fundamental character of American Jewish culture: its liberalism, flexibility, and openness to—indeed, fostering of—dissent.

Institutional leaders have embraced the Christian fundamentalist right—the only group that gives more support to Israel than American Jews. Never mind that their motive is ultimately anti-Semitic—the second coming requires the return to Zion of all the Jews, who will not be invited to the post-apocalypse party. As long as Billy Graham and Tom DeLay and Ralph Reed and Dick Armey and Family Research Council spokesperson Janet Parshall and a cadre of other high-up end-timers will shill for Sharon's hard line, they are being welcomed into the Zionist fold. In exchange, Jewish organizations are already showing a willingness to abandon long-standing support for environmental protections and even for immigrant rights.

Meanwhile, what a friend who works in a New York Jewish agency has been calling "Jewish communal McCarthyism" has chilled even the most measured critiques of the occupation. Members of the synagogue I belong to were spit on and kicked for carrying pro-peace signs at the April rally in Washington; a friend who was invited to submit an article to a journal suggesting what should be done with excess Nazi reparation money was told he'd risk his job in a Jewish organization if he published his idea that it should be used for Palestinian nation-building; a Hebrew school principal told me that if she simply neglected to send busloads of kids to her local annual pro-Israel parade—much less, made a statement opposing it—she'd be forever ostracized from her professional community.

Whatever happened to two Jews, three opinions? To the essential, shaping fact that Abraham argues with God? To the very idea of the Talmudic tradition? To good old Jewish disputatiousness?

In my darkest hours, I fear that the rightward-rushing, dissent-killing, tribe-narrowing proponents of a fortress American Zionism will shrink American Jewishness to a mean and little space. Those who don't toe the right-wing Zionist line will be so unwelcome in Jewish places as to abandon them altogether, leaving the right to define and delimit Jewish-American aspirations and expressions. They will make a culture that will continue to produce its Podhoretzes, Kristols, and

Morton Kleins, but not its Tony Kushners, Marshall Meyers, Marcia Falks, or Judith Malinas.

According to Zionist creed, in addition to being a safe haven, Israel was supposed to be the place where Jews could most assuredly live full Jewish lives, neither crushed by bigotry nor attenuated by assimilation. It's debatable whether that purpose has been fulfilled in Israel for anyone other than the ultra-Orthodox—and arguably their choosing to keep one foot in the eighteenth century rather restricts the fullness of their Jewishness. My Ber Sheva cousin's children, now in their twenties, don't primarily think of themselves as Jewish. They are *Israeli*, one of them insisted when she visited me in New York a couple of years ago. She couldn't understand why I recommended a visit to the Jewish Museum and was genuinely baffled that my partner would host a weekly radio program on Jewish affairs or that I would learn Yiddish or ever set foot inside a synagogue. These were quaint and pointless endeavors as far as she was concerned, harmless maybe, but passé, even embarrassing.

Perhaps she's not representative of her generation of sabras—though I've encountered the attitude among many of her peers—so best not to conclude that Jewish life has shrunk rather than expanded in Israel. In any case, there is no question but that Jews in America—at least those who have wanted to—have been able to build Jewish lives of infinite variety, matching the American imperative of self-invention with the ur-performativity of Jewish identity.

But today, American Zionism is doing nothing less than diminishing the polymorphous, exuberant, and myriad ways of being Jewish in America. Quite deliberately, it is weeding out the tribe. As Henry Siegman, once the head of the American Jewish Congress, lamented in an interview with the *New York Times* in early June, nowadays, according to the *macher* organizations, "If you do not support the government of Israel then your Jewishness, not your political judgment, is in question."

If that is so—if, after all these millennia, the Conference of Presidents really gets away with instituting a kind of Jewish excommunication over its rapturous rallying behind Sharon—then Zionism will forever distort, and even threaten to destroy, the creativity, the diversity, the genius of American Jewishness. Zionism, *khas v'kholile*, will turn out to be the greatest peril Jewish America has ever faced.

SHIRA WOLOSKY

ISRAEL AND AMERICA: REVISIONING HISTORY

There seem to be two threats to the survival of the Jewish people: persecution, and non-persecution. These have been, throughout history, interlocking. In Europe, the possibility of the second—hardly ever realized—always depended on the menace of the first. The condition and price of acceptance into society was the concealment or abandonment of the very difference considered unacceptable—an odd sort of toleration really, where one could stop being persecuted only if one stopped being who one was. Even the so-called Emancipation of 1870—which very partially extended into very few places for a very short time—led, as Gershom Scholem scathingly observed, not to the integration of Jewish into European life but to the opposite, with Jews rushing to throw their identities overboard like dangerous cargo at the first opportunity. But this betrayal was then itself betrayed. It is chilling that Emancipation marks the date for the one-grandparent definition of Jewish identity: that was the year Nazi archivists busily researched in order to unearth, unbury, Jewish antecedents long thought to be dead.

America is a different story. In America, non-persecution is an independent possibility, offered without veiled or overt threats of discrimination. Here is a genuine American exceptionalism, whatever prejudices or restrictions have been in place or shifted around. Besides lacking both the theological and nationalist histories of anti-Semitism of the European, or now, the Muslim sort, the whole integral structure of American identity stands as guard. To be American is a political definition, not a bloodline. It involves taking one's place in the particular constitution of the American polity, not on initiations by birth or cultural habits. In their 1958 comparative study of the bases for *Civic Culture*, Verba and Almond found that as against, say, the Italians, who named as their defining sources of national pride art and landscape, Americans named above all their governmental institutions. These structures are available to every citizen (although it is America's failure that they are not available to every citizen equally), regardless of such other considerations as, for example, their cultural past.

This heritage is just what Europeans find so bewildering, and so dislikable, about America. Alexis de Toqueville's *Democracy in America* offers one of the first anatomies of this dislike, and remains breathtakingly current, as I discovered in a seminar on American culture I taught at the Hebrew University, to a group consisting of Britons, Americans, Israelis (all Jewish), and one Arab Catholic. Here before my eyes I could witness the hostility and distaste Europeans feel when they gaze across the Atlantic, and the lack of understanding—and, largely, the refusal to take it all very seriously—Americans return in their answering gaze. (It is just this sort of cross-cultural experience, and the urgent sense that Israelis ought to be more deeply cognizant of American and other cultures, that makes teaching in Israel so distinctive and consequential.) To the Europeans, American culture is just thin. It is all about money. No echoing American songs reach back through a thousand years or more of continuous history. Americans can retort: these sorts of echoing songs sound best in marble vaults, in graveyards. De Toqueville, in a chapter called "How the Aspect of Society in the United States is at Once Excited and Monotonous" (Vol. II, ch. XVII), complains: "When the reverence that belonged to what is old has vanished, birth, condition, and profession no longer distinguish men; hardly anything but money remains to create strongly marked differences between them and to raise some of them above the common level." But American students notice that what de Toqueville's alternatives really come to are money as social mobility versus fixed social distinctions that make for thick but immobile class structures. Yes, the American cultural heritage is thin. But cultural heritage is not really what America is about. It is not the appropriate criterion, not the proper measure. When Americans look at themselves, in a vision that Europeans never behold, what they see is not the mere reduction of all value to money (although this is a very powerful impulse, in problematic and uneasy balance with other values), but the possibility of self-definition, of self-creation in a society open to each unencumbered person, to make of him- (her-?) self whatever he (she? these freedoms do not extend equally between genders) wishes to be. Both self and society are enterprises of active construction.

Which is to say: in America, identity is in the future, not in the past. Identity is to be constructed, accomplished, attained; not preserved, cherished, and guarded.

But this is a highly paradoxical notion of identity. It is as if what defines you doesn't even exist, as if it is somehow made up as one goes along—but then, who is one anyway, and who is doing all this doing? And where and how can a Jewish identity accord with this American one? For if Jewishness is anything at all, it surely must be connected in some way to a past identity, a history, being carried in some way forward. This contrast was dramatically brought home to me through one summer's itinerary. Some years ago I visited Florida's Disney World with my family. Of the many displays of Americanism there—and some are quite explicit, such as the Presidential facsimiles and the pavilion on United States history—the one that struck me as most quintessential was the exhibit on American household technology (which I remembered from my own childhood at the New York World's Fair). The presentation of changing household spaces and appliances was gripping, not least in its (unintentional) window into changing gender roles and their material base. But the accompanying jingle said it all: "There's a great big beautiful tomorrow, / Shining at the end of every day. / There's a great big beautiful tomorrow, / And it's just a dream away."

I then returned to Israel, where I have been living and teaching literature at the Hebrew University of Jerusalem since 1985, having resigned my position at Yale to do so. I was invited to a tour of the City of David—a politically controversial area outside the Old City walls that has been resettled by Jews. The guide was impressive. He had, it seems, devoted his life to the grounds and backgrounds of the City of David. Every step, every stone, was like a deep well to which he had the plummet. Jeremiah had walked in this spot, and had stood in this spot, and had said this and this and this in this and this spot. Here was a living typology—biblical story as immediate directive. The contrast with Disney World could not have been more complete. In one case, the future is pure, unanchored invention. In the other, the past is nigh absolute, determinative, ironlike. There is in this sense of the past enormous, resonating depth. But at the extreme, such a past can become a map to which the present and future are glued or, like a moth, utterly pinned.

These are poles of opposition, schematic no doubt, yet with powerful energies driving each world (that is, America and the others) in contrasting directions. The Middle East especially seems pinned to such maps of the past. Bernard Lewis remarks that in America, when you say "that's history" you mean it is gone, finished, irrelevant. In the Middle East, to say "that's history" is to lay nearly absolute claim, imposing, irrevocable. Is there then nothing but bleak choice? Is it possible either to be true to the future, or to be true to the past? And what is the meaning of such ultimatums for Jewish-Americans, Jewish-Israelis, Jewish-American Israelis? For each impulse has its costs. At times to be an American seems like being invited to an outspread smorgasbord buffet, free to choose among the many offerings, from many cultures, for many purposes, with the ultimate end of achieving one's own desire, direction, self-realization. Each may assemble any selection that suits the self and the moment; and the next moment and next self again. To be a Jew, in contrast, seems more like taking one's place at a ceremonial meal, formally and ritually served and with each selection rehearsed and savored. The first banquet lacks cultural depth, while the second is culturally restrictive. Yet how, without the existence of the ceremonial meal, is the banquet even possible? Without its distinction and devotion, wherefrom will the enriching diversity and variety be drawn?

America and Israel often seem to me to be mirror images of each other—which is to say, mirror asymmetries. In America, the self can tend to be too disconnected, too narrowly self-concerned. This, again, is how Europe often sees American behaviors. America seems to lack a sense of common ground or good. The community is ghostlike, a shadow cast by compulsive self-interest. Yet a fuller reading of American culture shows this to be a partial and distorted view. America is not founded on exclusive self-interest. Republican participation, voluntarism, and community activism are equally foundational. This republican tradition in a sense also gives priority to the individual, but as called toward joint efforts, civic virtue, community commitments. However, the balance between these principles is highly unstable. From the nineteenth century onward, personal wealth, as Emerson himself, no mere spokesman of the egocentric, warns, has challenged the commonwealth, with communal space requiring defense and support.

Israel traces an almost opposite course. In this tendency it is closer to Europe, although Europe's claims to moral concern all too often disguise what are really possessive defenses of its cultural past—a past with its own severe record of exclusionary intolerance against any people not embraced within its nationalist bosom. Of such exclusion the Jews stand as the longest instance. Israel, founded in a vision of national rebirth grounded in national death, gives the community priority. The needs of survival, the very existence of the state, called for raising the common over the individual. And yet from its inception, or even from before, there were questions as to which and whose community was to be constitutive. For of course the Jewish community was and is plural and diverse, not only demographically but also ideologically and intrinsically to Jewish identity itself. In Jewish tradition, the call to community is integrally balanced by a recognition of the self: of its individual integrity and the value of its uniqueness and diversity. Here an American model is clarifying and has especially much to offer: not only in its history, which, unlike Europe's (at best) toleration, was composed of ethnic diversity and religious freedom, but also in the very constitution and role of liberal American religion as participant and ground of that respect for each individual, that sanctity of each soul, that is the core of the liberal ethos itself.

It is my view that the bond of Jewish-American and American-Israeli has exactly the task of negotiating these directions. If America has tended too far toward the side of atomized self-interest, elements in Israel have tended too far toward religion as a form of political authoritarianism. This situation is partly pre-modern, as with other fundamentalisms; and is also Mideastern, where the remainder of the

Middle East has barely even begun to address such balances between self and state, individual and authority. Regarding such mirror-reflections of America and Israel, American-Jew/Jewish-American-in-Israel, one can perhaps speak of inverse challenges. Americans tend to sacrifice community to self. Israelis tend to sacrifice self to community. Each no doubt accords with the historical circumstances of each place. In the Israeli context, the need to rescue and create community has been genuine and impelling. But, besides these immediate political urgencies, there are also cultural-theoretical ones, with implications for Jewish identity (and American identity) as such. In each case, that is, there is a notion or model of the self at work. The American imagined self is of autocthonous birth, springing solely from itself, autonomous, self-defining, whose goal is self-fulfillment and self-realization—even if and when that is to be coordinated or directed through polis or community. But the Jewish imagined self has a different structure. That self is born out of community, shaped by culture, filled with history. This circumstance need not, indeed ought not, entail the negation or absorption of self into collective. Each self, as in the biblical tradition, remains autonomous, morally responsible, self-defining. And yet the very "self" that is "self-defining" is already a cultural, situated self. The fantasy of utter self-possession and the goal of self-fulfillment become transformed. Here, to possess a self is always to be inscribed within a cultural history; to fulfill the self is (also) to fulfill this cultural commitment.

Can this (Jewish) model of the cultural-self be sustained? In America? In Israel? In America, the lack of persecution is a positive enticement, not a negative danger. In America, you can (so it is promised) choose freely among and between identities, constructing unique combinations and versions. This may be a liberating dream for the individual. It is not, however, particularly sustaining for a historical culture, especially not for a culture itself rooted, by definition, in cultivating a particular history. This is not to say that to be American is in itself antithetical to being Jewish. America, as I see it, is also a site of Jewish history and ongoing cultural definition. Nor is this to say that living in Israel offers miraculous, or even reliably mundane solutions. As far as I can see, there is no solution to the question of Jewish identity. Indeed, I believe that solutions are the wrong things to ask for, the wrong terms to speak in. Nonetheless, being Jewish, and being American, are not identical identities, not even identical structures of identity, but instead coexist in exquisite tension and contention. To be devoted to the self and its realization is not the same as, and at some point may become incompatible with, being devoted to a particular civilization and its continued life.

To live in Israel counter-poses no less disturbing tensions. At first—I mean in cultural imagination, not merely in time—the refounding of the Jewish State seemed a miraculous deliverance: in fact, an End to Jewish history as it had so horribly been enacted in twentieth-century Europe and throughout most of its precarious sojourn in Europe over a thousand years. But the current, twenty-first century world has meant not the resolution, but rather the plunge back into Jewish history, which is to say into history as continued, often dire struggle. Here the threat to Jewish existence has become a political, military question. The Jews are no longer (mainly) an Other within the body of Christian Europe, but an Other as nation-state rejected by the Arab states that surround it. I am not claiming here, and certainly not predicting, the imminent destruction of the state of Israel. But there is no mistaking, not for me, the sadness of having failed to be accepted into the company of nations: the continued skating on the edge of outcast; the unbelievably hypocritical European claim to humanitarian interest (their eye on Israel, they somehow overlook that two millions of people have died in the Sudan; three millions of people have died in the Congo; Zimbabwe is starving; South Africa is an agony of AIDS—and that is only to take one continent) to mask oil interests and market interests, if not residual anti-Semitic distaste. Israel stands today as the Jew of the nations. Theological villain, mythologized demon, alien subversive, sacrificial scapegoat: all the time-honored Jewish roles are there, only now on a personified, national level.

And one clenches one's teeth each day for the attacks against civilians through which this old and new hatred takes old and new form. (I don't care whether these attacks are called terror or some other military nomenclature. What is essential is the intentional attack on civilian targets, that is, the purposeful intent to kill ordinary people such as children and students. This violence goes against every moral and military convention, and remains distinct from efforts to damage military targets, even when these, tragically, cause civilian deaths. It is as if Israel, or any other power, set out on purpose to bomb hospitals. Arguments that suicide-murders merely make use of such military power as is available are arguments that deny civilian status to Israelis altogether, that is, deny the very right of Israel to exist.)

Do the Jews deserve this treatment? Are we sufficiently guilty to explain (guilt is a master explanation, making every attack a punishment) the bombings of cafés, train stations, universities? Sorry, I don't think so. Of course, how the historical narrative looks is essentially determined by where you decide to begin it. Yet to me some basic lines stand clear. Looking backwards, the current intifada was begun as the refusal of an offer to return the occupied territories and institute a Palestinian State—an offer the Israeli public, all signs show, would have embraced and which a majority of Israelis favor. It is just incorrect to say this intifada is about the liberation of the occupied territories. The current war was launched to reject the Israeli offer to return territory. This intifada is no spontaneous outcry against oppression. On the contrary, it was carefully premeditated. The weapons were stocked, the preparations were made, the provocation awaited. While I consider the visit of Ariel Sharon to the Temple Mount an immense stupidity, I think it must also be noted that Yasir Arafat to this day denies that the Temple Mount has any genuine Jewish historical or religious importance, and that all Jewish religious sites that have fallen into Arafat's hands have been immediately destroyed. Arafat is not liberal. His regime is not dedicated to the mutual respect of difference in neutral public spaces, to the recognition of the rights of men—and women!—to personal self-determination, to the free exercise of religion or any other individual right.

The intifada was prepared, as was its conduct. Three days into the intifada—not after months of disappointed effort and ensuing despair—Arafat released from jail all the members of Hamas and other groups intent on attacking civilians. And he had already financed and set into play the purchase of weapons on the ship *Karin A*, with the goal not of negotiation but of a major military attack on Israel. And this account could go still further back, to the fact that the territories became occupied as a result of attacks on Israel—existential attacks—before there was any occupation at all—unless Israel with any borders is considered, as Hamas openly states, to be occupied territory requiring abolishment.

That is: the cause of the conflict is not the occupied territories, although I dearly hope they may help toward its resolution. The cause was and remains Arab anger at a Jewish presence in what they see—not wrongly but also not simply and not reconcilably—as their lands.

This is not to say the Israelis do not also have their uncompromising margin, who wish to hold on to the territories at all cost. I think they are deluded—although without a partner on the other side, there is little chance to check this delusion. Nor does it mean that the Israelis have not dealt very problematically with its own Arab citizens, nor that the Palestinian people do not suffer. There is, however, a general consensus in Israel willing to offer a two-state solution—as there are, I hope, Palestinians willing to put their anger aside to come to an agreement on two states, accepting the existence of a Jewish one as Arafat has not yet done. They are silenced, however, in fear of Palestinian authoritarian lawlessness. But there remains the problem of identity as iron map of the past, shadowing both sides.

It is my belief that Jewish-Americans, like Jews everywhere, have benefited enormously, measurelessly, from the establishment of the State of Israel. Erik Erikson includes, at the back of *Childhood and Society*, a gripping essay on German national identity. Reading it brings a vivid picture, now almost lost, of what it was like to see the Jews only as wandering, as piecemeal, the target of hatred and projection. To the Germans this dispersion was itself provocation, where "The Jew seemed to remain himself despite dispersion over the world, while the German trembled for his identity in his own country." The reconstitution of national self-determination in Israel has utterly transformed the image of the Jew for Jews everywhere. Yet the Jews remain caught in the extremities Erikson goes on to describe, that is, divided between the dogmatic and the relativistic, between the impulse to resist all change, as against the impulse to adapt at any cost. Both American and Israeli Jews stand between and facing these directions, within a world where identity seems to prevent the future while modernity demands abandoning the past, but where ongoing life requires both defense of what was and venture toward what may be.

In this world, we Jews are still inside history. Indeed, we seem in the last two years of Palestinian intifada and European hostility to have fallen with a vengeance back into Jewish history, after somehow apparently imagining—under what delusion? where did we think ourselves to be?—that history had Ended, that we had gotten past it, that we had climbed onto some sort of new plane beyond the fear of destruction or the struggle for acceptance. We Israeli Jews live this new/old history every day, as we steel ourselves hourly to listen to news broadcasts, as we witness Arafat twisting backwards and forwards to deny Jewish legitimacy, to forbid a place for Jews in the Middle East. The plight of the Palestinians is heartbreaking—my own view in fact is that this intifada marks not least the failure to found a Palestinian state under Arafat, where instead of a past of blood there could be a future of schools and courthouses, roads and, yes, boring things like sewers and waterworks. Every coin rendered to Arafat has gone either into pockets or into weapons, including textbooks printed not, as has been claimed, under Jordanian but under Palestinian authority, with the purpose of burying children's minds in a past of anger and a future stillborn before it is even conceived.

Do I condemn Israeli policy toward the Palestinians? Let me whisper a secret. We don't know what to do. We offered them a state (and check the maps, look at the reports: this was more than isolated cantons; but Arafat, according to those at Camp David and Taba, wasn't even interested in negotiating further lines. He turned the deal down flat). Speaking for myself and many, many others, I am pretty much open to considering any arrangement so long as it doesn't require my own suicide. In the last two years, we have lost our public spaces to fear. I have teen-aged children: try telling them they should never go out. Their will to independence has become life-threatening—almost a parable of the general politics of terror and authoritarian violence. And how can we allow the free passage of, say, ambulances, when Palestinians smuggle bombs under the stretchers of children? The suffering is terrible. But where are the Palestinian voices raised against attacks on civilians? Where are their voices for courts of law, rather than summary executions? Where are the voices of women, in a land where "honor killings" over sexual "dishonor" are a way of life/death; where a United Nations resolution condemning such killings was defeated because so many countries are in favor of them; where, to tell only one story, a girl was killed for dishonor by her family after being raped by members of the Tanzim, Arafat's own personal military faction? (And where are the European voices on these human rights abuses? Where was European pressure on Arafat to accept the lands Israel offered to return? Jacques Chirac advised against the offer.) Let's imagine that it was a blow for Arabs that lots of Jews showed up in the Middle East after World War II (there were always some living here) with no other place to go (something easy to forget, something difficult to remember, something that is still the case for most Israelis). Let's say that there is right against right. Still, we are here. Isn't it time to ask, not what's past, but, like Americans: what next?

There are voices, on both sides. I myself belong to a discussion group of women—Muslim, Christian, and Jewish—on gender issues in all of our lives. Here is where my own triple identity weighs in, although today an immeasurable chasm seems to have opened between my two worlds, once felt as continuous. There is a true divide between an America at peace and an Israel in war. It is difficult to describe the shock to my American ear of shooting and bombings—out my window, down my street, at my university. Here is where the mirroring between America and Israel might, just might, become not merely reflective but transformative, an image with effective power. The American-Jewish challenge resides in the promise of opportunity and possibility granted (at least ideally and ideologically) to each American, to abandon whatever past and imagine whatever futures he or she chooses—though perhaps at the risk of the very identity one is presumably pursuing. But the Jewish- (and Muslim-) Israeli challenge is to allow for new futures out of pasts that threaten to become entrapping. And here the American in me perhaps can point in other directions—as a teacher to students for whom knowledge of America is urgent and potent, as a mother of children;

as a member of community. Perhaps the American model can open space for a greater individuality, while the Jewish one guards against a loss of community, making possible a self grounded in, but not engulfed by, its cultural past, and a more liberal religion as against politicized religious authoritarianism, with the value of diversity itself a religious value. For truly, if God had wished to create everyone the same, surely He could have done so. If He had wished to found one religion or manner of worship, He could have established it. How else is the diversity of the world religiously accountable? Is it not irreligious, indeed blasphemous, to claim one divine truth?

There is a blessing: *Chadesh Yamenu KiKedem*—renew our days as of old, let our past times be renewed to us. This blessing is a never-ending paradox, in which neither future nor past is absolute, where neither demands the betrayal of the other—neither of past to future nor of future to past. It seeks not a release from history, but rather, continued commitment to it. The End of history is a longing born out of suffering and uncertainty; but for all that, it is seductive, dangerous, as are all absolute claims. Ultimate solutions tend to be traitorous, entailing both fulfillment and destruction, fulfillment as destruction. The way of history evades both complete destructions and complete fulfillments. In its courses, identities are never final, indeed never identical—just as in *Drash*, commentary itself renews, brings to new life, the text it engages, in ever-changing ways. What is needed is a new grammar, or rather, a new sense of identity as grammatical: not as fixed but as unfolding, through past and future cases, conditionals and indicatives, with each element built from what came before, even as it creates what will come after.

SHARON POMERANTZ

PLAYING THE ANGLES

My cousin Barry Vishniak's heyday in New York was the eighties. He was at home with the filth and corruption, high prices, dirty subway cars, and unlimited girls girls girls on 42nd Street. Back then, Ed Koch was mayor, Reagan was in the White House, and the high percentage of mental patients babbling and screaming on Manhattan streets made Barry feel saner, more secure. By the time I got there, New York was Giuliani-ized, Disney-fied. The Upper West Side, where Barry once lived, had become no different from Scarsdale. "That's why I moved to Jersey City," he told me as we walked up Broadway one warm afternoon in March, 1997. "I can't take how clean everything is anymore, and the smugness. The fuckin' YUPPIE smugness." He opened the door to Zabar's, and a rush of people spilled out the door, as if they'd been trapped in there for days. Barry wanted to whet his appetite, to inhale a little nova lox and sample fifteen different kinds of olives.

"Remember that night, back in '82?" he asked me, referring to when I'd come to New York as a teenager to interview at Barnard and he took me out for my first ever sushi dinner. I assured him I did, for he had, just as he was doing now, insisted on walking into Zabar's beforehand, to work up an appetite, the way two Irishmen might start their evening at the local pub. As he wandered up and down the aisles, pushing and shoving his way from cheese to candy to fish, I thought about that night and the bet he'd insisted on making with me: whoever ate and drank the most got twenty dollars. Not exactly fair, as I'd never had saki before, or much alcohol at all for that matter. At one point, I got up to go to the ladies' room and walked into a brick wall. Within moments a big welt formed on my forehead. In the cab on the way back to his apartment, I had to puke into Barry's ski cap.

"You still owe me twenty bucks from that night," he said. "I won fair and square."

"I overslept and missed my interview," I reminded him. "I almost didn't get into college because of you. Not to mention all the coke you were snorting beforehand gave you an unfair advantage." The coke part had only dawned on me years later. Back then, age seventeen, I thought he was just very energetic and prone to colds.

He shrugged. "A bet's a bet, kiddo," he said, as we exited the deli. "Everyone in New York learns to play the angles eventually. Except the suckers and the tourists."

"Uhuh," I said.

"So what are you up to tonight?"

It occurred to me that he might be expecting an invitation to dinner—I was on my way to meet some coworkers in Soho—but something stopped me from asking. I was no longer seventeen. Back then, it had been enough to me that he lived in Manhattan, slept two hours a night, and spent money like it was not his own, which was more or less the truth—he was a stockbroker. He had no boss or budget—two words which ruled our parents' lives—and all I wanted then was to be just that free. On my rare visits, I trailed after him from club to cab to restaurant, studying his tastes, hanging on his every word and gesture.

Those days felt long gone. Barry, once trim and dark-complected, with the charisma that came from tremendous drive and unlimited uppers, was now a short, balding man with an enormous belly, smelly cigars, tattered shirts, and a still unnamed profession. There was a slightly wild look in his eye, deep pouches of exhaustion on his face, a constant sniffle. I had only been at Hoffman and Hoffman a few months and was, at that moment, going to meet the other publicists in my department. People in Armani suits who drank Cosmopolitans and carried their Dunhills in small silver cigarette cases. How would they react to an evening with cousin Barry? Not well, I suspected.

On the other hand, Barry had just hooked me up with Jack Fingerhut, the real estate king, who, for a mere $2800 above first month's and security, had gotten me a rent-stabilized studio. Meaning affordable rent for life. Most people had more chance of being hit by the crosstown bus than they did of getting their name on a stabilized lease in the boom nineties. Wasn't that worth, at least, an invitation to dinner?

I felt a little ashamed as I kissed his cheek and told him I had to leave, but I couldn't invite him out with the crowd from Hoffman and Hoffman. My mother would point out, at this juncture, that this did not make me a snob, merely a survivor. The problem was, he was family, and from somewhere deep in the earth my grandmother was wagging her finger at me. My father was shaking his head. Barry was his favorite nephew. His gutsy nephew, he once called him. Gutsy and good to his mother.

"You have dinner plans?" I whispered, glancing down into the mouth of the subway. Tentatively, I put my foot on a lower step.

He shooed me away with his hand. "Go, go, earn that $2000 you owe Jack," he said.

"It's $2,800," I called back. I felt suddenly better; he had forgotten, momentarily, about what was likely his own kickback.

* * *

The next time I saw Barry was four months later, in the summer. He was sitting at a table off West End and 84th, around the corner from my new apartment, with two men. He was wearing a navy blazer, camel-colored pants, pale blue shirt. Usually my cousin was in baggy, wrinkled khakis and a tattered oxford. If he hadn't called to me, I wouldn't have recognized him. The café featured glatt kosher food. Outside, a giant photo of the Lubavitcher rebbe looked on blankly above the words "Get ready for *Moshiach*."

The men were introduced to me as Rabbi Davidman (beard) and Rabbi Perez (clean-shaven). Perhaps Barry saw shock in my expression, for he gave me a look that felt like a warning.

"Did I ever tell you, gentlemen, about my participation in Operation Moses?"

He began a long tale about his role in the airlift and rescue of several thousand Ethiopian Jews, a secret mission into a hostile dictatorship conducted by the Israelis in 1985, and then again in '91. Barry described how the army had used El Al planes, removing chairs and seat cushions to pack more people in.

"My parachute didn't work right," he said, "and I got lost from my unit, somewhere in the Sudan."

"Oh," I said, leaning forward. "And what exactly did you do then?" In 1985, my cousin was still a retail stockbroker in the two-person operation that made him a lot of money before he was hauled to court on insider trading charges. He'd gotten off on a technicality, a fumble by a young SEC lawyer. I was sure his travels that year had not taken him past Newark.

I looked at the two rabbis; they were riveted. Barry's abilities were inherited from his father, my Uncle Vishniak, whom he closely resembles. Uncle Vishniak was known for never telling the truth under any circumstances, except in cases where it didn't matter. Luckily, he always worked for the transit authority.

"So there I was, alone in the desert," Barry continued, "and within two days I was outta water." There was a black bird following him, he said, a strange kind of crow, which he shot. "That ugly bird saved my life. The feathers were wet enough that I could suck the water off them. The meat could be roasted. And then the eyes of certain wild birds. . . ." He paused for effect. "You can poke them out with a knife and eat them, they're full of iron."

"What can I get for you?" The waiter suddenly appeared at my side.

"Bring her a chicken sandwich," my cousin said, and waved him away.

"Really, I have to be going."

"Annie here is one of my only living relatives," Barry told the two men. "Most of our family is dead."

"Or in jail," I whispered. Barry pinched my leg under the table.

Somewhere in the middle of it all, I realized that my cousin, without anyone's knowledge, was about to become a rabbi.

"So when, exactly, have you been in school?" I asked. "At night? Is there such a thing as a rabbinical correspondence course?"

"I'm sure I told you about it," he said. "There's a new seminary, over in the sixties."

"Flexible class time," Rabbi Perez said. "For working people. We take on a lot of older students. Your cousin here has taken to Talmud study like a duck to water."

"Talmud is all about playing the angles," Barry said to me.

The two rabbis looked at each other, puzzled, but I was beginning to put a few things together. I got up, this time insistent on leaving. The rabbis rose, too, and Barry, suddenly the only one sitting, jumped up, dropping his napkin on the ground.

"Take care of yourself," Barry said.

"Be well," said each of the rabbis.

"Your father," I said to my cousin, kissing his pudgy cheek, "would certainly be proud."

* * *

Whenever I worked late that year, which was more often than not, I liked to walk home through the streets of Manhattan, to let off steam. I had my regular route, walking from 57th and Sixth over to Central Park South, up to Columbus Circle then up Central Park West. After ten p.m., the street itself was quieter than my apartment, plus the doormen were always out, silent and vaguely protective. You saw plenty of young and middle-aged women walking alone that time of night, their Ferragamo pumps making a click click click on the sidewalk. Their faces—our faces—were set in exhausted determination: Someday hard work would surely triumph over economics and we'd pay off our Visa bills and trade the nagging symptoms of Chronic Fatigue Syndrome for a down payment on something permanent. Meanwhile, our eyes darted here and there in the darkness, trying to separate the rapists from the eligible single men.

On one such evening, I spotted a building with a large cardboard star of David outside. This had to be Barry's seminary, I thought, walking toward the area of Lincoln Center where Broadway and Columbus unite. Halfway there, I saw my cousin in a crowd, coming out a side door.

I called to Barry, and he turned around and smiled, came toward me with his arms outstretched, a book in one hand.

"Let's walk this way," he said, going back toward the park.

"Don't you want to go out with your friends?" I asked.

"Friends," he said. "You think I have anything to say to that bunch of losers?"

"But you're going to be a rabbi," I reminded him.

"It serves my purposes," he whispered, taking my arm.

"When you applied, didn't they need to see a copy of your diploma?" I asked. My cousin had dropped out of college in his senior year, 1973, forfeiting his scholarship and briefly entering a commune in San Francisco.

"I got them a copy of my diploma."

"You sent a fake diploma to a rabbinical school? Jesus, you're going to hell. . . ."

"First off, if you knew anything about our faith," he said, a faint smile playing on his lips, "then you'd know that there is no real conception of hell. There's Gehenna, which ain't such a bad place. Heaven, on the other hand, what's heaven? A bunch of Jews waiting around in limbo for the Messiah? A shortage of cute blondes and no Eggs Benedict? Fuck that. Second, the seminary counts life experience. Something you could use a little more of, if you ask me."

I assured him that New York had already given me enough experience for several lifetimes, and that as it was, I was exhausted and discouraged. I had been in Manhattan about six years at that point, and was wondering who in the whole city could afford to live decently without a trust fund, a rich spouse or, as Barry had warned me, an angle to play.

"I got a letter from Robert last week," Barry said. At the mention of his older brother, he lowered his voice.

"Any chance he'll get out early?" I asked. "For good behavior?"

"No chance. They throw the book at attorneys. A wasted life. He was the smartest one in the whole God-damned family."

"I know," I said. "I know." If there'd been a horse race (which in a certain way there had been), Robert, the oldest of us cousins, Barry, his baby brother, and I, twenty years Robert's junior, were the front runners to break away from the family vocations—generations of postal and blue-collar workers and small-time crooks. I'd gone to college because they'd done it; applied for the same scholarships, done the same dance. But of the three of us, none was as handsome or brilliant as Robert. It couldn't have been easy for Barry, growing up in his shadow.

Once, when I was twelve or so, Robert came back to Philadelphia for a few days and the whole family showed up to see him. Thirty of us all stuffed into Aunt Stacia's tiny rowhouse. I was sure Robert didn't even notice me, but after dinner he insisted we go for a walk, just the two of us. I jumped up and practically ran to the door, for I rarely got his full attention when he came back, everyone wanted to see him, touch his fine suits and taste the caviar he brought from New York. He was the prodigal returned. Barry was likely out in some neighbor's car that night, getting high. He was just as bright, in his own way, but already known as the family fuck-up. Even I, who worshiped both of them, could see that Robert was the genuine article and Barry some kind of imitation. One had started college, the other had finished it and gone on to law school. One was physically promising, the other perfected. One chased women, the other was chased by them, and had married the daughter of an enormously wealthy man. When Robert was around, Barry was even more prone to say the wrong thing, be a little too affectionate or over-anxious, even crass.

We only went to the end of the block. Robert stopped there, silent. He took a bill out of his wallet, folded it in thirds and placed it in my palm. "This is a secret between you and me," he said. "Don't tell your mother. Don't tell anyone." It was a $50 bill, the first one I'd ever touched. I looked up at his face, towering over me: he had blue eyes and thick black hair, enhanced by what my mother called bone structure. "I'm only letting you have this money under one condition," he said. "You have to spend it on something useless and beautiful. Don't let anyone talk you into putting it in the bank. You promise?"

I nodded. There was something sacred about the oath. Perhaps I took it too seriously, because I walked around with that money for years, couldn't let go of something he'd given me. Everywhere I went, I looked for the perfect object, the one possession that would lift me into his realm of beauty, wealth, and culture. I never spent that money. Over two decades later, it was still in an envelope in my underwear drawer.

I tried not to think about what it was like for Robert in prison. We didn't understand the extent of his crimes, or why he was sent to a federal facility, incarcerated with gang members and murderers. By all rights, he should have gotten a year or two in a white-collar place; he was accused of embezzlement and money laundering. Amateur theatrics, Barry said. He was working night and day, he told me, to try to get Robert pardoned or his sentence commuted.

"When was the last time you saw him?" I asked. The two brothers had not gotten along for years: Robert's second wife, Crea, a Miss Porter's girl if ever there was one, couldn't stand Barry, had long ago banned him from their home in Greenwich.

"Six, seven years," Barry replied. "Hey, blood's thicker than water. We were close as kids, in our way. I don't blame him 'cause his wife had that thing about canned fruit."

I smiled, vaguely remembering an incident in which Barry, on his last visit to Robert and his bride, had made a late-night raid on the family refrigerator in nothing but his undershirt. Crea, hearing the noise, came in and found him in the light of the open door drinking all the juice out of a large can of imported Brazilian pineapple chunks, leaving the fruit to dry out and rot on the bottom. This, she pronounced, was the last straw.

I'm sure, for both brothers, that incident now felt like a universe away. For it was Barry who was out there acting on Robert's behalf, and Robert, the great white hope, who'd been rendered powerless. I wondered just then where I might end up. My own future felt like anyone's guess.

"Robert got the brains and the looks," Barry continued. "And you, Annie, you got the class. But me, I got none of that, you know. That's why I need to . . ."

"Go to rabbinical school?" I asked, cutting him off. "You need God on your side?"

"Yeah," he said, and put his arm around me, pulled me close and planted a wet kiss on my cheek. "You smell like a million bucks, kid. You always smell like a million bucks."

I didn't know what he was up to with this rabbi thing, doubted it was legal, but I was rooting for him. How could I not be?

About a year later, it all became clear. Barry was out in East Hampton, rabbi to the very rich and somewhat famous. I'd asked him, when he was ordained in a small auditorium on 122nd Street, if he knew enough Hebrew to carry this off. Enough? He'd laughed at me. Enough for the laity, he said. For none of them knew what was what anymore, and the richer they were, he added, the less they knew. A nice sermon every now and then, about the virtues of charity, or family values, was all that was needed. A good excuse to stand around eating and trading stock tips.

He led me out of the crowded reception of rabbinical students and their parents, and onto a high balcony that overlooked a courtyard. All around us were life-size bronze sculptures of men lost in prayer. Perched on top of their unusually wide shoulders were tiny, almost insignificant heads.

"Jacques Lipschitz," Barry told me. "He did these statues."

"I think you underestimate the demands of what you're getting into," I said.

"Hey," Barry said, lighting a cigarette and blowing the smoke out the side of his mouth. "All they want from me is weekends and holidays. Nobody else wanted a position that asked for so little." He paused. A certain intense twinkle came into his eye, almost but not quite lecherous. The force of it made his eyes water. A new scheme he'd thought up, or a wild, out of control desire for something he couldn't quite describe.

"What?" I asked. "What's that look about?"

He wiped a tear from his eye. "Schmucks!" He dropped his cigarette butt to the ground, stomping on it with great gusto. "They all thought part-time was below them. Perfect for me to swoop in and get the spoils. Do they even realize who my congregants will be?"

A few months later, I came to know exactly who they were. By then, opportunity had knocked for me in the guise of a project for Hoffman and Hoffman—beefing up the public image of a company called Double Vision, which made fitness videos and did a quiet underground business in soft porn. They had gotten some bad press of late and we were hired to fix it. So while Barry was bestowing Sabbath blessings out in the Hamptons, I was in the office until eleven every night, learning as much about the flesh-peddling business as possible, including the remarkably high profit margin and enormous revenue opportunities offered by international cable sales. Though much of Double Vision's product came through the standard channels, there was one independent porn director/producer whose name, Victor Lampshade, sounded remarkably familiar. I dismissed the observation immediately, for how would I ever have met such a person before? Eventually, Lampshade called me, after receiving a memo I sent him on the advertising and promotion of his new film, *Down Under*, about a group of Australian coeds hitching their away across the United States.

"Annie, Annie Lieberman?" he asked. "Jesus, could that be you?"

"Uhuh," I said cautiously.

"It's Vic, Vic Lampshade? Your cousin Barry Vishniak's college roommate." He paused and I searched my memory, but came up with no picture of him, nor any reason for him to remember my name. "I came to your family for Thanksgivings during school," he said, then reminded me, as if to prove his credentials, of Aunt Stacia's much lauded duck, of Robert's first wife, who everyone swore was a Rothschild, and of how Uncle Vishniak always smelled of ear wax. "You were a cute little girl," he added. "I used to bring you bath toys. Until Barry told me if I ever did it again, he'd wait until I was asleep and cut off my . . . "

"Are you the one who's very very tall?" I asked quickly. "Beard and glasses?"

"That's me. Seven feet," he said, and laughed. "Helps with the camera angles. I do my own camera work, you know. Creative control is very . . ."

"I'm sure." It was all coming back to me. Mother and Aunt Stacia had often complained about both his table manners and how much food he could put away. Barry's parents, though in a perpetual state of debt, always offered enough to eat, particularly at holidays, even if it meant that Aunt Stacia spent the next six months beefing up her coupon files and buying day-old. But Victor Lampshade was not a relative, and his invitations quickly came to an end.

"Have you been in contact with Barry recently?" I asked.

"Not in a year or two. I used to string my movie out-takes together—the ones that weren't allowed by the triple X rating system—and send them to him every year for Christmas. In return he'd send me . . ."

"He's a rabbi now," I interrupted.

While his secretary scurried around in the background, attempting to find a paper bag—I believe he was having trouble breathing—I quickly got off the phone. A few days later, I advised Double Vision to stop distributing Lampshade's work once his contract ran out. His porn, I pointed out, was not soft, nor was it art. It was simply in bad taste. It was Lampshade's earlier movie, *Turkish Delight*, about a group of Turkish coeds hitchhiking their way across the United States, that had garnered so much negative attention from both feminists and the Muslim Anti-Defamation League.

Things went exceptionally well after that. A series of interviews with major fashion and fitness magazines, and the removal of Victor Lampshade's films, cleared the air for our client and created a fresh buzz. There was talk at work of my being promoted as I had worked so hard on the project. I also began dating Bruce Barnett, the president and founder of Double Vision. He was that essentially Darwinian genus and subspecies: the Manhattan self-made man. He'd risen from the slums of Bensonhurst to own a full floor on 72nd and Central Park West plus a house on the beach in Bridgehampton, and he understood the value of everything he'd earned.

Bruce's house on the beach had a magical quality, the insides achieved by a rigorous team of decorators, and the outsides more or less put there by God Himself. Three stories with a balcony jutting almost into the ocean, the place felt at times like a giant luxury liner. Off the sun room was a tennis court, and underneath the balcony, for those who preferred chlorinated water, was an Olympic-size pool. Inside, the house was full of Dutch modern furniture, abstract expressionist art, and apricot-colored carpets. During my weekends there, I often thought of Robert, locked in his dark little jail cell with no view. He would have appreciated the house's teak baseboards, marble jaccuzi and proximity to the ocean. I was still trying to impress him, if only in my imagination. To make myself worthy of his tastes. An accomplished sailor, as well as fencer, golfer, horseback rider, and any other activity forbidden to us in childhood, Robert had always seemed a natural to this world, as if born into it, whereas I was only faking. Bruce was faking, too, in his way. It was something we had in common. That, and how much we both enjoyed his money.

The more I went to Bridgehampton that year, the more all roads seemed to lead not to the easy polished class of Robert, but to the harsh angles of Barry. It turned out that when Bruce was in the Hamptons, he occasionally attended Rabbi Vishniak's synagogue. I asked him about it once, never letting on that Barry was my cousin.

"The rabbi's an idiot," he said, for he was a direct kind of person, used to having his opinions listened to. "I don't understand how he gets away with it. Skipping half the service, sermons that sound like they come out of a cracker jack box. He pinches women's butts during the *Kiddush*."

The thing was, Bruce found it amusing. I think a lot of them did. Like so many of Barry's congregation, Bruce was there because once or twice David Geffen had shown up, and Michael Milken, even in the midst of his prostate problems, had been known to drop by. In his own strange way, my cousin was becoming the success he'd always wanted to be.

About six months after Barry came to Congregation Mikveh Israel by the Sea, Bruce and I were at the Union Square Café for dinner. It was a Friday night, when reservations had to be made six months in advance unless you knew someone, and Bruce did. We were at a private balcony table on the second floor—the equivalent of a box at the opera. Just after the appetizers, I thought I spotted my cousin and a woman at a corner table on the ground floor.

"Are you all right?" Bruce asked, for I was growing pale. He'd just ordered his second bottle of an expensive Cabernet Franc. Bruce was the kind of drinker who took cover behind the status of his hobby—he had a wine cellar in the country and a man who stocked it for him. After we finished the second bottle, I knew he'd order several samples of port, spread out in front of him in silver thimble-like shot glasses, so that I could pick one. He was always happiest when I pointed to the most expensive brand; he'd smile and say "that's my girl." But I had the feeling, were he not wealthy, he'd have happily downed malt liquor in his kitchen.

"I have to go to the ladies' room," I said. "Start the wine without me. I'll be back."

"Fancy meeting you here," Barry called out when he saw me. He stood up very straight in his navy blue suit and began to glance upward at the higher tables. "Is that your date?" he asked. "That thug up there? Old enough to be your father . . ."

"He's not a thug," I said. "*Cosmopolitan* magazine voted him one of the most eligible bachelors in America."

"That only means he's got alotta money," Barry said. "Oh, boy, I wish my brother was here, he'd laugh his ass off." He introduced the woman he was with as Claudine.

"Pleased to meet ya," Claudine said, and stuck out a profoundly manicured hand, long red fingernails decorated with stripes and stars, like tiny American flags. She was wearing a tight white cotton sweater and a suede mini-skirt. Her legs were unusually long and shapely and she'd outfitted them in clear stockings touched with bits of gold thread and suede boots that came up above her knees. It was a look, that was for sure.

"What," I whispered, "are you doing out on a Friday night? It's the Sabbath."

Claudine giggled.

“Is she a congregant?” I asked.

“More or less. She’s Jewish. That’s good enough. Now that it’s winter, and the season’s over out there, we only have services once a month. Can’t get a minyan together otherwise,” he said, reminding me that a minyan was ten people.

“I know what it is. Aren’t you afraid one of your congregants will see you?”

He gestured for me to come closer, then whispered that he was on his way out of the rabbinate, something very big was about to happen for him. When I asked him if he’d like to have dinner some night the following week, he told me he couldn’t, for he was full up with hospital visits. “*Bikur Cholim*, visiting the sick,” he said. “It’s an essential part of my job.”

I looked over at Claudine, who was just then digging something out of her fingernail with the toothpick from her martini olive. “Is that how you two met?” I asked. “Hospital visits?”

“I think your date is getting restless,” Barry said, peering into the rafters. “Better get up there before it’s past his bedtime.” Then he turned to Claudine and said, “This is a lesson for ya, honey. These days in New York, if you’re rich enough, even if you’re a thug and practically geriatric, you can buy pretty much any woman you want. . . .”

I didn’t hear the end of what he said, turned and walked away, my face burning. It was not what he said as much as the horrible way he said it, and to an audience. For even then I still believed there was a chance I’d fall in love with Bruce Barnett. That, I told myself, was what separated me from Barry—I could never marry solely for money. He, on the other hand, would jump at the first rich woman who crossed his congregational path. That must have been the reason he took the job in the first place. I retreated up the steps to Bruce and his three thimbles of port, convinced that I had finally reconciled myself to the truth: Barry was incapable of loving anyone but himself and his bank account. His attempts at good will toward me over the years were likely just another scheme, a ripoff I had yet to discover. He had crossed the line that night, humiliated and embarrassed me, and I did not intend to forgive him.

* * *

Not long after that, a small piece in the *New York Post* told of a seventy-five-year-old congregant of Barry's who had died of brain cancer and left him four million dollars. Just a few months before his death, this man, who manufactured semiconductors, had married for the third time. The woman, said the article, was only thirty and named Claudine Goldschmidt. Clearly, the same Claudine I had met. Because the will had been changed so close to the time of death, the family was contesting it, both in terms of Claudine's inheritance and Rabbi Barry Vishniak's. Barry had been fired from his synagogue but he would eventually be a rich man, assuming the will stood up in court. Knowing Barry, whatever Claudine inherited, he'd most likely taken a percentage for brokering the match.

When he called me, a year later, the nineties were coming to an end.

"Come on kid," he said, "I'm sorry I was such a shit to you that night at Union Square. I was drunk, and jealous of that rich old guy up in the good seats. But now I'm a rich old guy with all the good seats I can handle. And you've never been a grudge holder."

He was right, I can never stay mad, it's not in my nature. A new century was dawning, a fresh start, and forgiveness seemed the only alternative. That or turn my back on him forever.

"What are you doing with all that money?" I asked.

"It's invested. Most of it's in dot-com stock. How's the job going?"

"Fine, I just got a promotion."

"Yeah, what's that mean? Another eight grand a year before taxes? A window in your office?" Unfortunately, he was right. That was exactly what I'd gotten, plus a title change and much longer hours. "You still with that thug?"

"No, I'm with a friend of his. It's a long story."

"Maybe you didn't get the class after all," Barry said. "Maybe you're no different from me, or from Robert. What's this one's name?"

"Charlie. He's in venture capital. He says in a few months, the roof's going to fall in on all these dot-com stocks. I suggest you think that over."

"I got a broker," he said. "Listen, I'm calling to invite you to my wedding. Why don't you bring whatever his name is? It's out in Rhinebeck. You'll like this girl I'm marrying, she has a master's degree."

"I thought you were dating Claudine?"

"Claudine?" His laugh was high pitched and hysterical, like a smug hyena. "Well, I wouldn't call what Claudine and I did dating, not by a long shot. But she did help make the two of us much richer."

I hesitated. "You still being sued? For that man's money?"

"I won," he said. "A will's a will. It's going to be a blowout wedding. You being my only living relative who's mobile, I hope you'll be there."

"You know, there are a few others you could invite," I said. I didn't name names, but he knew who I meant. More distant cousins—mail carriers, department store clerks, receptionists—honest people with children, pumping their own gas and paying large mortgages.

"Them?" Barry asked, and laughed.

I came without Charlie, who did not need talking out of any event related to my family. Claudine was at the wedding, and so were the two rabbis I'd met with Barry on West End Avenue. I was shocked to see them; my cousin's suit had created a local scandal. They assured me it was all hot air, and besides, he'd just donated $150,000 to their seminary.

The bride approached me at the smorgasbord before the ceremony and asked if I was the cousin Barry often spoke about. She had a magnificent sweep of blonde highlights, and was several inches taller than her future husband. But what struck me most, as she put out her hand to grasp mine, was how fine and white her skin was, alabaster and poreless, soft as the finest imported silk.

"Are you a hand model?" I asked, keeping hold for several extra seconds. I'd never touched anyone quite like her.

"Oh, no," she said, and smiled. Her voice sent tiny chills up and down my spine. "I do take good care of my hands and feet though. Would you like the number of my manicurist?"

I took a lipstick liner out of my bag and handed it to her. She wrote the number on a cocktail napkin, all the while describing her new job—she had just finished grad school—as the head of a nonprofit that funded day care centers in poor urban areas. I couldn't imagine such a woman loving my cousin, even with some of his better qualities, but she didn't seem the type to marry for money.

"We'll have to have lunch some time," she said, and almost but not quite kissed my cheek. Her breath was like a whiff of mint ice cream. After she walked away, the two rabbis approached, assuring me she was Jewish, despite the fact that her last name was Christmas, Margo Christmas.

"The mother's Jewish, at least," said Rabbi Perez.

"Christmas is not her real name," said Davidson, piling some more raw tuna on his plate.

During the ceremony, held in a solarium with a view of the Hudson River, I sat next to Claudine, now the millionairess, who was wearing a white see-through strapless Versace dress and very little underwear. I wondered if she was trying to upstage the bride, yet she seemed sincerely moved throughout the ceremony, dabbing at her eyes from the moment the organist began. My cousin beamed as he walked down the aisle; I'd never seen him look so happy. I wished suddenly that Robert could have been there. Then I would have asked him the following: Was it possible I had gotten it all wrong? That Barry, of the three of us, was the one truly capable of love?

"Do you know how he met Margo?" I asked Claudine.

"I think he hired her," Claudine whispered.

"Secretarial work?" I suggested hopefully. "Catering?"

"Not exactly," she said. "She worked her way through grad school with a girlfriend, it was a clever business if you ask me. Very high end, very expensive."

I didn't say a word, but as the bride made her way up the aisle to Barry, Claudine could tell I was all ears. "They hired themselves out," she said. "You know, two girls?"

"Two girls?"

"It's not like they let anyone touch them or anything. More like a performance." She described to me the evening, six months earlier, in which my cousin had received a wonderful surprise phone call, out of the blue, from his old college roommate, Victor Lampshade.

"I'm familiar with him," I said.

Claudine looked not a bit surprised. She told me how, in celebration of old times, the men got enormously wasted and called on the services of two women whose number Lampshade knew by heart: Margo Christmas and her partner, Debbie December.

When Barry woke up the next morning, he didn't remember anything of the night before. "Everyone was gone," Claudine said. "Except Margo. She was sleeping right next to him. Isn't it romantic?"

* * *

After their honeymoon in Nice, Barry and his bride moved back into the city. Not long after, he lost most of his money in bad Internet investments. I have no doubt he'll get it back again, somehow. Through it all, Margo stayed with him, and they seem the happiest of couples. She has been an excellent influence on Barry; he speaks more softly, is less inclined to lash out or use crude language, and no longer talks of the rabbinate.

Recently I received my one and only letter from Robert, written from his jail cell. Barry, he wrote, had succeeded in getting him moved to a lower-security facility where he was much more comfortable, but he didn't want to talk about himself. "I'm deeply concerned about my brother," he said. He wanted me to confirm how Barry met his wife, was horrified that his brother would marry a girl he could simply pay for. He went so far as to ask about her family background, feared they might have children and then Barry would really be stuck. Robert was always a social snob, and it had clearly gotten worse since his incarceration and second divorce. Both his ex-wives had been socialites, his only daughter a member of Connecticut's horsey set.

I wrote back to the post office box and long series of numbers that my cousin had become. I told him of my recent break-up with Charlie, and my decision to leave New York and all its trappings. Lately I had been thinking a lot about that fifty dollars he gave me so long ago, and how I had been searching unsuccessfully for the perfect object ever since. That was the difference between us: my cousins wanted more, more, more, so much more that they'd never have to think about Aunt Stacia's humiliating economies. And I wanted one priceless acquisition, the one possession that would illuminate my life and separate me, once and for all, from everything desperate, cheap, or poorly made. In the end, the result was the same. Robert was in jail, Barry could not relax for a moment, always playing the angles, and I was stuck in middle management, maxing out credit cards and dating men mostly for their ability to pay for expensive dinners. In short, I told him, there is no talisman. The faster we run from what we come from, the more the past stretches out in front of us like a never-ending freeway.

I went on to assure Robert that I'd recently lunched with Margo Christmas Vishniak. An article in the paper had lauded the work her organization does for children in the South Bronx, and we toasted her success. Not only does she have a master's degree in public policy from Yale, I assured him, but in my opinion she is the nicest person to come into our family in a long time.

NANCY REISMAN

TEA

It wasn't always the handsome men Lillian wanted: she liked a certain assurance, a scent, the way ordinary men were transformed by desire. How beautiful they became, their bodies shimmering, muscular legs stretching, broad backs, and thick arms bending around her, cocks hard in the dimness of hotel rooms, balls delicate against her thighs. She chose men who only in private revealed their sweeter natures: all had unforgiving lives, all wanted forgiveness. Even, it seemed, begged for such a thing, not simply sex but the transcendence sex might confer, a wild impossible blessing. Was it delusion, seeing them this way? Imagining her fingers slipping past a man's ribs, palm cupping his heart. She wanted that and in certain moments, the men—their faces bathed in yearning—seemed to want it too. But for all their spur of the moment appearances and near-desperate fucking and orgasmic proclamations *I love you Lillian I love you Lillian Oh Lillian Lillian Oh*—the men quickly vanished, never left their wives. It was a story she'd heard elsewhere. How it became hers she did not know.

But one way or another, your life unspools. Lillian saw the ways it could go. Take her parents, her father oafish and generous and dead; her mother fish-pale and morose, an ineffectual, complaining woman. Carp under river ice, nibbling ancient disappointments. The smallest pleasures—hot bath, tea, orange dusk through the bare elms—dissipated in Lillian's mother's house. Lillian could, at least, choose her own loneliness: at seventeen she took a tiny flat, a job as a shop clerk.

Years tick. You pass certain men in the street. Some you pull into your body, briefly, always too briefly, singular tastes and scents with you even when you're sure you have forgotten. And then, at a holiday party, a wedding reception, there's the quick peck on the cheek, close enough for you to catch the scent again. A sexual thrill rushes through you: you have to brace against it as the next in line, maybe his wife, maybe his daughter, also kisses your cheek, and other men you have known and their wives look on.

In 1927, the year she turned thirty-five, Lillian was plush. Zaftig. Dark lipstick, flowery perfumes, plunge neckline blue satin and beautiful shoes. In a tiny shop on Main Street, Maxwell's, she sold stationery, fountain pens, account ledgers, dark leather diaries. When Abe Cohen appeared, she made no assumptions: for years he had lived on the outskirts of her thinking. Dull. Handsome. Relentlessly upstanding. A friend of her older brother's, respectable in ways her brother Moshe was not. A family man, which is to say he slaved to bring his wife over from Russia, then kept her pregnant for a decade, his life increasingly obscured by that strange brood of daughters, one pleasure-loving son. There had once been rumors—a romance with a Polish girl before his wife arrived—dusty now, insignificant. He himself insignificant, but for his jewelry store, display cases stocked with opals, rubies, diamond studs, pearls she could pull across her tongue.

"Hello." Abe Cohen smiled, removed his hat, and made a show of examining leather-bound account books and watermarked paper. He sorted through the ivory letter stock and asked, "Would you like tea?" as if in mid-conversation.

"Pardon?"

He gestured at the street. "Miss Schumacher, would you like a cup of tea?"

His thumb moved across the ivory paper in small deliberate circles. Cultured pearls, she thought, *tea*? He dampened his lips with his tongue, and his gaze was direct, chestnut. She'd forgotten his eyes were chestnut, if she had ever known. Bits of white in his hair now, charcoal overcoat like an unbuttoned pelt and beneath it the three-piece suit. Trim for his age, trim for any age except boy and the thumb circling and circling, and when had he unbuttoned the coat? Fedora in his left hand, deeper charcoal. "May I take you to tea?" A soft grit in his voice—this was what sold jewelry to women, of course, that landscaped baritone, and the three-piece suit with all the buttons suggesting their opposite, a continued unbuttoning, and those thumbed circles on the notepaper saying what he meant by tea.

His wife was ill, she'd heard, *failing*. "That's kind of you," she said. This was the moment to decline, or at least steer their meeting to a public venue, sanctioned commiseration: *How is your wife today? Is she feverish? Walking? Eating? Can she take soup?* Tea and pastry. He had beautiful hands. She wanted to touch his mouth, the point on his lip he reached for with his tongue. "I would like that."

She closed the shop early, aware of him watching her hands as she locked the windowed oak door, pulled on her leather gloves, wrapped her blue scarf around her neck. He stood out on the sidewalk a respectful distance, easily a chaperone sent by her brother. When did she decide? In a shopping bag, she carried a box of notepaper and a box of envelopes. The air smelled of snow, the daylight weak behind pillowing gray clouds. Wind pushed east from the lake. She hesitated. Paper in paper in snow, she thought. Wet scraps. He was pressing his tongue against his upper lip. "Would you mind if I stopped home?" She gestured at the shopping bag.

She didn't pause in the foyer of her building, even when he fell behind her, slowed, presumably readying to wait. He followed her up the stairs to the second floor and her apartment. And she was thinking then of the cold outside and the heat of her apartment, the charcoal coat and the buttons, forgetting already his larger life, almost forgetting the tearoom down the street. *Please come in*, she said, and he removed his overshoes and followed her into the small parlor. A reserved breathiness to him. Lillian touched her palm to his right cheek, and he kissed her hand, and then her mouth. There was no hesitation, only a brief awkwardness in the undressing: her fingers pulling open his shirt buttons *Oh*, his checked step back, as if he'd always undressed himself. His face bore the near drunk, desperate expression of men who have been fighting desire and given over to it—men who might later soberly admit *I have broken a commandment*—tiresome as that was. Best to see him with this expression, beyond caring. In her bed he entered her and moved slowly and then rapidly, climaxing quickly. He touched her for an hour, then rose and washed and kissed her forehead and left.

Two weeks later he reappeared, plied her with cakes from a

Polish bakery, good gin smuggled from Canada, moved his fingers over her face and kissed her on the mouth, all gratitude and lust, before running his hands over her breasts and belly and down between her legs, stroking then entering her: it was staggering and deeply pleasurable, bitter to relinquish.

In the first months, Abe's courtship seemed to her a kind of truth, his attentions and her pleasures contradicting all other absence. *Shana* he called her, beautiful one, and during their hours together she believed him. How easily she could forget all previous courtships, the fickle nature of men and romance, the impermanence of passion, the moment at which unalloyed sweetness begins to change. Abe liked ritual, and in the first months held to the rituals of cake and gin and tenderness, intense sex during which his desire seemed to meet her own. But in the spring Abe came to her restless and unhappy and without gifts. She offered him holiday wine, which he refused. What he wanted was hard and unsparing: he took her from behind, not kissing her, not looking her in the eye. It was something men did. *Oh*, she thought, *this*. She gave over to him and her body seemed a separate thing and she dissolved beneath him. He wanted her to say *yes, I like it*. "Yes I like it," she said, both lying and in some way meaning it. A strange release when he pinned her down, as if she had reached the end of fear. Her lungs refilled only after he'd left her apartment. He returned the next week with fruit and chocolate, kissed her, caressed her, and did not mention his previous visit.

No one seemed to notice the affair, Abe's biweekly visits to Lillian's apartment, although he was known in her neighborhood. Or perhaps no one would believe it of Abe, who after all was her brother's dear friend, a man suffering the burden and sorrow of his wife's illness. Lillian did not meet him in public or ask for more time. She did not want Rebecca Cohen's life: she wanted Abe as she had found him in her flat that first day, a man shaken loose from the world, immersed in the pleasures and wilder demands of his body and her own. For the first year, the trysts at her apartment were enough. For the first year she did not stop seeing other men.

And then another January. Rebecca Cohen collapsed on a streetcar and was confined to bed. This was the word from

Lillian's sister-in-law Bertha, the word in the markets and beauty parlors. A brief note from Abe: my wife is ill. And nothing. Slow ticking days, desire accumulating, a honeyed thickness becoming ever more dense, the surfaces of each day coated with the repeating question *where's Abe where's Abe where's Abe*, which did not stop when she drank or slept. And sleep was instead a drifting, the bed an ice floe, lake winds pushing her further and further into arctic realms. She tried the remedies she knew: bootleg gin, reefer, mechanical sex with other men, *not-Abe*, through which the thrumming persisted, without return or release. There seemed no end to her awareness of him in the world. Downtown, almost daily, she saw walking reminders: his daughters, a small army, everywhere. The sourest one, Jo, now worked in Moshe's law office; the strangest, Celia, wandered the city, regularly stopping at Maxwell's to touch and sometimes steal sheets of paper. The eldest was forever at the druggist buying syrups and pills for her mother; the married, stylish one appeared at dress shops Lillian preferred. Two daughters had his eyes, the others his mouth and brow but favored Rebecca, whom Lillian now thought of only as *her*. This required effort. At the butcher shop, the fruit market, in department stores and tearooms, in beauty parlors, in the post office, on the streetcars, in the lobby of the Hippodrome, women clucked and murmured *poor Rebecca*, and *Rebecca's girls look pinched* (hadn't they always?) and *Rebecca's Abe is so pale, poor Abe*.

By mid-February Lillian was half-eaten with desire and mute grief. What reprieve she found came late at night when the arctic drifting deepened and the night seemed a translucent haze, bits of other winters resurfacing as if new: a burgundy reading chair, air colored by men's voices—her father's, his friends'—boisterous and gravelly sweet, tobacco smoke, hot tea. Peppermints. Her father's tone of hilarity, his off-key singing, his callused hand resting on the crown of her head. The chair and voices and smoke blurred into a single feeling pulled from that other decade, a feeling as immediate as the streetlight through her bedroom window or her white duvet or the freckles on her forearm. And yet it was intangible, a feeling yoked to empty space.

The hazy merging of *then* and *now* quietly leaked from a night into a morning, and then into a day, and another day, as

Abe's absence solidified. On Main Street, Lillian would hear and immediately lose not Abe's baritone but a graveled laugh—perhaps the exact laugh she remembered, or a stranger's, or just a misinterpreted squeal of streetcar brakes. The burgundy chair would swim up at her while she restocked sheets of onion skin, as if it had been there all along, waiting for her, as if it might even restore the tea and tobacco smoke and peppermints, the gravelly voice, the hand on her head, all of what she could and could not name. Say the burgundy chair was waiting for her, say it was *that* chair—would the room and by extension the house it had occupied also wait for Lillian? There was a single Brunswick Boulevard address, a house her father had chosen and paid for, a house her mother inherited and from which Lillian had fled. Yet in her mind there seemed two separate houses, one she wanted to visit and one she did not. Was one hidden inside the other? Throughout the city, snow fell in thick flakes, day after day, and the wind came in off the lake, the air itself blurring, and on these, the blurriest of days, it seemed possible the Brunswick house was still her father's. On a Friday evening Lillian set out through the snow to the two-story wood-frame off Humboldt Parkway, the painted steps and snowdrifted porch and thick brass mezuzah in the doorway convincingly belonging to the house of memory.

Lillian's mother Isabel appeared in the doorway in a dark blue dress and glass beads, lipstick brightening her face, but the red mouth shifted between a flat pucker and a frown. She kissed Lillian on the cheek, an unfishy kiss. Lillian tried to decide what parts of her mother to believe: the kiss or the furrowed brow and intermittent frown. And what parts of the house to believe. The kitchen smelled of bread and roast chicken; in the dining room, the linen tablecloth was spread, the table set with her mother's wedding silver and white china and brass candlesticks. But the living room seemed eerie and hard to navigate: three card tables covered with picture puzzles—half an Eiffel Tower, and two scrambled landscapes—occupied the space between the sofas. Porcelain figurines of forest animals crowded the old bookshelf and mantel. And where was the chair? Had there ever been a burgundy chair?

Isabel lit the candles and murmured the Sabbath blessings,

and the frown and furrowing vanished. She must have been beautiful, Lillian thought, and it seemed a new thought, though her mother had been called beautiful and still sometimes was. During Isabel's prayer, you could almost see her as someone else, someone gracious. The house as that peppermint house. Then the blessings ended and Isabel's mouth reverted to a carp's and she took the carving knife to the chicken. "Nice you decided to visit, Lillian," she said. "And for Shabbat. Who would have guessed?"

"I wanted to see you," Lillian said, but the sentence came out as a question. The word "you" seemed to wobble.

"So you say. Shabbat shalom," Isabel said. "You need money you go see your brother Moshe."

Lillian felt a sharp prickle in her temples. Already, the beginnings of headache, her beautiful forgetting unraveling. How fast the turn—had it always been this fast? Had the Brunswick house ever been anyone's but Isabel's? In the dining room's flat cool, fishmouthed Isabel slapped potatoes onto wedding plates, and below the aromas of dinner lurked the house's trace scents of ammonia and talc and chicken fat. As always. The absence of deeper voices as always, a bitter, heart-stopping *always.* How could Lillian have thought otherwise? In her belly she felt a sharp pull, an impulse to hit. "I don't need money," she said, and reached for the sweet wine.

"You going to bring me more of that?" Isabel said. "I got that from Rabbi Greenberg."

"Moshe will. I brought you paper from the shop."

"Paper I can buy," Isabel said. "But thank you."

"If you don't want it, Ma, I'll take it with me."

"Did I say thank you? I like the paper. It's good what you bring."

And maybe *good* suggested another opening, slim, evanescent, but still a crack in a door through which Lillian might see through her mother to her father. She waited, ate in silence. The chicken tasted of rosemary and onion and salt, there were roast carrots, and Isabel set out honey for the challah. Poppy cake. Strong tea which Lillian cut with lemon.

"You met someone?" Isabel said.

"No."

"You going to tell me or not?"

"There's nothing to tell."

Isabel sipped at her tea with exaggerated care. "He must be no good."

"Ma, what did I just say?"

"Your brother Moshe, he's a good man. A schemer but a good man. Bertha too, you should take a lesson from her. Stop with the nogoodnik."

Had her father's friends actually visited? Lillian couldn't have made them all up. Couldn't have made him up.

"Lillian? You hear what I'm telling you?"

"What else do you want, Ma?"

"You already got pearls."

"What?"

"You think I don't know you. I know you. You want more pearls, you ask your brother Moshe."

She had not invented Abe Cohen, his hands moving over her, had not invented their coupling: these remained clear. What seemed slippery and opaque was the life he occupied without her. Lillian could only imagine it as a shell around blank air, the reasons for his absence spurious. And so, in the late weeks of winter, Lillian deliberately circled Abe's life, choosing the streetcar stop nearest his store, visiting his favorite bakery, buying from the pharmacy near his house. Twice she borrowed her brother's Packard and drove it up and down Abe's street. House lights on the first floor and often the second, occasional fluttery movements at the windows. Snow drifts buttressed the side of the house. The front walk was cleanly shoveled. Ice shone on porch rails and shingles. The interior remained impenetrable, a kind of shadow into which she and Abe had disappeared.

She waited until March before visiting the jewelry store. The son, Irving, minded the counter. Beautiful boy, spitting image of his father but still soft, irresolute, except for that glimmer, the same pleasure lust she saw in Abe's private moments. In Irving the lust was more public but more diffuse. "Can I help you, Miss Schumacher?" A light purr in the voice.

No sound from the back room, where Abe set stones, though the door was ajar. She asked to see bracelets, and Irving opened up the case, pulled out a velvet card with four, let her hold them to the light and try them on. For her sister-in-law Bertha, she said. She'd have to confer with her brother, she'd send him over to look. And would Irving please give regards to his family, all best wishes for good health?

Two nights later, Abe returned to Lillian's flat, defeated and sad, his hands redolent of illness. Complied when she asked him, first, to bathe.

One thing Lillian knew: open the door to risk and the room will widen and stretch. The work of caution—automatic at first—becomes over time onerous and boring, another chore in a too-long list of chores. You can't manage it all, defer whatever seems inessential. And this was how she explained Abe's about-face: almost nightly, he visited. Seemed, in fact, oblivious to risk, foggy with exhaustion and despair. He wept when she touched him, wept when she did not. The weeping, she knew, was hidden from his family. Seeing Abe this way—shaken down to boy, neck-deep in bewilderment and sorrow—moved her. But she also preferred him careless. He'd appear at her flat, late, and collapse on her bed, and after a time they'd make love without speaking. For an hour he might sleep. And though she knew better, some nights she'd meet him on Delaware, a few blocks from his house. Once, at two a.m, Lillian parked the Packard across the street from his house and he slipped out the back door and through the neighboring yard, crossing the snow-crusted lawns to the curb, her borrowed car.

They carried on this way until Rebecca died. During shiva, Lillian joined her brother and his wife when they paid their respects to the family. Red buds studded adjacent trees, crocuses bloomed in the Cohens' front yard, the bright greens of the new grass mixed with the winter browns. For the first time, Lillian entered the house on Lancaster. In the foyer the dark wood shone, wallpaper pattern of spray roses spilling down the hallway and into the parlor. There was a faint scent of cedar and baked sugar and tea, and in the parlor visiting relatives sat quietly with the daughters—the crazy one, the paper thief, Celia, perfectly still and paler than usual, Irving slumped beside her; the married daughter elegant in black, whispering to Abe, her husband standing guard beside them, adjusting his spectacles and surveying the room. The other daughters were ragged and red-eyed, Jo meeting Lillian's condolences with a scouring stare. The pattern of roses dropped behind the upright piano; sheet music lay open, a sonata. Lillian retreated to the hall which led in one direction to the fragrant kitchen, the other to the front staircase, with its fat maple banister and Persian runner, silent invitations to push farther into the house. She passed the formal dining room (more roses) before two synagogue women arrived, arms loaded with platters and casseroles, a jumble of piety and whispers, noodles and fish. Lillian stole outside to the empty front porch, away from the windows, and waited for Moshe and Bertha to finish with their sympathy.

Lillian would not have chosen that wallpaper: the clipped pink roses girlish, sentimental, falling in dainty lockstep. Still, the papered rooms felt like sugar bowls, and after she left that day the image of the spray roses returned to her. Davenport in dark wood, upholstery the color of biscuits and linen, Abe's reading chair a fine pale green. Upright piano, the scatter of black notes across the white pages of the open score. She pictured the parlor empty of visitors, the davenport clear of Celia and Irving, open, inviting, a place to let the day hush, to gaze up at roses, light patterned by budding trees, lazy piano softening the afternoon. That night, Lillian imagined her own bed as the davenport, lulled herself to sleep with the pretense of thick petals and buttery air and Abe's weight upon her.

That was the beginning of a more deliberate daydream, the trail of roses leading up and back to both glimpsed and unseen rooms: the wide white kitchen, the polished dining room table, and the tall glassed cabinets, company china and Passover dishes, thin-stemmed goblets, heavy brass candlesticks, silver Kiddush cup. And upstairs? The carpeted steps leading to an unlit pocket of space. And to pass through such space? Like passing through night, perhaps. Lillian knew about the windows, stout rectangles facing the street, a round moon of glass above them, smaller windows on the sides. She guessed at the floor plan: front and back stairways, the windows suggesting a division of rooms. In some of the rooms there would be beds, dressing tables, chairs. Cream walls? Some ought to be cream, a base that would hold the light but allow you to add color. And in the master bedroom, there ought to be violet and royal blue bedcovers and chairs, which would suit Abe. She imagined herself and Abe coupling in pale blue sheets, his broad back and thick arms wrapping her, intermittent dark freckles on the white skin, black eyelashes against the blue, and the steady rhythm and near ache of Abe moving inside her. Butterscotch and white for the front guest room, perhaps some fleur-de-lis.

She considered colors for other rooms, tending toward blues and greens, inventing a complete house the shape and size of Abe's house on Lancaster. Downstairs, the rose wallpaper stayed, the piano stayed, the parlor furniture stayed, and at moments the invented house and the real one seemed indistinguishable. In the fantasy house, Abe's children did not appear; presumably they had moved to another invented house, or, better, another city. That could happen, in the mind. The arrangement seemed beyond Lillian's will, as if Abe's house had chosen to occupy her and she could not refuse it. The invented house hummed, waiting to be manifest in the physical world.

You begin, of course, with where you are. Begin with the life you know, begin with sex. Try a simple request, and make the request late at night, after he has climaxed. A Thursday. Lillian and Abe were spooned together in her bed, Abe's hand still on her breast, when Lillian asked, "Shall we go to a restaurant next week?"

Simple and not simple, a meal in a restaurant. Or tea? Wasn't it what he had once proposed? A table, a waiter, a menu. Polite conversation. Nothing, compared to what they'd done. Tea but tea in public and now: a signal of earnest courtship or of scandal. He closed his eyes, sighed. She had seen him respond this way to Celia's incessant *could we will we can I* before he answered no. But to Lillian he said, "I don't know." To Lillian he said, "Perhaps in time."

A week later, she cooked a dinner at her flat. Abe arrived harried and distracted, and she poured him gin, set the table with a blue-bordered cloth, carried out plates. Roast beef and sweet potatoes, glazed carrots, salty bread. Tea and linzertorte. By dessert he was back to the Abe she wanted: alert gaze, body tipped in her direction, his cheeks slightly pink. "Does this feel like home?" she asked, and he answered yes.

She stroked the back of his hand. "You don't invite me to your home."

"Oh but Lillian. You know why."

"Good reasons," she said. "Before."

"*This* is our place."

She hesitated. The blue bordered tablecloth seemed part of a past life, and she thought of that other polished table, and the imagined linens and the glass bowls, a basket of pears. The invented house seemed wholly real and she did not know what this meant. "Not forever," she said. She loosened her fingers from his and rose, cleared the dinner plates and the empty serving platter and the used glassware. Then she offered him chocolate from the box he'd brought, square pieces decorated with waves of green.

"Tell me," Lillian said to her brother, "how a person buys a house."

Moshe had always been a big man, but here at his law office he seemed even larger than usual. An enormous, round-bellied suit, sighing at her. "Lilly, would you like a cigarette?"

She took one from him, allowed him to light it, noted the resemblance of his fingers to the cigar he lit for himself. "A little house?" he said. "Just for you?"

"Maybe that."

"Or maybe you're thinking a bigger house?"

"I think all sorts of things. Let's say any house."

"Are you asking can I buy you a house?"

"No. I want to know how a person buys a house."

"First," Moshe said, "a person needs to have money. Lilly, sweetheart, you do not."

"But if I did?"

Moshe squinted, as if he were adding numbers in his head. Pursed his lips, not unlike a fish. "A very large if. You understand that? You be careful, Lillian."

You cannot rush fate, Lillian told herself, no matter how sure you are of your path. For now, she was in God's hands; she imagined a light touch on the top of her head and refrained from talk of houses. Surprisingly, this seemed to work. In the spring of 1929, Rebecca Cohen's gravestone was unveiled, and two weeks later Abe again asked Lillian to tea. A

Wednesday afternoon. They took a table in Jocelyn's tea room, surrounded by middle-aged women. Abe bought tea and sweet cakes, inquired about her mother's health. Asked about the stationery business, where the paper was shipped from, if the shop owner traveled to New York, as Abe often did. Mentioned that her brother's law firm was growing admirably. Lillian watched his lips as he talked. This was a strange game, Lillian thought, but a pleasant one. She sipped her tea and folded her hands in her lap and spoke about her fondness for, of all things, gardens; she imagined kissing him in the tea room. After an hour he asked if he might secure a taxi cab for her.

Among the gossips there was murmuring the next day, there always would be murmuring about Lillian, despite the legitimacy of the tea with a widower. But Lillian's faith in God seemed justified. She felt a surge of hope: why shouldn't she be happy? Why shouldn't Abe? On his next visit, he brought flowers to her apartment, and there seemed a new lightness to his mood. Now he wanted to make small but definite plans: tickets to the theater, an afternoon at the Falls. In May he suggested a restaurant dinner with Moshe and Bertha, followed by dessert and coffee at his house.

The evening they went to Little Paris, Lillian wore black silk and pearls, her hair cut that day in shoulder-length waves. Abe brought corsages for Lillian and Bertha. At Moshe's house, they drank illicit champagne, then drove to the restaurant, Bertha carrying Moshe's gin in her handbag. A waiter arrived with savory tarts, then with soup. Four courses. They drank the gin over ice. Through the dinner, Abe joked with Moshe and squeezed Lillian's hand and seemed purely happy; by mid-evening, Lillian was awash in grand hope. The soft night air seemed a confirmation, and on the drive to Abe's house, she leaned her head out the side window—the elms and maples in full leaf, the breeze pushing her hair from her face, Abe holding her hand, kissing her on the cheek and pulling her back into the car. And when they reached Abe's house it was quiet, the lilacs swaying in the light wind, perfuming the parlor, which was as Lillian envisioned: falling roses, empty davenport, pale green chairs. There was a bakery cake, chocolate, and Bertha brewed tea. In the china cabinet, Lillian found dessert plates: gilt edged, the inner pattern a ring of grapes on the vine, the fruit precise and dense and violet blue.

Would the evening have gone any differently if, instead, she'd taken down the everyday china, left the grapevines dutifully in place, stubborn tribute to the dead? Abe and Moshe lighted cigars and patted each other on the back, and Bertha—round and affectionate and drunk—concerned herself with cake, which she served in thick slices. Lillian sipped the milky tea, savored the chocolate. Abe sat beside her on the davenport, and it seemed that another life was beginning, that grief had fallen away and time had stopped, leaving them forever in this bright soft evening, this parlor, this house. Abe's fingers circled and circled Lillian's palm, sweet measured pressure he might later move to the rest of her body.

If the others sensed the presence of Abe's daughters in the house, they didn't think much of it. Why would they? Moshe and Bertha commonly entertained, their children and housekeeper discreetly migrating to the upper floors. Here on Lancaster, there had been little entertaining for years, but Abe—admittedly flushed with alcohol—seemed completely at ease, affectionate and unworried. It was after all Abe's own house, his parlor, his evening with Lillian and Moshe and Bertha. And the parlor seemed fully the parlor Lillian had imagined.

They were still eating cake when Lillian heard steps on the back stairway, an uneven thudding, the steps approaching from the kitchen through the long hall to the parlor. A muttering. And then in the parlor doorway stood Jo and Celia—Jo in another of her mud-colored dresses, Celia puffy-eyed, her thick hair disheveled. They stared at Lillian, Lillian and Abe, Lillian again. Celia swung her left arm back and forth.

Jo snorted. "You seem pleased," she said to Lillian.

From across the room, Moshe cleared his throat, and Jo registered his presence and placed her hand on Celia's swinging arm. Moshe smiled his expansive, warning smile and gestured at the cake, "Would you girls care for some dessert?"

"Mr. Schumacher," Jo said. "Thank you, no. Hello, Mrs. Schumacher. We'll go upstairs. Celia?"

"Hello." Celia relaxed her arm, then fixed her gaze on the dessert plates, and in that moment the evening tipped. "Those aren't yours."

"No," Lillian said.

"Celia," Abe said.

Bertha, drunk, traced the grape pattern with her index finger. "Beautiful," she said.

And Celia stepped into the parlor, her arm swinging again. "Not yours." She yanked Bertha's plate from her hand, then Lillian's from the table, bits of cake still on them.

Abe, white-faced, standing, lurched toward Celia. "Celia, leave the plates."

But Celia grabbed the other cake-stained plates, tucking them against her dress and retreating to the hall.

"Enough." Abe's voice was louder now and harsh, and Celia unblinking.

"Not yours," she repeated, this time to her father.

Moshe licked his lips, a deliberately delicate gesture. Checked his watch, while Bertha glanced out at the swaying coned lilacs.

"You don't tell me," Abe said. "You do not tell me."

And now Celia turned back to Lillian. "You stay away from them."

"Celia you will apologize," Abe said.

Celia backed up to the staircase, the plates crushed against her, chocolate crumbs falling over the parquet floor. "*You* apologize," she said.

"Jo, take your sister upstairs," Abe said.

Jo crossed her arms over her chest and dropped her voice, "If she wants to go."

Would knowledge have mattered? Lillian did not yet know that Celia only slept in her late mother's sick room (a second floor room which faced the street and the tall elms, and from which a familiar Packard could be remarked); that Jo had suffered insomnia since her mother's collapse; that Rebecca Cohen had not been an Isabel. These were things you tried not to know, truths that might starkly appear and pin you down anyway.

Neither Abe nor Jo nor Celia moved. There was the chugging of a car on Lancaster, and Moshe rose, smiling, stretching, as if nothing had transpired in the mood. "What about a nightspot?" he said. Ashed his cigar. "I think we should. Lillian? Bertha love?" He set a hand on Abe's shoulder. "Abe?"

"What?" Abe said.

"Let's." Moshe ushered the Schumacher women to the front

door, nodding to Jo and Celia, "Good evening, ladies." And then Lillian was out on the lawn, stranded it felt, her sister-in-law murmuring *That Celia's a nasty one* and strolling past her to the Packard. The upper reaches of the house were lightless, remote. Lillian's palms were damp with sweat, and the lilac-scented air seemed a strange trick. How does one forestall what has already passed? Lillian counted the windows. The ember of Moshe's cigar marked his progress down the front steps and the walkway, Abe and Celia and Jo now fragmented silhouettes through the open front door. *Lillian?* Moshe's hand a warm weight on her shoulder. *Lilly, come with me.* Cake still sweet in her mouth, thin breeze nosing a sycamore, the Packard sputtering awake. Then the puzzle of silhouettes shifted, lush grass spilling over Lancaster Avenue, her fingers not exactly her own, her body close to dissolving in the fragrant air, and the night sky unspeaking.

JULIAN LEVINSON

IS THERE A JEWISH TEXT IN THIS CLASS?: JEWISH MODERNISM IN THE MULTICULTURAL ACADEMY

Are courses on modern Jewish literature good for the Jews? The question has become exceedingly relevant for me since, for one thing, these are the sorts of courses I teach, and, for another, I have a growing sense that my courses, listed under the rubrics of both English and Jewish Studies, may not fully satisfy my various constituencies—including some of my students, the donors who supply my salary, and the legions of demographers worried about Jewish continuity. Whereas these varied groups often seem intent upon arriving at some grounded and coherent "Jewish identity," the writers that I teach—ranging from S. Ansky to Saul Tchernichovsky to Henry Roth to Moyshe-Leyb Halpern—celebrate the energies that disrupt cultural continuities. Rather than supporting the sanctity of collective life, they champion imaginative freedom and idiosyncratic self-fashioning. The more I read and teach modern Jewish literature, then, the more I suspect that the word "Jewish" and the word "literature," so comfortably set beside one another in the course title, turn out upon examination to clash irreverently and inconclusively with each other. Hence the question: is there a Jewish text in this class? And if not, what is the course doing in a Jewish Studies curriculum?

I offer my thoughts not only to those who teach and think about Jewish writers, but to anybody sorting through the conflicting demands of the multicultural academy. The courses that a generation ago would have signaled a defiant assertion of identity—courses such as African-American literature and women's literature—have now become required. Yet even as marginal literatures have gained this sort of legitimacy, it is not necessarily clear what such courses actually assert. In treating the case of Jewish literature here, I do not wish to suggest that the Jewish difference is necessarily analogous to, say, the Chicano/a difference or the Asian-American difference. Far from it. We have thankfully moved beyond the reflex tendency of treating all "different" identities as some monolithic Other. Yet some questions bind us together; and the one I consider below—the relevance of literature (and of modernism in particular) to a scholarly agenda of reinforcing and promoting collective identity—resurfaces with faithful regularity. I have seen enough sparks fly from the confrontation between so-called Jewish texts and readers who look to literature as a mirror for the collective self to suspect that educators working in other fields have faced similar problems and have considered the need to rethink the relationship between literature and identity.

I. Jewish Studies: From Wissenschaft to Ethnic Studies

Since the 1960s, when Jewish Studies programs began proliferating throughout American colleges and universities, the discipline's borders have become increasingly porous. Once the domain primarily of historians and Biblical philologists, Jewish Studies has welcomed into its ranks sociologists, anthropologists, philosophers, and scholars of comparative literature. At the same time, the field's overall self-conception has changed. Inevitably, it has come to mirror the changes in American academia in general, particularly the emphasis on ethnic identity that has been a feature of college curricula for at least two decades.

The influence of the Ethnic Studies paradigm on Jewish Studies can perhaps be illustrated by the *scandale* that erupted at Queens College in the summer of 1996, centering around the Yiddish Professor Thomas Bird. Bird, who had been teaching in the Queens College Jewish Studies program for twenty-five years, was appointed to be the program's new director. He felt compelled to resign from the post after a mere two weeks, however, when another Queens College professor publicly criticized his appointment on the grounds that Bird is not Jewish. Elucidating his position, sociologist Samuel Heilman explained that the director of any Ethnic Studies program has responsibilities over and beyond purely administrative and academic ones. "Jewish Studies exists to give Jewish students a role model," he told an interviewer, "just like any other Ethnic Studies program."[1] He added that "the person who heads the program is more than just a teacher. He's someone who stands for the group."[2] According to this logic, Bird would inevitably fail as a role model because he is not Jewish; his appointment jeopardizes the fundamental mission of Jewish Studies.

Heilman's charges did not go without comment. Various Jewish academics and community leaders, indeed even Elie Wiesel, spoke out in defense of Bird. After all, in addition to being an expert in Yiddish language and literature, Bird has been a longtime advocate for the freedom of Soviet Jewry, testifying before Congress a number of times. Many have agreed that Heilman's charge reflected an unfair bias.

I do not propose here to weigh in on either side of this controversy so much as to marvel at the historical novelty of Heilman's charges. Until the Queen's College controversy, the most common anxiety voiced by Jewish Studies practitioners was not that the field was being overrun by outsiders, but that it was not sufficiently considered a part of the mainstream academic tradition. This sort of concern may be discerned in the early literature of the American Academy for Jewish Research, which was organized in 1920 and is the oldest of the Jewish Studies organizations in North America. Using a resonant political metaphor, the acting president Alexander Marx insisted in a 1928 publication upon the need to "put Jewish research in its right place in the republic of learning."[3] Similarly, when Brandeis University was formed in 1948, under the exclusive sponsorship of American Jews, the trustees were eager to emphasize that although it sought to give to Jewish learning a "rightful place in its curriculum" the institution was nevertheless thoroughly "non-sectarian." The rhetoric of the university's first General Catalogue emphasizes Jewish participation in a larger social network: "Brandeis came into being because of a desire of the Jewish community to make a corporate contribution to American higher education."[4] Many contemporary Jewish Studies scholars have similarly resisted making their discipline seem like a partisan or parochial enterprise, and, as Howard Adelman has pointed out, have consistently distanced themselves from the label of "ethnic."[5] By contrast, Heilman embraces what he sees as the analogy between Jewish Studies and other Ethnic Studies programs in the contemporary academy. His conception of Ethnic Studies informs an agenda of sustaining Jewish particularism, hence his uneasiness over the prospects of offering a non-Jew the reins of Jewish Studies.

These two impulses—to join the "republic of letters" on the one hand and to maintain an exclusive Jewish ethnicity on the other—reflect sharply contrasting priorities on the Jewish community's cultural agenda. The first goes back to the early nineteenth century, when many of the institutions of Western European society were becoming increasingly hospitable to Jews. At this transitional moment, a now-legendary group of young scholars in Berlin gathered to form the *Verein für Kultur und Wissenschaft der Juden* (Society for Culture and Science among/of the Jews). Fired by a self-assumed mandate to secure cultural legitimacy for German Jews during a period of renewed anti-Semitism, these figures—who included Leopold Zunz, Eduard Gans, and the young Heinrich Heine—sought to forge an ideology of Judaism that would provide the basis for a post-Enlightenment and essentially secular Jewish identity. In an intellectual milieu where "science" was the reigning value, they sought to transform Judaism into an object of research and thereby to ensure its survival under the sign of culture. Over and over they insisted that Judaism had never been solely a religion, but had at every stage constituted a culture. As a culture, it deserved to survive, even after the waning of faith. What developed was an ideology for urban, intellectual German Jews who, spurning the alternative of conversion, endeavored to return to Jewishness on their own terms. As Gans put it, "The enthusiasm for religion and the genuineness of the old relationships has vanished, but no new enthusiasm has broken forth, no new set of relationships has been built. We stuck fast in that negative enlightenment (*Aufklarung*) which consisted of scorn and disdain for the traditional without taking pains to give that empty abstraction another content." His solution is scholarship, which comes just in time to redeem a debased and corrupted race: "Arise you who set science, the love of your own people, and benevolence above all else; arise, attach yourself to this noble society of Jewish Science, and see breaking forth in the strong fraternal union of such good men the messianic age, of which the prophets spoke, and which only the persistent corruption of the race has made a fable."[6] Enlightenment had emptied the content of Jewishness; they would fill it again. Good Hegelians that they were, they saw their task as providing the synthesis to a Jewish identity, for which *Aufklarung* had been the antithesis. Their grand solution has ever since been known as *Wissenschaft des Judentums* (Science of Judaism).

Their chief method of inquiry was philological. In what is often called the foundational work of the movement, *Etwas über die rabbinische Literatur* (On Rabbinic Literature), Zunz sought to mine rabbinic literature for the literary and ethical gems it might contain. In his view, scientific research could make it possible to "know and distinguish the old which is still of use, the antiquated which has become pernicious, and the new which has become desirable."[7] While he never quite specifies what he means by "desirable," he implies that an adequately pruned rabbinic tradition could bolster a modern and socially acceptable Jewish identity. The reductio ad absurdum of this approach can perhaps be detected in a sermon published by a nineteenth-century Jewish preacher, entitled "Our Patriarch Jacob—the Model of a City Councilman." Gershom Scholem mentions this sermon in an essay called "From Reflections on the Science of Judaism," where he bemoans the appearance of "the prince of the nation in the guise of a petty bourgeois."[8] Yet from the perspective of the likes of Zunz and Gans, such a sermon could not have seemed entirely off the mark.

When contemporary Jewish Studies scholars express a resistance to being seen as "ethnic" partisans, they are voicing concerns reminiscent of the concerns of their Berlin predecessors. Even in present-day America, where the conditions of Jewish life bear little resemblance to those prevailing in early nineteenth-century Germany, there is a prevailing anxiety that Jewish Studies will be "ghettoized" and that Jewish respectability in the academy and elsewhere will suffer as a result. Nevertheless, since the 1960s, another impulse has made itself felt alongside this drive for legitimacy. Where the *Wis-*

senschaft des Judentums drew upon the vocabularies and methods of the Enlightenment, this recent development has cast itself from the language and overall vision of multiculturalism, which characterizes ethnic particularity as a good in and of itself.

The position of Jewish Studies within multiculturalist discourse is, to be sure, far from unproblematic. For one thing there is the equivocation over whether Jews are to be treated as an ethnic group or as a religious group. As a religious group, their cause would seem marginal to the main thrust of multiculturalism, which at least until now has emphasized the study of different *peoples* rather than different modes of belief or thought. However, even if Jewish ethnicity is asserted, Jews are often considered to be (or to have become) "white," whereas multiculturalist initiatives tend to focus on "people of color."[9] Moreover, insofar as such initiatives seek quite consciously to redress social and economic inequalities, the real and imagined economic success of Jews in contemporary America would make their case marginal to the cause of multiculturalism. Finally, to complicate the matter still further, there is the fact that some of the most prominent critics of multiculturalism and champions of the "Western canon" have been Jews, including Allan Bloom, E. D. Hirsch, Harold Bloom, Norman Podhoretz, and Richard Bernstein. Bernstein, the author of *The Dictatorship of Virtue: Multiculturalism and the Battle for America's Future* (1994), has been among those to maintain that multiculturalism is bad for the Jews, that it threatens to dismantle the merit-based system in which American Jews have thrived.[10] In short, Jews have often been seen as marginal to the multiculturalist initiative because they have been deemed too white, too rich, too conservative, or because they themselves have often avoided such inclusion.[11]

These factors notwithstanding, Jewish Studies has inevitably been influenced by the recent emphasis on ethnicity in American academia. Interestingly, just at the moment that diversity has been valorized by American academia, the Jewish community has for reasons internal to Jewish history committed itself to the goal of self-preservation. The specter of a dwindling American Jewish population has led to many alarmist prognoses (see Alan Dershowitz's *The Vanishing*

American Jew), with the effect that "Jewish continuity" has become a key topic on the community agenda. In line with these concerns, many practitioners of Jewish Studies have reframed their endeavor in terms of promoting Jewish learning for the sake of Jewish ethnic survival. The historian Eli Lederhendler, for example, has recently described the contemporary mandate of Jewish Studies as a response to the threat of cultural dissolution: "We stand after the catastrophe, and we are engaged—when viewed collectively—in a salvage project: to preserve and interpret the record of our parents' and grandparents' world for those who can never enter that territory themselves. . . . By doing so, we commit ourselves to a more-or-less explicit survivalist program."[12] To "salvage" a culture is of course entirely different from the effort to displace a "pernicious" and "antiquated" culture with a new "enlightened" one (in Zunz's terms). Indeed, Lederhendler's possessive pronouns ("our" parents and grandparents) suggest that Jewish Studies has taken over a role formerly played by families. If cultural transmission no longer happens in everyday life, he implies, perhaps it can take place in the academy.

It is doubtless the case that many of the Jewish students in today's Jewish Studies classes have come precisely to add some heft to an identity they find ill-defined or somehow incomplete. In some cases they want to supplement whatever Jewish education they may have had as children. They are, as it were, giving Jewishness one more try (or in some cases the one and only try). I will have to rely upon my own data to substantiate this point. In the questionnaires I distribute on the first day of my Jewish-American literature class, I ask what students hope to get out of the class. A common response involves some desire to understand their "roots" or to learn more about a world they associate with their grandparents. Once I even received the candid response: "to find out who I am." Also, I (as well as various colleagues with whom I have shared these reflections) have more than once been approached during office hours by students wanting to know "what I really think." During the course of these encounters, it often becomes apparent to me that such students are seeking insight into something beyond the material of the class. They seem to be fishing for a definition of Jewish identity to which they can subscribe, and, to be perfectly honest, who can blame them? Other groups on campus seem to have gathered strength and confidence from Ethnic Studies classes. Why not the Jews?

II. Literature and Insubordination

Seen in the context of this new mandate for Jewish Studies, the multiple stakes in the Thomas Bird controversy become clearer. But whether one emphasizes the older drive for Jewish legitimacy or the newer one for Jewish survival, it is unclear that a course on modern Jewish literature will necessarily fill the bill. Certainly, if one considers the matter historically, modern, secular literature written by and about Jews signaled danger when it first became widespread at the end of the nineteenth century. When asked about his parents' reaction to his decision to become a writer, Isaac Bashevis Singer recalls their skepticism:

> They considered the secular writers to be heretics, all unbelievers—they really were too, most of them. To be a *literat* was to them as bad as becoming a *meshumed*, one who forsakes the faith. My father used to say that secular writers like Peretz were leading the Jews to heresy. . . . Even though Peretz wrote in a religious vein, my father called his writing "sweetened poison," but poison nonetheless. And from his perspective he was right. Everybody who read such books sooner or later became a worldly man and forsook the traditions.[13]

From the perspective of Singer's father, literature is corrupting, a gateway to heresy. As such, it would hardly serve the needs of the survivalist project of contemporary American Jewry. And as for the older *Wissenschaft* project of securing legitimacy, modern literature seems hardly less deleterious. Philip Roth tells us as much when, in *The Ghost Writer*, his alter-ego Nathan Zuckerman finds himself scorned by the Newark Jewish community for revealing dirty secrets about the lives of real Jews. Zuckerman is called upon not to reveal their impulses, unruly desires, and aggressive tendencies, but to operate as a sort of public relations coordinator for the Jewish people.[14] Yet few writers have demonstrated much talent at public relations. Certainly in Roth's own case, he has far more frequently been excoriated for slandering the Jews than he has been celebrated for saving them from assimilation.

The conflict between the communal effort to affirm ethnicity and the effects of modern literature can be observed in the clash between the expectations of many of my students and the material of my classes. This can be illustrated with a poem by Moyshe-Leyb Halpern (1886–1932), the *poet maudit* of American Yiddish literature. The poem is a bitter send-up of shtetl nostalgia entitled "Zlochov, My Home" (1924). From a literary standpoint, the poem represents an exemplary study in irony and poetic inversion. He begins by setting up what appears to be a loving recollection of his hometown, the Galician shtetl Zlochov:

> *O Zlotshev, du mayn heym, mayn shtot*
> *Mit dayn kloystershpits un shul un bod*
> *Un mit dayne zitserkes afn mark*
>
> (Oh, Zlochov, you my home, my town
> With the church spires, the synagogue and bath,
> Your women sitting in the market place.)

But no sooner does he apostrophize his hometown in this lofty way (already suspect because of the prominent church) than he sharpens the focus of the poem, and what emerges is a defamiliarized shtetl, one in which grotesque images gradually come into view:

> *Un mit dayne yidelekh vos raysn zikh op*
> *Vi hint af dem poyer vos kumt arop*
> *Mit a koyshl eyer fun sasover barg*
>
> (Your little Jews, breaking loose
> Like dogs at a peasant coming down
> With a basket of eggs from the Sassov mountains.)

The Jews are suddenly transformed into voracious dogs, a pointed image given the heightened aversion to things canine that traditionally characterized Orthodox Jews. The peasant with a basket of eggs precipitates a mad dash for scarce resources, revealing the previously concealed desperation and greed of the shtetl Jews. In the course of a single stanza, the speaker's memory has moved from lofty invocation to indignanation.

Halpern's poetic speaker ends up recalling a traumatic event that has become inextricably bound up with his memories of his home:

Dayn erd iz an eydes, az ikh trakht nisht oys
Ven mayn zeyde hot mayn mamen fun hoyz
Aroysgeshtelt mit dey politzey
Hot may bobe in der breyt mit di fis
Geshmeykhlt shier azoy honik-zis,
Vi a shiksa vos shteyt tsvishn zelner tsvey—
Az farsholtn zol vern mayn sine in mir
Vos hot mikh dermont on ir un on dir,—
Mayn heym, mayn Zlotshev

(Your earth be my witness, I'm not making it up
When my grandfather called in the police
To chase my mother from his house,
My grandmother, her legs spread wide,
Smiled almost as honey-sweet
As a girl standing between two soldiers —
Cursed be my hatred inside me
Which reminds me of her and of you—
My home, my Zlochov.)

This stanza refuses to specify what has prompted the banishment of the speaker's mother, though one might guess it involves a transgression of a sexual nature, most likely an affair with a non-Jewish man. At any rate, her banishment at the hands of her parents offers a bitter commentary on the narrative of shtetl life according to which the sole cause for Jewish emigration was Russian anti-Semitism. In a surprising inversion, the sinister smile on the grandmother's face reminds the speaker of a non-Jewish girl—a "shiksa" in the original—flirting with soldiers. The old world Jewish family, so often idealized by Halpern's immigrant contemporaries (consider the anthem of immigrant nostalgia, "Belz"), is transformed into an alien and hostile force of expulsion.

Students find it easy enough to visualize the poem's first three lines, with its "women sitting in the marketplace." Halpern's opening accords with the contemporary idealized iconography of shtetl life, that collection of images and signs that has come to figure so prominently in popularized versions of the Jewish past. But when Halpern's women suddenly become dogs chasing down the peasants and the speaker's grandparents evict their own daughter, some students resist shifting registers along with the poem, arguing that the speaker is ultimately expressing tenderness for his home town. Perhaps such students find it difficult to reconcile their own longing for the shtetl—at least for that version of the shtetl which has come down through *Fiddler on the Roof*—with the scorn that Halpern's poem evokes. As a teacher of literature, I find it necessary to suggest that they look beyond their fantasies. As somebody cast in the position of an emissary from the "Jewish world," however, I must confront a sense of betraying a mission. Would I. B. Singer's father accuse my class of "leading the Jews to heresy" or at least into its milder contemporary version, unrepentant assimilation? If my mandate is to preserve and interpret "the record of our parents' and grandparents' world," why bother with the complex nuances of the poetic imagination? Why not stick to the official version of the story?

Unfortunately, Halpern's subversion of popularized versions of the shtetl is hardly an isolated phenomenon in the works I teach. Another ready example is Henry Roth's *Call It Sleep* (1934), written when the author was under the spell of James Joyce. Interestingly, Roth's novel was one of only two works to be unanimously chosen as among the hundred greatest works of modern Jewish literature in a survey sponsored by the National Yiddish Book Center (the other was Sholom Aleichem's *Tevye the Dairyman*, itself a dark comedy about the breakdown of the traditional world). Yet this is not to say that *Call It Sleep* supports the survivalist mandate of contemporary Jewish Studies any more than Halpern's work does. If the ostensible claims of Roth's novel are taken seriously, it is difficult to see it as anything but an argument for modernist vision and an argument against traditional Judaism. Not only does the novel feature as a comic villain that stock character in much modern Jewish writing, the hapless *Melamed,* but the novel's denouement powerfully asserts the primacy of subjective experience over any and all communal structures. In the novel's final triumphant paragraph, the protagonist comes into an awareness of his ability imaginatively to reassemble the fragments of his chaotic experience just before dropping off to sleep. He comes into a sort of visionary power, which the text calls "strangest triumph, strangest acquiescence."[15] The novel, then, traces a portrait of the artist as a young Jewish immigrant. It cannot end until the protagonist recognizes his creative powers, enabling him to translate the ruins of experience into illuminated vision.

Like Halpern, Roth subverts the popular narrative of Jewish immigration. The "old country" turns out to be anything but the site of familial stability and integrated communal life. As it turns out, the protagonist's mother has been banished from a Galician shtetl, shunted off to America to conceal her affair with a non-Jew. Like Halpern's poem but more explicit, Roth's text raises the specter of the Jewish woman's promiscuous longings for a gentile man. Like Halpern's text, *Call It Sleep* calls upon the reader to feel solidarity not with the forces of cultural continuity and tradition, but with the banished mother. Her illicit longing for the romance of the gentile world becomes a symbolic analogue for the artistic imagination of the sons.

From these examples, we begin to discern a dominant impulse in much modern Jewish writing: the impulse to critique and displace the myths and institutions that have structured traditional Jewish communal life. Other salient examples include Saul Tchernikhovsky's early poems, Nietzschean meditations decrying the "life-denying" import of rabbinic Judaism; Mary Antin's autobiography, *The Promised Land* (1912), written with the expressed purpose of liberating its author from the "weighty dress" of her Jewish identity; Anna Margolin's lyrics, with their transgressive appeal to the world of paganism; S. Ansky's *The Dybbuk* (1921), which displaces the folk motif of exorcism with a narrative of triumphant romantic love; and nearly every page in the opus of Philip Roth, for whom transgression and defilement have almost become a sort of counter-*Halakha*.

Geoffrey Hartman has emphasized a somewhat different tendency in modern Jewish writing, a practice of rewriting previous texts in a mode that recalls the rabbinic form of midrash. But Hartman also calls attention to the way this practice dislocates the tradition. "Modern Jewish literature," he writes, "arises as an involuntary or insubordinate midrash:

We do not find free-standing works of art but the retold tale, the recycled motif."[16] His main example is Edmond Jabès, who in his *Book of Questions* playfully invokes the rabbinic mode of attributing one's insights to an earlier source. But the operative term here is "insubordinate." The ostensible function of classical midrash, we must recall, is to amplify and draw new meanings out of a text that is regarded as authoritative. The performance of midrash upon a canonical text reinforces the centrality of that text precisely by discovering in it a plenitude of readings. Rabbinic midrash is at least in this sense at some remove from modernist pastiche; in the latter, authority has shifted over to the organizing mind of the artist. A tradition once considered the repository of all significance becomes a plaything for the idiosyncratic modern sensibility.

III. Conclusion: The Smithy of the Syllabus

All of this is perhaps no more than to assert that the basic work of literature—at least since the emergence of the modernist sensibility—is to untie solidities, to stray from home, to confront the settled and the known with the unpredictability of subjective consciousness. The works that define the canon of modern Jewish literature gain their impetus in one way or another from this modernist spirit of revolt. In celebrating such writing at our cultural moment—with an ethos that celebrates cultural retrieval and restored continuity—one would seemingly be undermining one's ostensible project, rebuilding the house with defective tools, as it were. Yet Modernism, as more than one commentator has remarked, is Janus-faced, and one need look no farther than the very same Joyce who fueled Henry Roth's rebellion for a rather different formula for the literary: "Welcome, O life! I go to encounter for the millionth time the reality of experience and to forge in the smithy of my soul the uncreated conscience of my race." Here we discover a creative project alongside a rebellious one. The question is whether and to what effect Stephen Dedalus's anthem might be brought into the Jewish Studies classroom. Phrased in a different way, what kind of a conscience is forged in the soul of the Jewish writers I have invoked?

In 1967, the former Trotskyite Isaac Deutscher delivered a

talk at Hebrew Union College in Cincinnati entitled "The Non-Jewish Jew." Deutscher proposes that at least since the redaction of the Talmud, there has been a heterodox sub-tradition within Judaism. As exemplars of this tradition, he cites figures ranging from the Talmudic personage known as Aher to the Enlightenment thinker Solomon Maimon to the hermeneuticists of suspicion Marx and Freud. All of these heretical figures, Deutscher argues, are linked in their animosity to traditional Judaism; and the regularity with which such figures appear suggests that they constitute a sub-tradition of their own. The proposal of Deutscher's talk is simply that negation can come to acquire the substance of a tradition.

Students who enroll in a class on modern Jewish literature gain access to something resembling Deutscher's "non-Jewish" Jewish tradition. Even if Deutscher's claim is rejected, even if his "tradition" is dismissed as too disparate to constitute any sort of unity, the very mechanism of the college course—with its course title, requirements, its intricately mapped syllabus, its structured beginnings and endings (punctuated by midterms and finals)—makes the tacit assertion that the works under consideration adhere to one another. The college syllabus, in short, performs the cultural work of affirming continuities even where they may not necessarily exist.

Lest those engaged in the work of a "salvage project" find such a heterodox tradition too marginal to what has hitherto been considered the main thrust of Jewish culture, it should come as a relief that the logic of negation requires a confrontation with what has been negated. To flesh out the critique of Jewish collective memory in the texts by Halpern and Henry Roth, to grasp the ironies informing Jabès's invocation of rabbinical discourse, one must retrieve other versions of the past, "salvage" a series of cultural norms and foundational texts, if only by way of explication. One can even imagine a new, reverse itinerary of Jewish Studies that would begin with a writer like Halpern and move on to a study of Yiddish, and subsequently to Hasidic storytelling, and perhaps end up with rabbinic literature and the Bible. Of course these "foundational" texts would then be read through the lens of their subsequent, modernist subversions—not a bad idea since it would remind us that our own desires and ideological investments mediate our grapplings with tradition anyway. What we salvage, we adapt to our needs.

Such a version of Jewish Studies—merging heterodox and orthodox strains—finds a curious emblem in the first post-Communist era edition of Isaac Bashevis Singer's novel, *The Magician of Lublin*. On its cover, the publishers have put a picture of Menachem Schneerson, the former Lubavitcher Rebbe, gazing fixedly through his dense beard. This is a certainly an odd choice for a novel about a consummate Don Juan who eventually shuts himself off from the world in frantic hopes of saving his corrupted soul. But the Russian publishers seem to realize that the cultural significance of a work of art can transform the work's ostensible, internal meaning. For post-Communist Russian Jews eager to recapture some sort of Jewish heritage, I. B. Singer seems to provide an avenue of cultural return, his profound idiosyncracies notwithstanding. Thus, to advertise his text, the Russian publicists used a portrait of Schneerson, a semiotic guarantor of Jewish authenticity. Certainly, Singer's father would never have imagined that one of his son's "poisonous" writings would be categorized as rabbinic script. But when a new generation sets to work reformulating a tradition, using the materials of the past to understand the present, the most ready-at-hand is often the first to get pressed into service. The Torah, according to a common rabbinical dictum, speaks the language of men and women.

NOTES

The author wishes to thank Jonathan Boyarin and Lisa Makman, who read drafts of the article.

[1]Quoted in Pam Belluck, "Gentile Professor, Citing Bias, Quits as Head of Jewish Studies." *New York Times*, 16 July 1996, B:1,1.

[2]Quoted in Mohamed Bazzi, "After Prof Quits, Questions Raised." *Newsday* (Queens Edition), 17 July 1996, A3.

[3]Alexander Marx, "Address." *American Academy for Jewish Research Proceedings*. Vol. I, 1928–1930. (New York: Kraus Reprint Corporation, 1966), 5.

[4]Maurice Zigmond, "Brandeis University Is One Year Old" in *The Jew in the American World*, ed. Jacob Rader Marcus (Detroit: Wayne State University Press, 1996), 454.

[5]Howard Adelman, "Jewish Studies: An Ethnic Program or Part of Academic Tradition?" *The Chronicle of Higher Education,* 3 August 1988, A36.

[6]Quoted in Michael A. Meyer, *The Origins of the Modern Jew* (Detroit: Wayne State University Press, 1967), 167, 165.

[7]Ibid, 161.

[8]See David Biale, *Gershom Scholem, Kabbalah and Counter-History* (Cambridge: Harvard University Press, 1982), 3. In twentieth-century America, the endeavor to find suitable models in rabbinic literature has played itself out in the retrieval of Hillel as a kind of liberal humanist *avant la lettre*.

[9]For an interesting discussion of the relationship between "whiteness" and the Jews, see Karen Brodkin, *How Jews Became White Folks and What That Says About Race in America* (New Brunswick: Rutgers University Press, 1999).

[10]Bernstein made this comment at a public debate at the Jewish Theological Seminary of America on 10 May 1994.

[11]See Sara R. Horowitz, "The Paradox of Jewish Studies in the New Academy," in *Insider/Outsider: American Jews and Multiculturalism*, ed. David Biale et al. (Berkeley: University of California Press, 1998).

[12]Eli Lederhendler, *Jewish Responses to Modernity: New Voices in America and Eastern Europe* (New York: New York University Press, 1994), 195–96.

[13]*Conversations with Isaac Bashevis Singer*, ed. Grace Farrell (Jackson: University Press of Mississippi, 1982), 13.

[14]Philip Roth, *The Ghost Writer* (New York: Farrar, Straus & Giroux, 1979).

[15] Henry Roth, *Call It Sleep* (New York: Farrar, Straus & Giroux, 1991), 441.

[16]Geoffrey Hartman, "Imagination," in *Contemporary Jewish Religious Thought*, ed. Arthur A. Cohen and Paul Mendes-Flor (New York: The Free Press, 1987), 461.

JONATHAN FREEDMAN

"WHO'S JEWISH?": SOME ASIAN-AMERICAN WRITERS AND THE JEWISH-AMERICAN LITERARY CANON

> While conversation becomes increasingly global and one's sense of space . . . unstable and fluid, we do not automatically all get delivered into the same world by the processes that globalize and hybridize us. Conversing across differences is the art we have to learn.
>
> —Dipesh Chakrabarty

A few years ago, I started writing about Jewishness. This turn in my work was not due to a quest for a lost, more authentic identity, nor was it a sign of a midlife religious conversion. And, given the prevailing winds in the American academy, it was hardly a canny career move. Indeed, it was barely a turn at all—more of a sidelight in what I thought of as the real project, a study of the interplay between middlebrow and academic cultures. But as I began that work, I also started thinking about how oddly obsessed so much of fin-de-siècle American writing is with the figure of the Jew, and how odder still that critics, many of them Jewish, glossed over that fact. I started to give talks on these phenomena and received surprisingly positive responses, responses, in fact, more positive than any garnered by the work I was *supposed* to be doing. And so, being no fool, I dropped the middlebrow and started writing about Jews (which turned out to be more or less the same thing.)

The result was a book, *The Temple of Culture*, and along with it a newfound respect for the ability of Jewishness to unsettle my received ideas about everything, including, I found, me. For I discovered myself in the weird position of having an identity for the first time, at least as far as the '90s academy was concerned. Up until then, that is to say, I felt myself to be a fairly typical academic of the balding, bearded white-male variety. But I noticed gentile colleagues treating me with a slightly different attitude when I started to do this work, an attitude which one of them clarified one day as he was lamenting, in a fairly good-natured way, the problems his own sense of white privilege posed him in writing about matters of race. When I responded sympathetically, he looked at me and exclaimed "but . . . you're Jewish!!" (I am still trying to figure out what this meant, but guess it must be something like, "you're OK—authentic, ethnic, '*real*'—and, darn it, I'm still not.") And I found myself in an even more complicated position with fellow Jews. Whenever I give a talk now, for example, I anticipate hostile questions not from gentiles but from my co-religionists (fellow ethnics?), some of whom attack my understanding of Jewishness as an endlessly complicated, and constitutively complicating, muddle from the Right (what about the Holocaust? Anti-Semitism? Israel?) or the Left (what about Jewish racism? Jewish whiteness? Israel?).

None of this should be surprising to anyone except this Candide-like critic. But it does pose the question of what might logically follow from my interests and positions. For like many critics of my generation—regrettably, given the importance of the subject, too *many* of them being Jewish—I found that invoking the example of Jewishness enabled me to ask better questions about the issues that stand in the center of our professional, cultural, and social lives. After a generation of simply remarkable work in a number of fields—that, for example, of Sander Gilman, Daniel Boyarin, Jonathan Boyarin, David Biale, Bryan Cheyette, Paul Gilroy—it is or at least ought to be indisputable that Jewishness is inseparable from the ways we think about such crucial issues as sex, gender, race, populations, nations, otherness, cosmopolitanism, Diaspora. The logical next step is to extend this rich discursive matrix to a consideration of contemporary America. For the issues of our moment—how to negotiate an identity for yourself in the midst of social and cultural pressures to define you; what it is like to be ethnic (whatever that means) in a culture that is obsessed with race; how to think about an identity in terms that transcend the lineaments of the nation in which you live; what the relative claims of religion, culture, and community of origin might prove to be in a relentlessly individualistic society—these and more would seem to have deep and even renewed complexity when they are brought into explicit context with the theoretical, historical, and cultural conundrums raised by Jewishness. Exploring these possibilities seems all the more crucial at the current time, at which our society comes to terms with the remarkable changes that the recent waves of immigration have wrought in the body politic and social imaginary alike.

But I see little realization of this potential. To be sure, some moves to engage with the larger discourses of racial and ethnic identity formation have enlarged the terrain of Jewish studies, including an interesting anthology entitled *Jews and Multiculturalism* and a trenchant study of the same issue, from the perspective of Jewish fiction, by Andrew Furman.[1] And much work has emerged from what one might broadly term American cultural studies, largely focusing on the question of the Jew's assimilation by means of whiteness.[2] But each, while commendable, has displayed a conspicuous lack of attention to the possibilities raised by the discourses in and around Jewishness for deeper critical and cultural analysis of a multiracial, multiethnic, polyglot America—and, of equal importance, vice versa.

In what follows, I want to advance this process by suggesting that the experience of Jews has a unique, because dialectical, relation to this hybridized vision of the U.S., bearing in mind that this relation is one as marked by divergence as it is by concord. My examples will be drawn from one specific arena: from the response of first- and second-generation East and South Asian-American writers to the representational strategies and structures of Jewish-American writers of a previous generation. My suggestion will be that this literary relation is tangled and intense, crackling complicated cathexes and revisionary energy, for two reasons. The first has to do with the dynamics of literary succession—and, perhaps more cynically, the exigiencies of the publishing industry. These latter-day writers need to surmount the massively successful examples of Henry Roth, Bernard Malamud, Saul Bellow, Philip Roth, Grace Paley *inter* an abundance of *alia* in order to establish their own authority, all the more so in a culture which created in the 1950s and '60s a box called "ethnic writers" on the basis of the Jewish example. "Perhaps not since the mainstream 'discovered' Jewish American fiction in the 1950s has such a concentrated, seemingly 'new' ethnic literary wave come our way," wrote *Publisher's Weekly* of Amy Tan, Gish Jen, Gus Lee, Frank Chin, and David Wong Louie's "arrival" on the literary scene.[3] The bizarre conflation of such disparate writers alone would be enough to make them fretful; all the more troubling, then, was the suggestion that this new "wave" of ethnic writers could be conflated with the previous one.

But a second, perhaps even greater reason for the intensity of this engagement is that many Asian-American writers wish to bring a different model of acculturation, with a different ethno-racial dynamic, to the fore. This pattern of response is far from universal in East and South Asian-American fiction, to be sure; I foreground it not to draw conclusions about the phenomenon of ethnic writing or to draw comparisons between the East or South Asian- and Jewish-American experience across the board. (Many accounts of East and South Asians as "the New Jews" circulate in popular culture; they are by and large overdetermined and, frequently, incoherent.[4]) I do so because I want to suggest that thinking through this different model of acculturation/assimilation might just save contemporary Jewish-American culture from its own tendencies toward triumphalism and self-congratulation—and point to a future more fully engaged with that of the nation at large.

Beyond *Seinfeld:* Jewishness and Multiculturalism in the New Century

All is not well on the Jews-and-multiculturalism front, and it's perhaps best to begin with the bad news, the revanchiste tendency of much of Jewish self-representation in both Jewish culture and the mass media. To be sure, given the long history of exile and persecution to which Jews have been subjected, given the overt and subtle prejudice they faced in America, and given the recrudescence of the most invidious forms of anti-Semitic slurs in Europe and the Middle East, the triumphant affirmation of Jewishness that Stephen J. Whitfield affectionately traces in "Why America Has Not Felt Like Exile," is something that one doesn't wish to quarrel with—overmuch. Indeed, even more than Whitfield, I think we are living in a Golden Age of American Jewish social and cultural achievement, one marked by a remarkable success of Jews in the public sphere (Cabinet officers, presidents of the Ivy League universities that once tried to limit their admission); a revival, particularly among more youthful congregants, of traditional Jewish practices and beliefs; a flurry of self-identified Jewish cultural production in a number of media (literature, music, art). And this marks a revolution in Jewish self-conception in an America that has oscillated between benign ignorance of and lazy hostility to its Jewish citizens.[5]

To restrict my argument to the cultural sphere alone, consider the difference between the Pulitzer Prize-winning play of 1949, Arthur Miller's *Death of a Salesman*, and the Pulitzer Prize-winning novel of 2001, Michael Chabon's *The Astonishing Adventures of Kavalier and Klay*. Miller is a New York-born Jew whose most famous work avoids locating its hero in any one ethnic location or identity. Willy Loman's fate might be seen as a tragic version of the process Ruth Wisse has discerned in comic Jewish fiction of the 1950s in which the *schlemiel*, the Jewish loser, is redefined as an American everyman, a tragically deluded dreamer of the American dream.[6] Indeed, Miller goes even farther than de-ethnicizing Loman. The play's very form places him in an irrevocably Christian context: its closing scene is subtitled a "Requiem," that is, a piece of explicitly Christian liturgy. Chabon's novel (much of which takes place in the New York in which Miller grew up and lived while writing *Salesman*) is a fantastical extravaganza based on the Jewish origins of the creators of all-American comic books like *Superman*. It involves as well the entire sweep of Jewish history in the '40s, from that taking place in the slums of Brooklyn to that of the Holocaust-shadowed streets of Prague, and references an entire ensemble of Jewish-inflected cultural texts, like the Golem myth, and experiences, like the novel's trope of escape. To put it perhaps a bit too simplistically, in Miller's moment a Jew had to be an Everyman; in Chabon's, Everyman can be, and frequently is, a Jew.

And what's true in what's left of high culture in America is even more spectacularly true in popular culture, most notably, its most consummate expression, the television sitcom. As Jon Stratton (among others) has shown, when Jews made their way into mass consciousness in the 1950s via the new medium of situation comedy, their Jewishness was either exaggerated (*The Goldbergs*) or evaded (in the pilot of the *Dick van Dyke Show*, Carl Reiner played Rob Petrie but was replaced by Van Dyke at the insistence of a studio that deemed Reiner too ethnic).[7] This situation is the precise opposite of that classic contemporary example of the form, *Seinfeld*, whose run of five years was exactly the same length as that of *The Dick van Dyke Show*. The show's co-creators, Larry David and Jerry Seinfeld, are both Jewish; most of the stars of the show are Jewish; the milieu—the Upper West Side, Long Island, Florida—is deeply, one might even say quintessentially, Jewish; so too are its situations: neurotic, urban singles with crazy parents.

Indeed, *Seinfeld,* far more than even other '90s shows that demonstrated ease with Jewishness (e.g., *Friends*, in which Monica and Ross Geller or their friend Rachel Green date and mate easily alongside Chandler Bing and Phoebe Bouffée—and in which a WASP, Courtney Cox, plays a Jewess rather than, as is more typical, the other way around), pushes Jewishness to the point of ubiquity. The joke of *Seinfeld* is that with the exception of Jerry and Kramer, the rest of the characters are ethnically marked as non-Jewish even as they are placed in situations coded Jewish. Jerry's best friend, George Costanza, is, despite his own last name, a recognizable Jewish character-type—the nebbish—and is linked to the stereotypically Jewish practice of masturbation when, in a scene that out-Roths Philip Roth, he is caught masturbating by his own mother. And he is conjoined to two other Jewish stereotypes (the miser, the exploiter of gentile women) when his cheapness causes the death of his WASP wife Susan by poisoned wedding invitation. His parents, played brilliantly by Jerry Stiller and Estelle Harris, are recognizable stereotypes, too: quarrelsome, overbearing father, neurasthenic, doting mother. Jewish characters, on the other hand, are represented as being painfully at odds with the world of their fathers (and mothers). Jerry usually dates exogamously, with hilarious exceptions, like the time he is caught making out with a girl at a screening of *Schindler's List* and barred from seeing her again by her horrified parents. Kramer, who would seem in appearance to be as Jewish as Jerry, is horrified by the quintessential, one might even say definitional, Jewish ritual of circumcision.

The effect of *Seinfeld*, then, is to render a world in which every other form of ethnicity has collapsed into Jewishness, in which Jewishness has become the baseline condition of contemporary, urban life—something that non-Jews aspire to and Jews rebel against. Or at least of white ethnic life. For the flip side of *Seinfeld*'s creation of an entirely Jewish white world is the evocation of a uniformly hostile one composed of Latino-, African-, Asian-, and Middle Eastern-Americans. And more: these ethnic others are all as stereotypical in their manifest Otherness, to the point of embarrassment: an Indian named Baboo whose immigration papers Elaine loses and who returns from deportation to testify against Jerry and crew; a Johnnie Cochran look-alike named Jackie Chiles; the entire Puerto Rican population of New York, whose Independence Day parade frustrates Kramer so much that he ends up inadvertently burning the Puerto Rican flag. In all of these cases, a white New York in which everyone is Jewish comes problematically face-to-face with a non-white world in which no one is—and whose sole purpose would seem to be to frustrate the efforts of Jerry and friends to get a good table at a restaurant, to make it across town, to date.

The show has been condemned for its racial and ethnic insensitivity, which I too would find offensive if it weren't thoroughly misanthropic with respect to its own characters (self-defeating neurotics who end up, in the final episode, in jail) and particularly satirical of white desires to escape whiteness: Elaine, for example, dates a white man thinking he is black, only to find that he is dating her because he thinks she is a Latina; Jerry becomes obsessed with a woman named Donna Chang then finds out that she is a Long Island Jew formerly known as Changstein. But what I do find problematic here is what *Seinfeld* tells us about Jewish experience in the United States in the late '90s: a sense of Jewish disconnect not only from the experience of African-Americans with whom Jewish popular culture has long been complexly and problematically intertwined, but also that of the "new immigrants" (as Gayatri Spivack calls them)—those who have come, largely from Asia and Latin America, since the revised immigration laws of 1965—whose experience chimes (at times harmonically, at times discordantly) with that of immigrant Eastern European Jews. It's perhaps not too surprising, in the context of the closing-the-door-they-just-passed-through behavior of successive waves of immigrants to the United States, to see the children of generations afflicted by the Immigration Restriction Act of 1924—whose quotas limited possibilities of escape from the Holocaust—making light of the situation of a figure caught in the INS bureaucracy. But it's sad nevertheless, and provides an ironic counterpoint to the triumphalism *Seinfeld* enacts.

Interestingly, and tellingly, this complex relation between Jews and newer modalities of immigrant experience has *not* been kept alive by contemporary Jewish writers like Nathan Englander or Allegra Goodman. Although their focus on traditional Jewish communities in contemporary America rejects the assimilation plot that has long been the focus of Jewish-American fiction, their work has the tendency to isolate Jews from the American ethno-racial hurly-burly in ways that are analogous to *Seinfeld*'s triumphalism. Rather, it is in contemporary writers of color—particular people whose family of origin are from East and South Asia—who have turned to thinking about the relation between Asian diasporas and the Jewish ones in ways that are provoking for both. To be sure, this very conflation is worrisome. It disguises the ways Jews and Asian-Americans are equally the victims of the model minority myth; discredits the tremendous diversity of each community, downplays their economic and social reticulation; and constructs oppressive identity strait jackets for both. But a remarkable degree of work gets done through the invocation and parsing of this relation—work which can locate the endeavor of this generation of Asian-American writers more precisely and, more relevantly for my concerns, can help overcome the more complacent sorts of Jewish self-conceptions that *Seinfeld* both hilariously critiques and problematically promotes.

The Discourse of Diaspora and (vs.) the Anxiety of Influence: Bharati Mukherjee

A fine example is provided by the Calcutta-born novelist Bharati Mukherjee, now Professor of English at the University of California, Berkeley, author of a number of novels about the trans-locational experience of exiled, hyphenated migrants in a world of loss, exile, political revolution, terrorism: in short, the world we have always lived in, and now, post-September 11, know we live in. Particularly in the early phases of her career, Mukherjee frequently defined herself in relation to Jewish-American writers. "The book I dream of updating," she writes in the introduction to her first collection of stories, *Darkness*, "is no longer *A Passage to India*—it's *Call It Sleep*." *Darkness* is dedicated to Bernard Malamud (a teacher of her husband, the Canadian novelist Clark Blaise), and she consistently mentions Malamud as a prime influence on her early writing, the one who gave her her new, true subject, the lives of immigrants:

> I see a strong influence between my writing and Bernard Malamud's, in spite of the fact that he describes the lives of Eastern European Jews and I talk about the lives of newcomers from the Third World. Like Malamud, I write about a minority community which escapes the ghetto and adapts itself to the patterns of the dominant American culture. . . . Immersing myself in his work gave me the self-confidence to write about my own community.

Gestures of literary affiliation are, however, complicated, and Mukherjee's are especially so: this is, after all, a woman who wants to displace first Forster, then, in her 1993 novel *The Holder of the World*, Hawthorne. So it should come as no surprise that Mukherjee invokes Malamud's example in order to challenge it. In the same interview she is asked how her writing differs from his and responds: "When you are from the third world, when you have dark skin and religious beliefs, mainstream America responds to you in ways you can't foresee. My fiction has to consider race, politics, religion, as well as certain nastinesses that older generations of white immigrant writers may not have had to take into account."

Fair enough—and as we shall see, not only Mukherjee, but

also Gish Jen uses the example of Jewish-American fiction to measure the ethno-racial and religious nastinesses that dark-skinned, non-Judeo-Christian immigrant communities face. But there's another moment in this interview that suggests just how complex Mukherjee's engagement with the Jewish-American tradition is. Mukherjee claims that the title story of her signature collection, *The Middleman*, developed as follows: "When I was working on [an uncompleted novel], a character with a minor role, a Jew who has relocated from Baghdad to Bombay to Brooklyn, took control and wrote his own story. He attracted me because he was a cynical person and a hustler, as many immigrant survivors have to be."[8]

As this language may suggest, Mukherjee's character Alfie Judah is about as far away from Malamud's protagonists—and, more important, those common to Jewish-American writing—as can be imagined. From Henry Roth's David Schearle through Saul Bellow's Herzog through Philip Roth's Alexander Portnoy, the archetypal Jewish-American narrative has been of the assimilation of a sensitive Ashkenazic man, tied to the world of his parents but struggling to find his place on the bustling, commercial American stage upon which he is too fine by nature to flourish. That Jewish man, moreover, is defined by a powerful sexuality but loaded with guilt for his expressions of it—largely because that guilt is incestuous, or miscegenating, or both, in nature. And, finally, that figure is frequently, if not triumphantly, victimized by those less morally scrupulous than he, a victimization which grants him a moral superiority even as it denies his practical efficacy. Alfie is the polar opposite of this figure of the Noble Schlemiel. He is Sephardic—Iraqi-born, and dark-complected (a fact which makes him acceptable to the Central American revolutionaries among whom he finds himself: at least he is not a *gringo*). And rather than assimilating, he is in flight from America by virtue of some shady deals which have landed him on the wrong side of the law. Alfie is deeply amoral, both in his business practices ("there's just supply and demand running the universe," he muses) and, perhaps more pointedly, in sexual ones as well: indeed, he is remarkably free of the sexual guilt that defines the Jewish-American quasi-hero. "I must confess my weakness. It's women," announces Alfie, and the story details his dangerous, and adulterous, lust for Maria, the consort of his American host, Clovis T. Ransome, and former mistress of the unnamed country's President. Alfie's amoralism crosses between his business and his bedroom practices, as does Maria's. Indeed, she uses him to help her deliver some of the supplies to the guerillas, led by her lover Andreas ("I have no feeling for revolutions," Alfie muses, "only for outfitting its participants") then rewards him with sex. Afterwards, Alfie listens to Maria detail the multiple violations of her life, responding with pragmatic comfort. The story ends with Maria killing Ransome in the midst of a guerilla intrusion, then briefly pointing a gun at Alfie before lighting out for the jungle with her lover; he realizes that only his intimacy with her—his compassionate response to her in bed—has saved his life. It closes with Alfie plotting his next move: "someone in the capital will be happy to know about [the guerilla attack]. There must be something worth trading in the troubles I have seen."

A more un-Malamudian/Rothian/Bellovian Jew I cannot imagine.[9] Indeed, Alfie is not just unlike, but the polar opposite of, the sensitive Ashkenazic Jewish man: he is the embodiment of the worst nightmares of the generation that produced that figure. After all, the specter haunting assimilating American Jews of this period was not only the Holocaust, but also the anti-Semitic projections of the Jew as the horny trader standing outside national and moral borders alike. Memorialized not only by anti-Semitic pamphlets of the 1890s but by the spirited endeavor of Henry Ford—whose *Dearborn Independent* editorials on Jews and Jewishness were collected in a widely-circulated tome called *The International Jew* in the 1920s—and high-art literature by the likes of T. S. Eliot and Ezra Pound, the concept of the hyper-phallic, dark-complected Asiatic or non-European Jew as morally corrupt and corrupting cosmopolitan, frequently associated with exotically corrupt (and hence covertly attractive) sexual practices, suffused Middle America and high-art modernism alike. If Alfie Judah seems like a literal embodiment of such a figure it is surely not because Mukherjee wants to revive the Ford- or Eliot-sponsored anti-Semitic notions of the Jewish man, but rather because she wants to invoke—if not make her own—all that the Great Tradition of Jewish-American fiction had to expel in order to make its successful march into respectability.[10]

In this light, Mukherjee's desire to "update" *Call It Sleep* takes on a new salience. She doesn't so much bring its immigrant narrative into the contemporary scene as suggest, from a contemporary perspective, all the things that were missing from that narrative in the first place. I will have more to say about this effect and its implications in the conclusion to this essay; for now I want to suggest what Mukherjee gains from this transaction. For she gathers not only a revisionary purchase on the tradition she is "updating," but a base upon which to build her own career. It's no coincidence that she moves forward from *The Middleman* to conflate Maria and Alfie in her most commercially successful novel, *Jasmine*. For in that novel's morphing protagonist Jyoti/Jane/Jasmine, she constructs a Maria-like woman who kills her rapist, dumps her crippled husband, and lights out for the territory—California instead of the Central American jungle—who is also an Alfie-like survivor, looking for and finding something to leverage in the multiple troubles she has seen.

In Mukherjee's 1980s work, I am suggesting, the discourse of diaspora manages what might be best described in Harold Bloom's tropology as the anxiety of influence: it allows her both to place herself in a powerful tradition and to remake it. And, as Bloom's paradigm would suggest, Mukherjee seems to have successfully internalized and then moved on from the tradition of Jewish-American immigrant writing she invoked early in her career; her most recent fictions, like *Dutiful Daughters* (2001), juxtapose Indian and American destinies in the transnational, postmodern, globalized economy stretching from Silicon Valley to Bombay. But her path in the 1980s, it seems to me, has important salience for a new generation of Asian-American writers, not only South- but also East-Asian, not only immigrants, but also first- and second-generation Americans, many of whom engage themselves in rewriting the immigrant narrative in ways that deal with Jewishness with the same revisionary energy that Mukherjee so fiercely displays.

"The New Jews" in the Promising Land: Gish Jen

The classic example of this tendency is the work of Scarsdale-born, Harvard-educated Gish Jen. Jen often speaks of the mixed generic and experiential relation between Jewish-American fiction and her own. Sometimes this expresses itself as a kind of a benign inspiration: "The biggest influence on my work has come from Jewish-American writers. . . . It's partly Scarsdale and partly the sympathy I see between the Jewish and Chinese cultures." Sometimes, on the other hand, her attitude seems to be touched with irritation: "What we [Asian-American writers] don't want is to be lumped together, ghettoized. I hope that twenty-five years from now, we'll achieve the kind of standing that Jewish American writers have—that is, we'll just be judged as writers." Throughout, there is a sense that both as a writer and as an *ethnic* writer—especially one who has parsed the interconnection between Chinese-American and Jewish-American identities in *Mona in the Promised Land*—the relevant judges of her work for better or worse are Jews: "I was very happy when Cynthia Ozick reviewed [*Mona in the Promised Land*] and presented, really, a banner take. I was thrilled just to have attracted the notice of a writer whom I admire as much as I admire Cynthia Ozick. But in addition I was thrilled to have passed muster with her."[11]

This mélange of conflicting affects—admiration, resentment, competitiveness—structures Jen's fictional response to her Jewish-American predecessors as well. Her first novel, *Typical American*, as Rachel Lee has nicely noted, draws "upon a hodgepodge of eighteenth- and nineteenth-century literary references; [her protagonist] Ralph Chang emulates Benjamin Franklin, believes in Emersonian Romantic individualism, encounters a Melvillian confidence man, and lives a rags-to-riches life made familiar by Horatio Alger."[12] But on the structural level, it seems most deeply engaged with fictions like Saul Bellow's, particularly that of the classic phase of the 1950s and early 1960s (the period *Typical American* describes; the period in which Gish Jen grew up in Scarsdale). The plot of *Typical American* is familiar from Bellow's great picaresque fiction *The Adventures of Augie March* (1956). A callow, relentlessly optimistic outsider on the fringes of American society undergoes a number of comic misadventures on the way to becoming a fully credentialed—a typical—American. In Jen's novel, as in Bellow's, these adventures turn on the protagonist's encounter with a number of ambiguous, and at times outright hostile, mentors. In Bellow's early work, these are as likely to be women as men; in Jen's (as in Bellow's later work) they are almost always older and male. The first in *Typical American* is, significantly, a thoroughly assimilated Jew: Ralph's aristocratic, cane-carrying, mansion-inhabiting thesis advisor, Pinkus, who having heard an erroneous rumor about his student, transforms poor Ralph into a walking embodiment of the Yellow Peril, even to the degree of accusing him of stalking Pinkus's daughter. (The irony here, of course, is multiplied by the fact that precisely this language and these allegations—that they lusted after "white" gentile women—were made against Jews as well as Asians as late as the 1930s.) But, tellingly, Pinkus is less important for Ralph's fate than two Chinese-American men: Old Chao, a slightly senior colleague, and, even more important, Grover Ding, a rascally entrepreneur. Both, in some sense, cuckold Ralph as they help advance his career. Old Chao, although married, is in love with Ralph's beloved sister Teresa. He uses Teresa's concern for her hapless brother to seduce her: feeding her information that helps him earn tenure as he advances, inexorably, toward a sexual relation. Cuckoldry is more explicit still in the relation between Grover and Ralph. Grover is a classic self-made entrepreneur *cum* petty crook who fills Ralph's head with Dale Carnegie-like nonsense, enmeshes him in criminal schemes, and even sells him a building for his restaurant that is quite literally falling apart—all in the hopes of seducing Ralph's beautiful, sensible wife Helen, as Grover ultimately does.

Even more than her plots, then, Jen's *dramatis personae* fit into the pattern of Jewish-American writing, most specifically that perfected by Bellow not only in *Augie March* but also *Herzog* and *Humboldt's Gift:* the *schlemiel,* his head in the clouds, encounters a number of near-criminal rascals who teach him valuable lessons about life in America even as they bamboozle him. Bellow's term for these figures is "reality instructors, [those who] want to teach you—to punish you with—the lessons of the Real," and in Bellow's case, as in Jen's, these figures frequently cuckold the protagonist not only as an act of sexual domination, but as part of the latter's reversal of the Horatio Alger story ("how I rose from humble origins to complete disaster," is Herzog's description of his own life, one which more or less applies to Ralph's as well). In Bellow's case, this narrative turns quite rapidly to the comic in the deepest sense of the term. Augie concludes the story of his life with a deep, affirmative laugh of the *animal ridens*; Herzog ends, purged of anger and hate, in his house in upstate New York, there to revive his life beyond the neurotic if brilliant *kvetching* in which he has been indulging for most of the novel. Ralph Chang, too, is by and large a comic character, one whose own bumblings are orchestrated by his seeming friend, Grover, and part of the fun of the novel is to witness his sublime cluelessness as Grover leads him to one harebrained scheme after another while his wife and sister attempt, loyally, to clean up after him. And, near the end of the novel, Ralph snaps, as does Herzog (who stalks his ex-wife and her lover with a gun). Ralph drives off with his wife, threatening her until she confesses her relation to Grover. Returning to the house, Ralph attempts to run down the dog he has named after Grover but hits his beloved sister Teresa instead.

Jen claims in an interview that this swerve from the comic high spirits of the rest of the novel to its sober conclusion (Teresa remains in a coma for much of the novel's final chapters) has much to do with the miscarriage she suffered while writing it. But it seems to me also a willful swerve (in Bloomian terms, a *clinamen*) from the kinds of ideological structures that Bellow's text exemplifies. For in Bellow's novel, the ultimate service of the reality instructors is to return Herzog to his roots, restore him to his family. After he is arrested and his gun—significantly, his father's weapon—confiscated, Herzog calls his estranged brother to bail him out, reestablishing a relation that he had severed long before. In *Typical American*, the situation is precisely reversed. Ralph's murderous rage at his wife and Grover leads him to eliminate neither of these two tormentors, but rather his own sister who has in typical immigrant style been living too closely with the family for anyone's comfort.

Swallowing up the Jewish-American example, in other words, Jen proposes a tragic variation on it: she uses the comic plot of transcendent schlemielhood to tell a profoundly different kind of story, one at once more sinister and more troubling than the one that Bellow has to narrate. Ties to the traditional family have to be severed, however violently; the "reality instructors" pass over the edge into outright criminality and threaten to bring the assimilating outsider with them; the bumbling protagonist actually does harm. Jen's lesson would seem to have as much to do with the inadequacy of the Jewish immigrant narrative to her Chinese-American protagonists as its relevance. Indeed, that narrative, however ironically represented (as it surely is in Bellow's hands), has become just one more fallible American construction, like Emerson's or Melville's or Dale Carnegie's, that exists as a bane and a lure the Changs must overcome—as, one senses, must Jen.

A completely different take on this issue is suggested in Jen's next book, *Mona in the Promised Land*, which offers a delightfully comic series of riffs on the Asians-as-the-New-Jews topos (Jen invokes it directly on the first page of the novel). But here, Jen's thematic interest is in complicating the idea of ethnicity tout court. When Mona Chang converts to Judaism, that act puts into stark relief not only the complexity of Jewishness but also, as her rabbi suggests to her, her own Chinese-ness. "The more Jewish you are, the more Chinese you will become," says the hip if not hippie Rabbi Horowitz, by which he means many things: that she will come to recognize her own ethnic identity by affiliating with that of others; that she will discover her own difference *from* Jews by affirming religious solidarity *with* Jews; that being Jewish means being something—anything at all—in a culture which enthusiastically deracinates its participants. As Mona says, fliply, at one point: "In America, you can choose to be whomever you want, and I choose to be Jewish."

But it turns out to be not quite so simple—and the complexity rapidly extends to what it is to be Chinese-American. For these questions of voluntary vs. involuntary identity (consent vs. descent, in Werner Sollors's typology) become yet more complicated when race is factored into the ethnic mix. Bearing out the truth of Rabbi Horowitz's words, Mona confronts her own sense of inhabiting a racialized body when she begins to think about her nose, skin color, and breasts as ethnic markers as her Jewish friends discuss their own nose jobs, or when the customers at her family's pancake house chant, "Grow your nose! Grow your nose!" after she announces that she is now Jewish. And, similarly, her increasingly Chinese-identified sister's Harvard roommate, an African-American woman named Miranda, identifies Mona as a person of color—"yellow," not white—an identification Mona first accepts, then balks at, then edges away from. But other, angrier African-Americans like Alfred, the cook in the pancake house, identify Mona as white, much to Mona's chagrin. While Alfred may be wrong in the sense of skin color, he is clearly onto something when he starts to twit Mona for being from a family that keeps a black gardener and relegates all the African-Americans in their restaurant to the kitchen.

Mona's conversion to Judaism leads to a failed or unsuccessful translation into Jewishness, and the force of the ironies that both generate is useful to Jen in the ways it brings, simultaneously, all forms of racial and ethnic identity-formation to the fore, there to play uncertainly against each other. To answer the question with which Jen begins the novel—are Chinese-Americans the New Jews?—they are not, except insofar as they, like the Jews, are struggling to reconcile divergent predications of identity (religion, culture, skin-color, physiognomical accouterments like noses) in a culture intent on classifying them according to simple, if not simplistic dichotomies. Near the end of the novel, Mona says to Seth/Sherman that she's having trouble figuring out what it is to be "not wasp, and not black, and not as Jewish as Jewish can be; and not from Chinatown, either." Seth/Sherman responds in classic American terms, telling Mona that she's best defined as an individual ("a sore thumb . . . sticking out by yourself"), but the point remains as true in relation to ethnic identity as it does in relation to individual identity. Chinese-Americans like Mona fit into none of the available boxes our culture has created; neither white nor black nor "jewish as Jewish can be," and not even, for that matter, Chinese-American, at least in the terms in which the cultural imaginary creates Chinese-ness. But this is not to say that she isn't Chinese-American in some compelling and important way; it is to suggest, rather, that that Chinese-Americanness is defined only in differential terms, in relation to all these other, equally factitious, identity boxes.

In order to communicate this insight, Jen turns to a different representational structure than the one she used in *Typical American*: to Shakespearean comedy, with its rapid-fire transformations of costume, identities, and affiliations. What

Shakespeare does with and to gender, it might be said, *Mona* does to ethnicity—a nexus made clearest in Seth's successful wooing of Mona in the guise of Sherman, a feat worthy of one of Shakespeare's trickster heroes. What this would seem to represent is a move similar to the one that Mukherjee makes, through Jewish-American fiction and beyond it, to other representational forms and agendas. One would therefore predict, as with Mukherjee's work, that Jen's work would move beyond the narrative that this form engages with—the assimilation/acculturation narrative—to ones that stress hybridity, free-floating recombinant diasporism. And this indeed is where it seems to be headed: her most recent collection, *Who's Irish?*, as its title indicates, seeks to interrogate the relation between Chinese-American and other, non-Jewish ethnic identities. But the connection with Jewishness, I want to conclude this section by suggesting, endures here in a different guise—in that of form, which, like *Mona*, raises questions of ethnic identification on the terrain of race but in a deeper, more troubled aspect.

I am thinking here of her acclaimed story "Birthmates," first published in 1995 and included not only in the *Best American Short Stories* volume for that year, but in the *Best American Short Stories of the Century* (1999). Jen's protagonist is Art Woo, a fifty-one-year-old traveling salesman for a company in an unnamed "dinosaur" industry. Ambitious but frustrated, facing racist taunts by his boss (who blames the "Japs" for everything wrong in the industry but then consoles Art by telling him he knows he's a "Chink"), worrying obsessively about a white colleague, Billy Shore (who shares his birthday but seems to be doing better at the firm than he), mourning the loss of his girlfriend and of the fetus they aborted, Art is mistakenly booked into a welfare hotel next to a convention he is working. Entering the hotel, he is first greeted by an enormous black man at the desk, then mugged by a crowd of children as he goes up to his room. He wakes up while being tended by an African-American woman, a nurse turned heroin addict named Cindy, who keeps him safe from the crowd outside. After feeling a pang of desire for her, he returns to his work, only to find that his birthmate/competitor has moved on to a more promising job in California. His sense of loss and his confrontation with his own mortality combine at the end of the story, where he too contemplates a move West, and, seemingly for the first time, expresses his sense of loss for both his lover and their almost-child, aborted, we now learn, because it would not have been viable outside the womb.

There are no explicit references to Jews, Jewishness, or the canon of Jewish literature in the story, but in many ways this is the one work of Jen's that engages most intensely, and with the greatest degree of contesting energy, with that tradition—and in such a way, I think, as to make us read it differently, just as Mukherjee does. The tale of the failing salesman who is being passed over by the Home Office, for example, inevitably recalls Arthur Miller's *Death of a Salesman*, a text rich in family dynamics that resonate, ironically, against the context of Art's family-lessness. Even richer effects are created by the story's echoes of Grace Paley's *The Long Distance Runner*. In that story, Grace's pseudonymous protagonist Faith goes for a run in the Brooklyn neighborhood where she grew up and returns to the apartment house in which her family lived. There, she is at first an object of curiosity, then an object of anger and potential mob violence until she is rescued by the woman who occupies her former apartment, Mrs. Luddy, who hides her under the bed until the crowd disappears. She stays with the family for many weeks, until finally she returns to her own grown children who have barely noticed her long disappearance.

The echoings of Paley's story in Jen's are subtle but unmistakeable: the plot arc is the same, the incidents chime with each other. But the effect of those echoings, as it is in the explicit invocation of the black/white divide in *Mona*, is to suggest how complex the position of Asian-Americanness is on the American terrain of race. The point of *The Long Distance Runner* is to emphasize the curious admixture of intimacy and distance that exists between Jewish characters and those African-Americans who now occupy their former terrain. When an Art Woo enters a welfare hotel—already a significantly different space from an apartment—he is treated, like Faith, as if he were white by the hostile African-American inhabitants, even though at work he is treated as if he were not by his complacently racist bosses. And when he encounters Cindy, these shifting definitions collide:

> "This ain't no place for a nice boy like you," [she says]. That stung a bit, being called *boy*. But more than the sting-

> ing, he felt something else. "What about you? This is no place for you, either, you and your kids."
>
> "Maybe so," she said. "But that's how the Almighty planned it, right? You folk rise up while we set and watch." She said this with so little rancor, with something so like intimacy, that it seemed an invitation of sorts.

Complex as the moment may be in terms of defining the shifting racial identification of Asian-Americans vis-à-vis African-Americans (a dynamic which resembles in many ways the half-racialization of Jews in the first decades of this century[13]), it gains further intensity through Jen's echoes of Paley's story. As with Faith and Mrs. Luddy, a kind of intimacy seems to be established between Art and Cindy; and as with Faith, Art moves out to some kind of reconnection with his own would-be family, even if that family consists of his ex-girlfriend, whom he thinks at the end of the story to call and invite to move with him to California. And as with Faith, this act would seem to happen through his encounter not just with an African-American, but with the complex historical and ontological facts of black experience itself. But the point of the echoings in the story, it seems to me, is to measure the difference between Art's and Faith's experience: the one defining the long distance that Jewish-Americans have run from their past, the other suggesting that, just as Art has not yet come to terms with his own personal trauma, he has not yet come to terms with historical ones as well. At the end of the story, his rivalry with his jocular birthmate Billy Shore, and the inability to imagine a new life for himself symbolized not only by his dead child but also by his failure to mourn for that child continue to press on Art, even if he seeks to solve the problem by moving to California. Faith can return from her ghetto experience to her family. Gish Jen measures Art's greater alienation by having him (like Mukherjee's Jasmine) light out for the territory, assimilating to Americanness only in his desire to flee from the site of personal and historical humiliation, loss, and pain.

Conclusory

Mukherjee and Jen, then, reference Jewish-American writing and respond to it in ways that, I have been suggesting throughout and may now explicitly say, comport to Harold Bloom's anxiety of influence model, and these, I want further to contend, are productive for cultural as well as literary analysis. That is, their struggle (the term is Bloom's, and the suggestion is that it is inevitable, not contingent) for creative authority involves them in a match with powerful precursors whose example they play with, transform, and ultimately transcend, in two different ways: in Mukherjee's case, toward a discourse that stresses diaspora rather than assimilation; in Jen's toward an interrogation of the up-for-grabs racial identity of the Asian-American in a field of definition hitherto inhabited by narratives associated with Jews and African-Americans.

The point of invoking Bloom here, however, is ultimately in the service of something Bloom resists: that is, in contributing to the *sociology* of literary influence, of the study of engagements these writers perform as well as the kinds of literary interventions they wish to make. There's much more to be said about this development in Asian-American fiction[14] and criticism.[15] But of more importance, I think, is what the revisionary example of writers like Mukherjee and Jen can do for Jewish-Americans' understanding of their own cultural situation at the current moment. One of the effects of the resolution of the anxiety-of-influence scenario, Bloom suggests, is that organized by the trope of *metalepsis*, the trope of reversal of cause and effect—one in which the belated poet switches places with the precursor, in which we hear the echoes of a successor in his predecessors: Wordsworth in Milton, or Keats in Shakespeare. Something similar happens when we rethink the Jewish-American precursor texts—and the cultural arrangements their narratives shaped—in the light of the revisionary narratives I've been describing here. When Alfie Judah gets layered against David Schearle or even Alexander Portnoy, all that got repressed in assimilating Jewish fiction and in Jewish culture—the image of the "black" or Levantine Jew, the association of the figure of the Jew with sexual license and financial chicanery—comes flooding back into our accounting of that fiction, exerting a presence and a pressure on it by its very absence. Similarly, when Mona Chang affirms her racial identity as a Chinese woman in the presence of Jewish women discussing their nose jobs, the effect ought not only to make us think about Asian-American difference and the costs it exerts, but also that confronted by Jewish women whose bodies—and psyches—bear the scars of assimilation.

All these and more—violence, the multilayered and problematic racialization, a persistent and even structural anti-Semitism in the cultural imaginary that caused even the most cutting-edge Jewish fiction to repress its most problematic avatars—are elements of the Jewish-American experience that its rise to social respectability has caused it to ignore, marginalize, silence, or forget, and that the fictions I have foregrounded have forced it to remember. As America slides toward recognizing its multiracial, multicultural future, the recognition of the salience of those elements of the Jewish-American experience might help lower the barriers to an honest dialogue between Jewishness and the larger culture that seem to be erected on all sides at precisely the moment when they are least needed. And it might do something more: it might return Jewish-Americans to that state of structural alienation in which they can find, I hope, a proper sense of community with a culture struggling to encompass the alienness of its own increasingly multiple populations. Even if America has not for most Jews felt like exile, even if America has palpably not *been* for most Jews a place of exile, the salience of these narratives to American Jews at the moment may be to remind us of how complicated a relation we have—and ought to maintain—to the idea of home.[16]

NOTES

[1]*Contemporary Jewish American Writers and the Multicultural Dilemma: Return of the Exiled* (Syracuse, New York: Syracuse University Press, 2000).

[2]I am thinking here of Michael Rogin's argument in *Blackface, White Noise* (Berkeley: University of California Press, 1996), an argument that has shaped such recent formulations as that of Matthew Frye Jacobsen in *Whiteness of a Different Color: European Immigrants and the Alchemy of Race* (Cambridge: Harvard University Press, 1998). To my mind, Rogin's critique is valuable but extremely selective; while it offers an important corrective to liberal banalities, it courts a nyaah-nyah style of exceptionalism (see? Jews were no better than any other "white" folks!) that downplays the precarious situation in which American Jews found themselves in the 1920s and 1930s; fails to address white expectations vis-à-vis Jewish difference (there was a certain dimension of minstrelsy even in the Jew's performance of their identity as *Jews* in that era that makes their perfor-

mances in blackface more complicated than those of other Americans); and fails to offer a comparative perspective on blackface performances across ethnicities and races. For an account that is no less critical of Jewish blackface but avoids the tendencies I've noted above, as well as one that adds a considerable degree of complexity to the story, see Jeffrey Melnick, *The Right to Sing the Blues: African-Americans, Jews, and American Popular Song* (Cambridge: Harvard University Press, 1999).

[3]*Publisher's Weekly* 238 (9 Feb. 1991), 25.

[4]For an example of this confusion, see Eric Liu, *The Accidental Asian* (New York: Random House, 1998) and responses to Liu in *Slate* magazine by Jewish liberal Nicholas Lemann, who endorses his argument and seeks to apply it to his own slacker kids whom he wishes were more Asian and hence more "Jewish"; and arch-conservative Elliott Abrams (son-in-law of Norman Podhoretz and Midge Decter, and plotter of Reagan-era Latin American policy for the State Department), who complains about Liu's endorsement of intermarriage.

[5]I don't mean to underestimate the degree of prejudice and generalized ill-will that Jews have faced in America, one which rose to the surface on a number of occasions (e.g., the Leo Frank lynching, Henry Ford's anti-Semitic campaigns) and which I suspect will continue to do so in such marginalized but still potent guises as the survivalist movement, and which may be influencing the anti-globalization movement as well. But going along with this tendency is an alignment, particularly powerful among evangelical Protestants, between the Jewish narrative and that of a Christian America, one which is currently being exploited by the Christian and Israeli Right. Neither of these, I should not have to add but will, strikes me as being particularly good for the Jews.

[6]An "emphasis on intensity," Wisse writes, "is one of the basic components of the schlemiel-character in American fiction and indicates his main point of departure from European sources. . . . He is an expression of heart, of intense passionate feelings in surroundings that stamp out individuality and equate emotion with unreason. The schlemiel is used as a cultural reaction to the prevailing Anglo-Saxon model of restraint, inaction, thought and speech. . . . The American schlemiel declares his humanity by loving and suffering in defiance of the forces of depersonalization and the ethic of enlightened stoicism." *The Schlemiel as Modern Hero* (University of Chicago Press, 1979), 82.

[7]*Coming Out Jewish: Constructing Ambivalent Identities* (London: Routledge, 2000), 296–97. Stratton also offers a reading of *Seinfeld* that is similar to my own, but which is more interested in the ambivalence of the show's Jews than their ubiquity.

[8]All of the quotations from Mukherjee are from Alison Carb, "An Interview with Bharati Mukherjee," *Massachusetts Review* 29 (1988), 645–54.

[9]Jonathan Raban makes a version of this point in his perceptive *New York Times Book Review* response to *The Middleman*: "Her characters have a good deal in common with their Jewish counterparts: they're heroes to themselves, a size larger than life. And they see the surfaces of American life with the bug-eyed clarity of the greenhorn afloat in a gaudy new world. Yet they're not tired, huddled, or even poor: they own motels, work scams, teach in college, breeze through on private funds. Their diaspora is a haphazard, pepperpot dispersal. With no Lower East Side to keep the manners and morals of the old world alive, they're on their own and on the make. How the introspective and overmothered sons of the ghetto, from David

Levinsky to Alexander Portnoy, would have envied Ms. Mukherjee's new Americans, their guiltlessness, bounce, sexual freedom, their easy money. Unlike their Jewish literary ancestors, Ms. Mukherjee's people are no more troubled by conscience than butterflies." (*New York Times Book Review* 93 (19 June 1988), 22. My own view below is that what's important about Mukherjee's work in the Jewish-American context is that she might allow us to remember just how much of this conscienceless, scam-perpetrating, sexually free behavior circulated throughout Lower East Side culture, and why these writers had to repress that side of their own experience or encode it in rascally, usually non-Jewish "reality instructors."

[10]The fiction of Philip Roth might seem an exception here—what is Alexander Portnoy but a literal embodiment of such a figure, at least sexually? But, I would argue, Portnoy and the figures who follow embody one half of this tradition—the Jew as lascivious luster after Christian women—just as, at the beginning of the century, Abraham Cahan's David Levinsky embodies the other—the Jew as trader. Portnoy, after all, pursues a thoroughly ennobled profession (he is the New York Assistant Commissioner for Human Rights) while also pursuing forms of degradation in his erotic life.

[11]*Publishers Weekly* 238 (9 Feb. 1991), 25; Interview in Powells.com, 2001.

[12]Rachel Lee, *The Americas of Asian-American Literature: Gendered Fictions of Nation and Transnation* (Princeton: Princeton University Press, 1999), 44.

[13]For this pattern in Asian-American identities, see the very interesting work of Gary Okihiro, especially *Common Ground: Reimaging American History* (Princeton: Princeton University Press, 2000). Okihiro's understanding of the Asian-American as occupying a liminal position between white and black (as well as male and female, gay and straight) is interestingly cognate to the position in which Jews (themselves often categorized as "Oriental" as well as "Levantine") were placed during the same period, albeit without the same barriers to citizenship. For the Jew as "Asiatic" or "Oriental" in racializing discourses of the early twentieth century, see Robert Singerman, "The Jew as Racial Alien" in David Gerber, *Anti-Semitism in American History* (Urbana: University of Illinois Press, 1986).

[14]As far as fiction is concerned, the last ten years have witnessed a striking prominence of a new generation of South and East Asian-American writers (some immigrants, many first and second, or third-generation), many of them trained in the finest universities and/or MFA programs in the country. I am thinking here of, just to name a few, Vikram Seth, Jhumpha Lahiri (winner of the 1999 Pulitzer Prize, one year before Michael Chabon), Chang Rae Lee, Susan Malka Choi, Lan Samantha Chang, Christina Chiu, Don Lee, David Wong Louie, Min Jin Lee. These writers have a strikingly varied relation to the traditional canon of Anglo-American literature, ranging from Seth's masterful use of the sonnet form to the crucial engagement with Ralph Ellison's *Invisible Man* (and the less fully acknowledged one with Alfred Kazin's *Walker in the City*) undertaken by Chang Rae Lee to little or no engagement at all. These writers also evince a varied relation to the Jewish predecessors, again ranging from no interest at all to a rich relation. As an example of the latter, Lan Samantha Chang claims a Mukherjee-like affinity with the work of Bernard Malamud: "When I was learning to write I was very personally affected by his early work: in its deep sorrow, its humanity and ruthlessness, its hints of the fabulous. Overall, I found the post-World War II Jewish writers to be

very inspirational." But notice the implicit claim here—as in Mukherjee's and Jen's writing—that this is an influence that has had to be overcome on the way to full artistic mastery. See "A Penguin Guide to *Hunger*" in *Hunger* (New York: Penguin, 2000), 9.

15The paucity of comparative work with Jewish-American texts is striking and I think tactical. If the foundational book of contemporary Asian-American studies, Lisa Lowe's *Immigrant Acts: On Asian American Cultural Politics* (Durham: Duke University Press, 1996) eschews comparative work with Jewish experiences, that omission only serves to emphasize the unique nature of the laws that barred Asians from citizenship and to wrest the very discourse of "immigrant" from the Jewish-American example that dominated the very construction of the field in the 1950s and 1960s. To be sure, newer work—like David Eng's *Racial Castration: Managing Masculinity in Asian America* (Durham: Duke University Press, 2001)—invokes comparisons to Jewish discourses, invoking Boyarin, Jay Geller, and Sander Gilman on the racialized Jewish subtext in Freud. But Eng is less interested in the fact that the hypersexed/undersexed stereotype afflicted Asian- and Jewish-American men in strikingly similar ways. The point, however, is not to map the Asian onto the Jewish-American or collapse the two into each other, but to explore the ways that comparative work might open up new ways of self-imagining for both critical traditions. The paucity of consideration of Asian-American issues in, say, Jewish immigration scholarship is equally striking.

16This essay has been long in the making, and I'd like to thank with particular warmth the following: the Modernist Group at Oxford University, and particularly Ron Bush, who invited me to present the paper which grew into this piece; Abigail Licad, who generously shared her own ideas on this topic with me; Min Jin Lee, with whom I discussed much of this material and who saved me from some embarrassing missteps; Rachel Lee, whose work on Jen and whose lecture on Chang-Rae Lee provided the impetus for much of this work; and Susette Min, whose work on Lee and flânerie also led, through odd processes of rethinking, to some of my formulations here. None of them, needless to say, are responsible for my confusions. Sara Blair has responded to and edited too many versions of this essay to escape full responsibility, although her sufferings at the author's resistance to her critiques should grant her some absolution.

STEPHEN J. WHITFIELD

WHY AMERICA HAS NOT SEEMED LIKE EXILE

A decade ago I was invited to participate in an American Studies program at a university in Thailand and was expected to lecture on the history of this academic field as it evolved in the United States. So I recounted the half-century of the formal discipline from its origins at Harvard at the end of the Great Depression through the height of the myth-and-symbol school in the 1950s and down to the emergence of multiculturalism beginning in the 1980s. At no point in the course of the presentation in Bangkok did I ever refer to Jews; my remarks were confined to an overview of the interdisciplinary ideas that have shaped American Studies. My audience consisted entirely—I assumed—of Buddhists, in a religiously monolithic society; and indeed the first question afterwards came from a specialist in Buddhism in south Asia: Would you please explain how it is that Jews have so much power in the United States?

About a decade before September 11, 2001, revealed the extent of conspiracy theories, I did not believe that the intent of the questioner was malign. It was, I still believe, innocent, and seemed unencumbered by associations with anti-Semitic resentment. Though the query came from left field, an answer was required; and I propose to expand upon that response in this essay. Jews have been, after all, an excruciatingly tiny minority of the American population, hovering now at 2.2%. Yet in this past century in particular, their place in American society and culture has been conspicuous. According to a 1992 poll, only 10% of Gentiles realized that Jews numbered less than 5% of the population. The median estimate of their proportion was 18%, or about six times the correct figure.[1] At the moment both U. S. Senators from California are members of Hadassah; and both of Wisconsin's Senators are their co-religionists. Indeed, the Senate no longer permits roll call votes on Rosh Hashanah and Yom Kippur because too many of its members (ten) would be absent. In his two terms of office, President Bill Clinton had the opportunity to appoint only two Supreme Court Justices. Both—Ruth Bader Ginsburg and Stephen Breyer—are Jews; and on the doorpost of her chambers is a mezuzah. That object is also affixed to the doorpost of the office of Steven Spielberg; and during my visit to Bangkok, there was some consternation among Thai academics because a poll revealed that fewer of the city's teenagers could name their mayor than could identify Mr. Spielberg. That there was also a mezuzah on the doorpost of the office of the ex-president of the University of Notre Dame, Father Theodore Hesburgh,[2] also provides a clue about the status of American Jewry.

The nation's most influential woman, according to a poll in the *World Almanac*, was the late Ann Landers. She and her identical twin sister, Abigail Van Buren, have been the most popular syndicated columnists on the planet; both have showed up on the lists of "most influential women" and "most admired women" as well. Esther Pauline ("Eppie") and Pauline Esther ("Popo") Friedman were born on the Fourth of July, 1918, in Sioux City, Iowa. They have gone beyond the wildest ambitions of Nathanael West's "Miss Lonelyhearts" in shaping popular attitudes and behavior. As Ann Landers (based in Chicago) and as "Dear Abby" Van Buren (based in Beverly Hills), they have reached almost 200 million readers, in over two thousand newspapers in the United States and abroad. The sisters have been guides to the perplexed and bedeviled, instructing them about relating to their parents and children, their friends, and the opposite sex.

To be sure the authority of Ann Landers and Abby Van Buren did not stem from the Book of Proverbs or from the *Pirke Avot*, or even from a desire to sustain the tradition of the "Bintel Brief" column of the *Jewish Daily Forward*. Nevertheless "Popo" Phillips picked her *nom de plume* from the Book of Samuel, which invokes the blessedness of Abigail's advice; and "Eppie" Lederer, who became an advice columnist three months ahead of her sister, recalled growing up "in an atmosphere electric with Yiddish adages." Their Jewishness is not irrelevant. Their Midwestern roots familiarized the sisters with the verities of what another journalist of Jewish birth, Joseph Kraft, called Middle America, so that its values could be picked up as though by osmosis. Yet the minority status of Popo and Eppie may have immunized them against an uncritical subjugation to those conventional norms, may have made them wonder how experience, *sachel*, and common sense might modify certitudes which once seemed as square as the couple portrayed in *American Gothic*. They have liberalized the heartland without straying far from its core.[3] Their impact in loosening up the attitudes of Middle America bears comparison only to the effect of another, very different figure, the author of *The Feminine Mystique* (1963), Betty Goldstein Friedan of Peoria, Illinois, in ending the rigidity of sex roles and the constraints upon relations between men and women.

Nor did Yiddish entirely disappear, even though the mother tongue of the immigrants could hardly be transmitted intact to the native-born. Indeed, Yiddish insinuated itself in the vernacular of millions of gentiles, who seemed to find no more apt words for their distress, their anger, their frustrations than what Yiddish made available. The literary art which had been mastered in only a couple of generations—from Sholom Aleichem and I. L. Peretz down to Isaac Bashevis Singer—was reduced to the punch lines of stand-up comics. Some parts of the vocabulary became indispensable to anglophone speakers. For example, the most recent edition of *The American Heritage Dictionary of the English Language* defines *schmuck* as "a clumsy or stupid person; an oaf." Humorist Calvin Trillin has observed that "as a smattering of Yiddish is passed on to out-of-towners, pronunciation has become a great problem. In an entertaining *Wall Street Journal* piece a few years ago, Jon G. Auerbach talked about a house speaker in the Georgia legislature who got so angry with a representative in a floor debate that he called him a 'smook.'"[4] Yiddish is a language older than Chaucer's English. Yet such has been the brevity of Jewish experience in the New World that it was scarcely more than a century ago that this "jargon" came to be understood historically, when Leo Wiener of Harvard wrote a *History of Yiddish Literature in the Nineteenth Century* (1899). Such has been the velocity of history that his son Norbert helped invent the theoretical system that he called cybernetics, which sanctioned the birth of computers.

Writing overwhelmingly in English, American Jews significantly affected the formation of literary taste, and as authors of fiction they seemed numerous enough to constitute a "school" in the decades immediately after the Second World War. So noteworthy had the efflorescence of Jewish writing become, so voluble were its exemplars proving themselves to be in every genre, that one volume of memoirs, published in 1970, tried to find a niche that would be distinctive. The book was entitled *Memories of a Non-Jewish Childhood*. (Robert Byrne, its author, had received a parochial school education in a Midwestern town.) One of the earliest and most famous of the memoirs of a Jewish childhood was Mary Antin's. Published in 1912, *The Promised Land* was something of a sensation, a best-seller which measured the distance from the tsarist Pale of Settlement to the hospitality of New England. The standard was primarily psychological, as a new identity was formed: "All the processes of uprooting, transportation, replanting, acclimatization, and development took place in my own soul." Antin became both an assimilationist who had married outside the faith (and did not raise her children as Jews) *and* a Zionist. Her memoir was a gesture of gratitude for civic inclusion, though Harvard professor Barrett Wendell would privately complain of Antin's "irritating habit of describing herself and her people as Americans"—a term that he wished to reserve for folks like his wife and himself, "who have been here for three hundred years." *The Promised Land* could nevertheless be read as a membership application, a desire to belong to "one united people," as John Jay formulated it in *The Federalist*, "a people descended from the same ancestors." (Never mind that this Founding Father's own grandfather had been a Huguenot immigrant or that his mother's stock was Dutch.)[5]

Antin had so many successors that some gentiles seemed to need breathing space. So emphatic did the Jewish imprint upon American letters and other features of culture become that signs of paranoia could be detected. After writing *Big Sur* (1961) at the Mach 2 speed of ten days, Jack Kerouac told his agent that the novel contained "flashes of the greatest prose" of which the Beat writer was capable. But then he also warned his agent ("just between you and me") that "my ideas are being lifted left and right . . . by Jews, I should really subtitle *Big Sur: Another Idea for the Jews to Steal*." But the novelist abandoned the subtitle ("dont wanta be blackballed").[6] In an interview a dozen years later, an embittered Truman Capote denounced "this god-damned Jewish Mafia." He tabulated that "the entire cultural press, publishing . . . criticism . . . television . . . theater . . . film industry . . . is almost 90 per cent Jewish-oriented. I mean, I can't even count on one hand five people of any importance—of real importance—in the media who aren't Jewish. I can't."[7] That the interview with the novelist was conducted in *Rolling Stone*, founded and published by a Jew (Jann Wenner), inadvertently strengthened Capote's point. So did the publisher of his fiction; Random House was run by Bennett Cerf. The editor at *The New Yorker* upon whom Capote relied was William Shawn; and a major patron was the founder of CBS, William S. Paley. So the novelist was not utterly deluded, however inexact his arithmetic. (The Reverend Billy Graham and President Nixon once put Capote's estimate even higher. Early in 1972 the evangelist and the President privately discussed "the terrible problem arising from the total Jewish domination of the media." According to H. R. Haldeman's diary, the two figures agreed "that this was something that would have to be dealt with.")[8] Yet the "entire cultural press" to which Capote referred covers too much terrain for so tiny a minority—however enterprising—to monopolize.

Yet so deeply implicated in the nation's culture had "this god-damned Jewish Mafia" become that its civic credentials could not be disdained as inauthentic. It might be resented, but it could not be impugned as un-American. Jews could not be isolated or targeted as alien, as rootless; and the consequent mildness of anti-Semitism is perhaps the most obvious explanation for their impact in the United States. By 1965 the authoritative *American Jewish Year Book* no longer provided a separate listing for the subject of anti-Semitism in the United States;[9] and, if anything, anti-Semitism has in fact dramatically receded since then. Elsewhere, at least until recently, there has been something ubiquitous about this prejudice. Anti-Semitism seeped fully into the very foundations of Christendom, and—like racism, like sexism—should be historically considered atmospheric, taken for granted, like inhaling oxygen. Deicide has been the most terrible crime of which Jewry—or probably any people—has been accused. Even though medieval massacres were not repeated in the United States, nor the pogroms and blood libels that stemmed from hatred of "Christ-killers," the slur lingered; and the rougher Roman Catholic neighborhoods were once risky for Jewish kids to enter. Deicide also had its political uses, whether against Jews seeking or holding office in an overwhelmingly Christian society, or in reinforcing suspicions directed against outsiders or aliens. In 1941, for example, the Honorable John Rankin (Democrat of Mississippi) took aim at Wall Street bankers and cosmopolitan journalists, none of whom voted in his congressional district, like Walter Lippmann. These "international Jews," Rankin intoned, "are making the greatest blunder since the Crucifixion."[10] On that crime the statute of limitations expired only in 1965, when Vatican II "exonerated" the Jewish people. Manifestations of anti-Semitism in the United States can certainly be tabulated. But there has been something exceptional about those outbursts. Despite some stridency in the voices of hostility, the dog did *not* bark.

There is a paradox here, since anti-Semitism has been so deeply entangled in the history of Christianity itself. Americans tend to be much more pious than western Europeans (other than the Irish), and therefore anti-Semitism should have been *stronger* in the United States rather than the reverse. But perhaps Judeophobia could be traced to motives other than religion. In the twentieth century the nation's most influential anti-Semite was also its most legendary manufacturer. But deicide hardly figured in the evils that Henry Ford ascribed to Jews; and his hostility is better understood as a cranky villager's populism that was basically anti-cosmopolitan and anti-urban. (In a different context, the famous *New York Daily News* headline got it right: "Ford to City: Drop Dead.") The demagogues of the Depression era, like Father Charles Coughlin, the Reverend Gerald Winrod of the Defenders of the Christian Faith, and Gerald L. K. Smith (*The Cross and the Flag*), plucked from religious imagery to defame Jewry. But such hatemongering is a patrimony that the contemporary religious right, which has been pushing the axis of American politics starboard, has discarded; and its leaders are quick to repent when vestiges of anti-Semitism are uncovered.

If diarist H. R. (Bob) Haldeman can be believed, the Reverend Billy Graham told President Nixon that the real problem that he faced originated among "Satanic Jews."[11] But even if spin-controllers would explain that the republic's most consistently admired citizen was not warning the Chief Executive against *all* Jews, no one seriously believes that the evangelist belongs in a survey like Leonard Dinnerstein's *Anti-Semitism in America* (where he is, rightly, unmentioned). Would anyone argue that, say, the cockamamie opinions of Representative Rankin reflected Christianity with greater fidelity than the philo-Semitism of the Reverend Martin Luther King, Jr.? Nor, on the Jewish Question, could Martin Luther King's own divergence from Martin Luther be sharper. As Christianity has evolved, it has managed to produce its own antidote to the toxin of anti-Semitism.

Of course the diversity of the American population and the dis-establishment of the church also tempered the imperatives toward homogeneity that Christianity earlier and elsewhere promoted, and secularism has shown its superiority to religious commitment in maintaining civil peace. The growth of pluralism has also sanctioned a desire to bury the hatchet—other than in the hides of one's enemies. Nevertheless, Christian triumphalism has played its part in imperiling the status of a minority that has been skeptical of the Resurrection. Whether Christians or Jews are correct on this point cannot, for the moment, be resolved empirically. Both theologies could be wrong, though both cannot be right; and only at the End of Days can the Redeemer or Messiah be asked if this is a first visit or a return trip. Because the Son of God whom Christians worship was historically incarnated as a Jew, feelings about the co-religionists of Jesus are likely to be complicated. The right word here is "ambivalence," which has often characterized gentile attitudes.

For even Judeophobes have also admired Jews, and could distinguish good from bad individuals, or a distant or abstract Jewry from their own neighbors and associates. It is rather difficult to tell the story of anti-Semitism in the United States without also telling the story of philo-Semitism (a far less studied topic, by the way). For example, the thrust of Mark Twain's essay, "Concerning the Jews" (1899), is incontestably positive; it defends their honor. Yet Twain did admittedly accept some canards. Cotton Mather and Booker T. Washington exhibited both positive and negative views as well. Christianity itself is too entwined with Judaism (and its adherents) for hostility to be analyzed as though it could be hermetically sealed from other attitudes and motives. Anti-Semitism differs from other prejudices in that it has often been means-tested, springing less from contempt than from envy—at the Jews' prosperity, their enterprise, and their success (even though, to confirm the truthfulness of Christianity in the Middle Ages, they were supposed to be accursed). That sneaking admiration was revealed in a 1936 political manifesto entitled "Schimbarea la Fata a Romaniei" ("Romania's Transfiguration"), by the pro-Nazi, pro-Iron Guard Romanian writer Emil Cioran, who called the Jews "the most intelligent, the most gifted, and the most insolent people in the world." As a journalist summarized Cioran's argument, "the Jews are a people of such fanatic gifts and genius that they strangle the national aspirations of all other nations around them. . . . They do so through the curse of their 'abominable melancholy and their ironies born of the obscurity of the ghetto.'"[12]

Yet in America hostility to Jews could gain little traction in part because no version of Christianity had constituted the official religion. American Jews have needed no Edicts of Emancipation, nor, for that matter, Edicts of Toleration, because they could flourish under the aegis of a free-exercise clause of the First Amendment. Perhaps more important has been another part of that Amendment: "Congress shall make no law respecting an establishment of religion. . . ." In banning any Congressional act respecting an establishment of religion, the proponents of a Bill of Rights shared an understanding that establishment referred to government support, whether of one church, many churches, Christianity, or religion generally, and that Congress lacked jurisdiction in religious matters. No deity is even mentioned in the Constitution, which is therefore quite literally godless; and the delegates to the convention which drafted it made a choice to skip prayers in opening and closing their deliberations. The Enlightenment had already exerted such an impact that perhaps only about 4% of the American population could claim church membership; probably nowhere else in Christendom was religious affiliation so low. Almost half the signers of the Declaration of Independence could be classified as skeptics or deists. It was their misfortune to have been born only once—unlike 41% of all Republicans, who have told Gallup pollsters of having been "born again." As members of "the party of humanity," the Founders minimized the role of the divinity and maximized the value of reason in human affairs.

The Constitution erects a barrier that Jefferson and Madison considered necessary for the preservation of civil peace (in a far more homogeneous society than ours). Such a wall both the Baptist minister Roger Williams and the astute foreign observer Alexis de Tocqueville believed would enable religion to thrive (as it has here, more vigorously than in virtually any other Western industrialized nation). The United States has been spared the gusts of fanaticism that blow through much of the Third World in particular. Teheran has not become the model for Tulsa, where the forces of desacralization have penetrated. Tulsa is the capital of the ministry of Oral Roberts, who has "consistently raised more money than any other religious association" in the United States in the second half of the twentieth century. Early in 1987 he warned that he would die were his fund-raising goals not met: your money or his life. But bumper stickers were soon spotted in Tulsa advising against donations to his City of Faith medical complex: "Send Oral to Heaven in '87."[13] The United States has been safeguarded from the wars of religion, the blasphemy trials, the inquisitions, the lethal *fatwas*, and other cruelties and follies that punctuate the history of holiness. But faith has operated openly, easily, and effectively throughout American history because the services of an umpire from Washington were not required. Non-interventionism has been a way to finesse the vexing problem of diversity, when absolute truths clash in a pluralist society.

It is that wall that all sorts of religious minorities—but especially Jews—have found indispensable to their sense of feeling at home in the United States, which is a Christian society but not a Christian nation. The Jews have been the inadvertent beneficiaries of a lucky historical accident, which is that the birth certificate of the republic was written and approved during the Enlightenment. Indeed, one colonialist historian has even interpreted the Constitution as "the eighteenth-century equivalent of a secular humanist text."[14] Of course not everyone has agreed. For instance, Jerry Falwell once claimed: "The idea [that] religion and politics don't mix was invented by the Devil to keep Christians from running their own country."[15] Such assertiveness may help explain why only 76% of Americans have a favorable view of evangelical Christians, according to a Pew Forum poll. By contrast, 88% of Americans have a favorable view of Jews, slightly ahead of Lutherans, Episcopalians, and Catholics.[16] By the dawn of the twenty-first century, Falwell's fellow Protestants were no longer a majority even on the Supreme Court, though—of the four most energetic foes of a high wall—three happen to be practicing Catholics (Antonin Scalia, Anthony Kennedy, and Clarence Thomas). Scalia and Kennedy also attended parochial schools. It cannot be coincidental that the two justices who favor the highest wall are Ginsburg and Breyer.[17]

It is easy to understand why their co-religionists have overwhelmingly favored strict separationism and the narrowest interpretation of the Establishment Clause. In 1988 three out of every four Jews opposed a Constitutional amendment that would have permitted prayer in public schools; nearly the same percentage of white gentiles *favored* such an amendment. A little more than a third of Jews favored erecting a menorah in a public space. But four out of five white gentiles favored the idea, and three-fifths of black Americans approved of a menorah in a public place.[18] More subject to the ravages of modernity than others, less likely to be found in houses of worship than their neighbors, Jews are peculiarly an ethnic as well as religious minority—"a certain people." But they are far from certain about the validity of their own faith, and are hardly animated by ancient verities and Biblical certitudes. They have felt safer when the wall is high. Though Ginsburg and Breyer are outnumbered, the state of Ohio is still not permitted to use the phrase "With God, All Things are Possible" on the official seal (or anywhere else), since the phrase was uttered by Jesus and appears in the New Testament (Matthew 19:26). "In God We Trust" can still be printed on legal tender, however, since the phrase is Francis Scott Key's, from the National Anthem.[19]

Besides the weakness of anti-Semitism and the barrier of the establishment clause, a third explanation can be advanced. This society has also become increasingly tolerant and open and has made striking advances in abandoning the prejudices of the past. One minority among many, Jews are less likely to stand out, to become targets of bigotry. The United States has often defined itself as "a nation of nations" (in Walt Whitman's phrase), or what Ralph Waldo Emerson in 1845 called a "smelting pot"—getting in one consonant too many and thus leaving it to Israel Zangwill to coin the phrase, "the melting pot." Even Frederick Jackson Turner, the celebrant of westward expansion and of the democratizing effects of the frontier as the key to understanding the national experience, described his native land as a "crucible," into which the immigrants were poured, becoming "a mixed race, English in neither nationality or characteristics."[20]

But the sense that the diversity of the populace was a source of strength probably did not get fully articulated until the Second World War. Until then the virtually uncontested ideal was homogeneity rather than pluralism. But in the battle against Axis powers which exalted a unity founded upon race, the ideal of democracy seemed increasingly to entail not only the right to be equal but also the freedom to be different. That particularism was of course possible even before Pearl Harbor. In 1939 seven-year-old Mike Nichols and his brother arrived in New York from Danzig, from which their departure had been delayed because of a traffic-stopping Hitler speech. On their first night off the ship, Mike Nichols saw a sign in Hebrew and asked his father (in German): "Is that allowed here?"[21] But the Second World War accelerated the process by which ethnic groups like the Jews felt themselves to be fully included in the American experiment.[22] Over half a million served in the military; eight thousand lost their lives in combat. Among them was Rabbi Alexander Goode, one of the four chaplains who gave up their life-preservers in 1943, so that others on the military transport, the *S. S. Dorchester*, could be saved. The four self-sacrificing clergymen were memorialized on a 1948 postage stamp as personifying "Interfaith in Action." Diversity could be empowering against the Japanese aggressor, even if it meant—for the sake of inclusion—the demonization of the non-white enemy. A popular song, for example, confidently predicted doom "when those little yellow bellies / Meet the Cohens and the Kellys."[23]

As the historian Edward S. Shapiro has pointed out, World War II was the first American war—and, so far, the only American war—in which the fictional representation of the global conflict was almost a monopoly of Jews. Each service had its own novelist who was a veteran of the war. The Army had both Norman Mailer's *The Naked and the Dead* (1948) and Irwin Shaw's *The Young Lions* (1948); the Navy had Herman Wouk's

The Caine Mutiny (1951); the Marine Corps had Leon Uris's *Battle Cry* (1953); and the Army Air Force somewhat later had Joseph Heller's *Catch-22* (1961). Anti-Semitism did not evaporate in wartime, however, and may even have worsened. In February, 1942, Americans were asked which minorities among them were "a menace." Twenty-four percent picked Japanese-Americans; 15% named Jews. Do the Jews have too much power, pollsters asked Americans in 1945. Fifty-eight percent of them answered affirmatively.[24]

But should World War II prove in retrospect less significant than it now appears, the legitimation of heterogeneity could not be forestalled indefinitely. To be sure, white ethnics got incorporated into the mosaic in a way that heightened the sense of exclusion of the descendants of African slaves. But the logic of equality could not permanently deny the claims of non-whites. We know we're not in Kansas anymore—at least not the Kansas of *The Wizard of Oz* of a century ago—when school teachers face polyglot pupils who speak Kurdish, Farsi, Urdu, Russian, Bengali, Khmer, and Spanish. We know we're in California, which has recently accepted more permanent immigrants than any other *nation* (other than the United States itself). Nearly one Californian in four is foreign-born, and only one in two can be classified as Anglo. Or perhaps we are in Birmingham, Alabama, which now boasts of over sixty Chinese restaurants—almost ten times the number of only a decade earlier? Sales of salsa outstrip ketchup, the chairman of the Joint Chiefs of Staff was named Shalikashvili, and more high school students know who Harriet Tubman was than can identify a white male named Sir Winston Churchill. *The Dictionary of Global Culture* (1997) has space for such writers as Zora Neale Hurston and Alice Walker (but not, it so happens, for a white male named Saul Bellow). The history of Hollywood is now conventionally told in terms of an earlier concealment or sublimation of a Jewish inflection. But by the end of the twentieth century, it was possible to buy a Haggadah based on the animated film *The Prince of Egypt* (1998), with stills serving as illustrations of enslavement and exodus. Not until the formation of Dreamworks SKG had a Hollywood studio imagined the publication of a Haggadah as an opportunity to plug a cinematic product, itself—in a backward loop—inspired by the text that inspired what participants at the seder read. The American kaleidoscope makes Jews seem less odd, less exotic, less foreign than elsewhere. In Ottawa in 1969, Mordecai Richler stepped forward to accept a literary prize, the Governor-General's Award, for *Cocksure*. A puzzled representative of Her Majesty asked the novelist: "*Êtes-vous Canadien*"?[25]

Ever since 1937 Gallup pollsters have been asking citizens about their willingness to vote for a Jew or a Catholic or a woman for President. In that year only 46% said that they would be willing to vote for a Jew; that proportion presumably included the 4% who were themselves Jewish. Only 33% of the populace would have been willing to vote for a woman; 60% was the proportion willing to vote for a Roman Catholic. The figure for Catholics had climbed to 94% by 1999. A year before Joseph Lieberman was nominated as Al Gore's running mate, the percentage willing to vote for a Jew was up to 92. Only 6% told Gallup pollsters that they would not vote for a Jew, no matter who the candidate was. In 1999 the number that claimed to being willing to vote for an African-American candidate rose to 95%. That proportion is, somewhat implausibly, higher than the number willing to vote for a Jew (perhaps because racial bigotry has been so explicitly stigmatized in recent decades, perhaps because the number of blacks polled is inevitably much higher than the number of Jews). Only 49% of the citizenry could imagine themselves voting for an atheist, which is the least popular religious category which Gallup pollsters have found. Only 79% of our fellow Americans would vote for a Mormon for the Presidency; 17% insisted that they would not. Only 37% would vote for a homosexual.[26]

Jews have also benefited from the broadly democratic character of American society and culture. Upward mobility was more likely when bastions of privilege were less formidable than elsewhere. A naturalized citizen who had an aristocratic French name—Sanche de Gramont at birth, Ted Morgan suggested the following contrast, doubtlessly heightened for effect: Rudeness can be done with impunity in Europe, because of the certainty that people of a lower "social background . . . will never extricate themselves from the mire. They will remain what they are, the objects of your snub." Yet "in America there are so many surprising reversals that it makes sense to be nice to people," since "the office boy may someday be board chairman." Appreciating such upward mobility, Morgan became an American in 1977, even though in the United States "whoever you kick on the ladder on the way up is going to kick you back when he reaches your rung. In Europe there isn't even a ladder."[27]

In the New World nobody quite knew what vocational options were available, and for immigrant Jewish parents the ambitions of their sons could seem unfathomable. Aaron Copland was born in 1900, in a Brooklyn tenement two floors above a dry goods store owned by his Lithuanian-born father. Copland never bothered to attend college; but when he informed his father of his desire to compose classical music for a living, the small businessman was baffled: "Where did you get such a strange idea? Can you make a living at it?"[28] The second question was legitimate. How could Harris Copland have ever encountered a classical composer—much less a financially secure one? Born in Minsk in 1880, Morris Raphael Cohen was brought to America at the age of twelve. His father was unlearned; there were virtually no books in the house. "It was taken for granted," Cohen wrote in his autobiography, "that in a few years I would join my father in some phase of tailoring."[29] Instead he became a philosopher, a renowned teacher at the City College of New York, a thinker who impressed Bertrand Russell. Lewis Selznick was born in Kiev in 1870, before there were any movies, and belonged to the first generation of Hollywood moguls, who were producing 90% of the world's films by 1926. After the 1917 Revolution, Selznick cabled the deposed tsar: "When I was boy in Russia your police treated my people very badly. However no hard feelings. Hear you are now out of work." Selznick offered to put Nicholas II "in pictures. . . . Reply my expense. Regards you and family."[30] The last of the Romanovs did not reply. He may have been offended by Selznick's last-shall-be-first chutzpah.

In such a society, the possibility of making something new was not discouraged; and the established hierarchies of Western culture could easily be suspended, or even upended. Culture itself could be redefined, for the sake of creativity and innovativeness. When George Gershwin was seeking singers for his new "folk opera," one name in particular came to his attention. Todd Duncan, a music teacher at Howard University, had recently won acclaim in an all-black *Cavalleria Rusticana*; and Gershwin had to plead with the baritone to come up from Washington to audition for the role of Porgy. Duncan was unenthusiastic. After all, "I thought of George Gershwin as being Tin Pan Alley and something beneath me." But a wary Duncan showed up at Gershwin's New York apartment anyway, assuming that there would be an accompanist for him. There wasn't. Would Gershwin himself be able to accompany him, Duncan wondered. (After all, the most famous, versatile, and prolific of all the Tin Pan Alley composers, Irving Berlin, could not play any musical instrument besides the piano— and even that only in the key of F#. He needed a special piano that would mechanically transpose keys by shifting a lever; and since he could neither read music nor notate it, a trained musician also had to sit next to him to write down what Berlin was playing by ear. He exemplified the untutored commercialism of Tin Pan Alley for which classical musicians had such disdain.)

But Gershwin offered to try to accompany Duncan, who handed the pop composer the sheet music to a piece by an obscure nineteenth-century Italian, Benedetto Secchi, entitled "*Lungi dal caro bene*." Another act of one-upmanship for Duncan, but Gershwin played while the baritone sang several bars. But then the composer wanted to see how Duncan might look on the stage as Porgy, and asked him to sing the aria without looking at the sheet music. Duncan proceeded to sing it again, and was astonished that Gershwin was playing Secchi's piece from memory. After eight bars Gershwin stopped and asked Duncan: "Will you be my Porgy?" Still reluctant to attach himself to music that he feared might not be up to the glories of European opera, Duncan demurred: "I'll have to hear your [new] music." The following week Duncan returned to Gershwin's apartment, where his lyricist-brother Ira joined them as well as selected guests to listen to the score of *Porgy and Bess*. When the brothers got to the second act, George told Duncan that this aria would make the baritone famous. "Aria?" Duncan replied in puzzlement, hardly imagining that he would be singing "I Got Plenty o' Nuttin'" all over the planet for the next four decades. By the time the brothers got to "I'm on My Way," Todd Duncan was weeping; and the Gershwins' effort to cast him in their "folk opera" had paid off.[31]

The first Porgy taught at a university and devoted himself to classical music. The composer had dropped out of high school at the age of sixteen, and yet faced no significant barriers in his own artistic aspirations. They collaborated on what became the only American addition to the operatic repertory, even though the most prestigious music reviewer of the era, Virgil Thomson, dismissed *Porgy and Bess* at its premiere as "a piquant but highly unsavory stirring-up together of Israel [and] Africa," flawed by "gefiltefish orchestration."[32] But the mixture of Israel and Africa is one way of summarizing what is peculiar about American vernacular culture. One of its most indelible ornaments would be *Porgy and Bess* itself, the first American opera to be performed at La Scala. Less obviously than in the Old World, culture in America did not consist of a lock that needed to be picked, and suggested unpredictability, fluidity, instability. American culture is unfinished.

But for most of the twentieth century, there was a price to be paid, which was the soft-pedalling of Jewish identity itself. Born in Ostrin, Lithuania, in 1887, Harry Austryn Wolfson was so astonishingly erudite that he was given the first chair in Jewish studies at Harvard. Wolfson nevertheless asserted that society imposed limits on the ambitions of Jews, whose identity was as inescapable as it was disabling. Indeed, a pamphlet he published in 1922 compared Jewish identity to a physical handicap: "Some are born blind, some deaf, some lame, and some are born Jews."[33] The burden of anti-Semitism, he believed, was as insoluble as physical deformation, a birth defect. But Wolfson was wrong. Jews did not have to limit themselves, or surrender their hopes, or make significant sacrifices, for the sake of their faith and their heritage. This freedom was not understood in the first half of the twentieth century, however. It was still too early to realize that Jews did not have to resign themselves to a constricted fate, or even have to give up anything in the yearning to become American. But how that surrender to the host society was transacted can be illustrated perhaps most vividly in the history of one family. It owned the newspaper which—more than any other—has been seen as emblematic of Jewish power in the United States.

In 1896 the financier and communal leader Jacob Schiff had supported the effort of Adolph Ochs to get control of the *New York Times*, because the new publisher "could be of great service to the Jews generally."[34] This hope would be dashed. The *New York Times* long exhibited an equivocal relationship to Jewish life. Ochs and his family feared the identification of the *Times* as a "Jewish newspaper,"[35] and upheld the ideal of impartiality instead. Thus the journalists themselves have usually been insulated from business pressures, and the separation has been respected between the editorial writers on the Fourteenth Floor and the staffers whose diligence in gathering the news became so notorious that magazine publisher Henry R. Luce called the *Times* "the best unedited paper in the world."[36] Though Ochs fervently defended the rights of Leo Frank, the Atlanta factory manager who was wrongfully convicted of murder in 1913 and lynched two years later, so much criticism was heaped on the newspaper that its publisher was determined never again to make the blunder of fighting anti-Semitism so conspicuously. Early in 1933, two years before his death, Ochs banned the publication of letters on the subject of the *Führer*. Otherwise the *Times* would have been obliged to publish pro-Hitler letters to the editor. But that also meant that anti-Nazi warnings could not be posted in defense of the Jewish people—a phrase that Ochs also banned, by the way, preferring "people of the Jewish faith" instead.[37]

Flaunting neither its power nor its wealth, the family generally avoided ostentation. Keeping a low profile was just what Ochs had advised his fellow Jews in Chattanooga, before he moved to New York City: "Don't be too smart. Don't know too much."[38] In the elevated atmosphere that wealth provided, however, blood became thinner, emotions were expressed parsimoniously, and ancestral allegiances were easily abandoned as well. Dorothy Schiff, the publisher of the New York *Post* and granddaughter of the venerable Jacob Schiff, opined that "once you reach a certain financial level, people don't think of you as anything but very rich."[39] In the family which Ochs founded, Jewishness was no more emphatic or direct than any other feeling.

In the nineteenth century, the Reform colleagues and followers of Rabbi Isaac Mayer Wise dramatically reduced the definition of the Jews. Neither a "race" nor a people, they were only adherents of a faith. But a paradox resulted: since piety itself was not enhanced it shriveled too. Ethnicity did not suffer at the expense of religion, which was also absent. Thus Ochs's daughter, Iphigene Ochs Sulzberger, was raised by parents who celebrated Christmas but did not participate in a seder. Ochs himself was so surprised by the bravura of his nephew John's "confirmation" at Temple Emanu-El that the publisher, with uncharacteristic fancy, offered the bar mitzvah boy a $10,000 bribe to become a rabbi. He declined, and under the name John Oakes—a change in spelling due to the anti-German hysteria of 1917—exercised far greater influence as the chief editorial writer of the *Times* than he ever would have enjoyed in the pulpit. When Ochs's beloved nephew Julius Ochs Adler died, his daughter was baffled that the funeral rites at Temple Emanu-El did not allow for a rendition of the favorite song of the deceased: "Onward, Christian Soldiers."[40]

The children of Iphigene and Arthur Hays Sulzberger grew up with the disabilities of Jewish identity; a few hurtful snubs were administered within the rarified class which the family had joined. But without any offsetting advantages, such as warm memories or secure faith or deep learning or a sense of collective history, the Sulzbergers were culturally deprived. On Rosh Hashanah and Yom Kippur, Arthur Ochs (Punch) Sulzberger and his siblings were kept home. Though Arthur Hays Sulzberger was even a trustee of Temple Emanu-El, nobody bothered to explain to the children why they were absent from school.[41]

Such wariness and indifference partly account for the record of the *Times* from 1933 until 1945. The newspaper minimized both the significance and the distinctiveness of the Holocaust, and failed to grasp the ferocity with which the Third Reich was fighting the war against the Jews. Nor did the newspaper see the point of Zionism; during the terrible crisis of European Jewry, Palestine was portrayed as one optional haven, but nothing more. Arthur Hays Sulzberger restrained his enthusiasm, even after 1948, for the Jewish state—another phrase which he kept off the editorial page.[42] "My attitude toward Israel," he reassured an interviewer, "is the same as my attitude toward Indonesia."[43] He also thwarted the ambitions of able Jewish employees who might have merited higher positions. Even columnist Arthur Krock, an Episcopalian whose father was Jewish, was stymied. He could not persuade his boss that, for purposes of genealogy, Judaism counted only maternal descent.[44] The ethnicity of Sulzberger and his father-in-law was enough to generate queasiness about particularist claims and to intensify the dedication to the ideal of objectivity which the newspaper upheld. But the Jewishness of the family was too weak to be of any genuine service to an imperiled people during the haunted years of the Holocaust in particular.

The ascent of Sulzberger's son "Punch" in 1963 coincided roughly with a nationwide legitimization of diversity. He shared his father's and grandfather's self-designation as an American of the Jewish faith, but kept the *Times* from falling behind the times. By appointing A. M. (Abe) Rosenthal as executive editor in 1969, the publisher risked the stigma of a "Jewish newspaper" which the family had so sedulously tried to elude. As a result of such a commitment to merit, the coverage of the *Times*, by common consent, got even better. Rosenthal himself was succeeded by two other Jews: Max Frankel, born in Saxony, and then Joseph Lelyveld, the son of a rabbi who was also a Zionist activist. Resilience and adaptation are therefore part of the story of the ownership of the *New York Times*. But there is continuity too, though Sulzberger, Jr., is not of the Jewish persuasion. "*The Times* . . . [is] my religion," the current publisher has remarked. "That's what I believe in."[45] That is a faith which has made a huge swath of American Jews, especially the most literate and politically alert, into his co-religionists.

America has done more than to provide a relatively open society in which anti-Semitism has been minimal, a state that has been uncoupled from an official religion, an economy relatively free of barriers to entry, a relatively democratic culture. America has also put Jewish history out of its misery, and has given Jews an opportunity to pursue happiness and to discredit the "lachrymose" conception of their Old World origins. This promise has constituted something new in the experience of the Diaspora. In 1950 the star of *The Jazz Singer* (1927) died in Los Angeles, where he was eulogized at Temple Israel. There comedian George Jessel summed up what Al Jolson had symbolized, indeed what mass entertainment had done to burnish the American promise. Jessel stressed what "a sad lot" the Jewish immigrants had been when they arrived at the dawn of the century. "And then there came on the scene a young man, vibrantly pulsing with life," the comedian proclaimed, "who marched on the stage . . . with a gaiety that was militant, uninhibited and unafraid, and told the world that the Jew in America did not have to sing in sorrow but could shout happily about Dixie."[46] Jolson had not been born there but in Lithuania. Yet the

"World's Greatest Entertainer" must have felt right at home in a land where "alabaster cities gleam, undimmed by human tears." Jefferson had made happiness the measure and the proof of civilization. For Freud, on the other hand, happiness was the price to be paid for civilization. Despite his notorious anti-Americanism, he contemplated moving to the United States in the 1880s, and kept on the wall of his study a copy of the Declaration of Independence—the very document that affirmed the pursuit of happiness as a right that President George W. Bush has hailed as "uninalienable."[47]

In so optimistic a setting, the pursuit of happiness could elide into the right to achieve it. One positive thinker, George Mason, wrote that new entitlement into the Virginia bill of rights; and not to be outdone, even the crusty John Adams put it into the Massachusetts bill of rights (five times). From the American Revolution until the very end of the nineteenth century, about 120 state constitutions were written. About two-thirds of them, according to historian Henry Steele Commager, "provide some kind of guarantee of happiness. . . . Most of these guarantee not only the right to seek it but the right to obtain it as well. In the United States happiness is not merely a moral but a legal right."[48] Commager did not comment on how many lawsuits were brought against these state governments by plaintiffs who remained glum. A. Alvarez, a London-born and -based critic, visited the former colony for the first time in 1953. He was surprised that his first American cabbie wished him a nice day. "It had never crossed my British mind," Alvarez recalled, "that a nice day could possibly be an option."[49] Defecting to the United States in 1967, the daughter of Joseph Stalin explained that she was tired of her "grim" compatriots; Svetlana Alliluyeva had experienced enough of "pessimism."[50] Walt Disney claimed to have dedicated himself to providing happiness for the millions. At California's Disneyland and at Florida's Disney World, a pledge of glorious progress is made in the section called Tomorrowland. But at the European counterpart to these theme parks, Disneyland Paris, Tomorrowland does not exist. Sexual pleasure has been defined as a right in the United States as well. The wife of John Wayne Bobbitt told the arresting officer why she had dismembered her husband: "He always have orgasm and he doesn't wait for me to have orgasm. I don't think it's fair so I pulled back the sheets and I did it."[51]

Jews besides Jolson were bound to be affected and eventually went from Saturday morning services to Saturday matinees, before getting inflamed with Saturday night fever.

They too have wanted to believe that desires can be satisfied, that life will turn out "all right"—which is the first English phrase that young David Levinsky—the protagonist of Abraham Cahan's canonical novel—learns in this part of the Diaspora.[52] Jews too have yearned to feel entitled to stroll "On the Sunny Side of the Street" (lyrics by Dorothy Fields, the daughter of vaudevillian Lew Fields). Or take what belongs on the short list of the most bizarre puberty rites in the several millennia of Jewish history. In 1978, following the ritual in a Conservative shul in which Harvey Cohen became bar mitzvah, the celebrants took over Miami's Orange Bowl, rented for the occasion. While the scoreboard flashed "Happy Birthday, Harvey," a sixty-four-piece high school marching band entertained the two hundred guests, who were served by waiters dressed as referees and by waitresses dressed as cheerleaders. One of Dade County's leading rabbis, Dr. Irving Lehrman of Temple Eman-El, complained that "in this case there is more bar than mitzvah"; and indeed the compliant City Commission had been persuaded to pass a special ordinance allowing liquor to be served in the stadium. Standing on the fifty-yard line after watching young Harvey say the *motzi* over bread and light the candles, grandfather Robert Cohen assured an interviewer that "it doesn't matter, I guess, where a bar mitzvah party is held, as long as there is love and family and joy."[53]

Of course hedonism has never been a monopoly of Americans. Nor have they always pursued happiness so ardently. They have, after all, lived for centuries in the "land of the Pilgrims' pride." Wanton pleasures were few in rural and small-town America. The nation "was born in the country," historian Richard Hofstadter proclaimed, "and has moved to the city."[54] There the citizenry has shifted increasingly from production to consumption, as its favorite reading matter shifted from the *Farmers' Almanac* to *TV Guide*. Nor is the glorification of joy exclusive to American Jewry. The Hebrews were worshipping the golden calf even as the Torah was being transmitted to Moses; Jewish history discloses that ancient revels coincided with revelation. The fun and games at the very foot of Mount Sinai may even be interpreted as an early version of Club

Méditerranée, founded in 1954 by a French Jew named Gilbert Trigano.

But a lavish and unmodulated commitment to the pursuit of happiness should at least be recognized as a rupture of Judaic tradition. Religion is itself a lifelong set of duties—Ten Commandments, 613 *mitzvot*, tractates full of laws, endless inconveniences. To be a Jew no longer brings much trouble; but it takes trouble to practice Judaism, which is a product of both the ancient world and of the Old World. The ethos of felicity and the relentless quest for self-gratification therefore pose a problem for Judaism. When Freud denied that "the intention that man should be 'happy' is . . . included in the plan of 'Creation,'"[55] this "godless Jew" had the authority of tradition behind him. The life of a believer is not supposed to be duty-free, and an ideal of sensation which endorses self-satisfaction wreaks special havoc on those expected to form "a kingdom of priests and a holy nation" (Exodus 19:6).

American values and the Jewish heritage are not entirely without friction, though perhaps that tension can be creative and healthy. But however Jewish life in the United States will evolve, this community will continue to matter. It is possible to foresee it as one of the only two centers of Jewish life that might sustain a critical mass. After Israel the third largest Jewish community is in France, though its Jewish population (521,000) is smaller than the Jewish population (637,000) of the Sunshine State which hosted the bar mitzvah party of Harvey Cohen.[56] On medieval and early modern maps, Jerusalem was the center of the world and—for reasons beyond the scope of this essay—remains so in the imaginative life of world Jewry. But in terms of sheer numbers, the *New Yorker* cover which Saul Steinberg drew—which may be more famous than any map from Rand-McNally—communicates a certain truth. The rest of America may be barely discernible from the perspective of New York City, which has harbored the biggest concentration of Jews of any city since Abraham left Ur of the Chaldees. (Warsaw was second.) Claims for the centrality of *eretz yisrael* need not be invoked here. But surely America merits consideration as another center of Jewish history, though the struggle to conceive of America in such terms still needs to be developed and refined.

A start was made in 1978 by Nathan Zuckerman, writing to

his brother Henry, a born-again Zionist, of American Jews "seething with confidence and success. And maybe that's a world-historical event on a par with the history you are making in Israel." Philip Roth has his alter ego conjecture that "one can play a role in history without its having to be obvious, even to oneself. It may be that flourishing mundanely in the civility and security of South Orange, [New Jersey] more or less forgetful from one day to the next of your Jewish origins but remaining identifiably (and voluntarily) a Jew, you were making Jewish history no less astonishing than theirs, though without quite knowing it every moment, and without having to say it. You too were standing in time and culture, whether you happened to realize it or not."[57]

NOTES

[1]David Singer and Lawrence Grossman, eds., *American Jewish Year Book 2000* (New York: American Jewish Committee, 2000), 247; Seymour Martin Lipset, *American Exceptionalism: A Double-Edged Sword* (New York: W. W. Norton, 1996), 151; Alan M. Dershowitz, *The Vanishing American Jew: In Search of Jewish Identity for the Next Century* (Boston: Little, Brown, 1997), 343.

[2]"A *Moment* Interview with Father Theodore Hesburgh," in Leonard Fein, ed., *Jewish Possibilities: The Best of Moment Magazine* (Northvale, NJ: Jason Aronson, 1987), 300.

[3]Jan Pottker and Bob Speziale, *Dear Ann, Dear Abby: The Unauthorized Biography of Ann Landers and Abigail Van Buren* (New York: Dodd, Mead, 1987), viii; "Advice for the Lonely Hearts," *Time* 117 (19 January 1981), 56; Judith Wax, "Dear Ann Landers: Is Incest Hereditary?", *New York Times Sunday Magazine*, 13 October 1974, 114, 116; Christopher Buckley, *Wry Martinis* (New York: Harper Perennial, 1998), 209–12.

[4]Calvin Trillin, "Carrying a Big Shtick," *Brill's Content* 4 (June 2001), 27–28.

[5]Mary Antin, *The Promised Land* (Boston: Houghton Mifflin, 1912), xix, xxii; Barrett Wendell to Sir Robert White-Thomson, 31 March 1917, in *Barrett Wendell and His Letters*, ed. M. A. De Wolfe Howe (Boston: Atlantic Monthly Press, 1924), 281–82; Werner Sollors, "National Identity and Ethnic Diversity: 'Of Plymouth Rock and Jamestown and Ellis Island'," in *History and Memory in African-American Culture*, eds. Geneviève Fabre and Robert O'Meally (New York: Oxford University Press, 1994), 105; John Jay, Number 2, in Alexander Hamilton et al., *The Federalist*, ed. Benjamin Fletcher Wright (Cambridge, MA: Harvard University Press, 1961), 94.

[6]Jack Kerouac to Sterling Lord, 9 October 1961, in Jack Kerouac, *Selected Letters, 1957–1969*, ed. Ann Charters (New York: Viking, 1999), 300–01.

[7]Quoted in *Truman Capote: Conversations*, ed. M. Thomas Inge (Jackson: University Press of Mississippi, 1987), 287–88.

[8]H. R. Haldeman, *The Haldeman Diaries: Inside the Nixon White House* (New York: Putnam, 1994), 405.

[9]John Higham, *Send These to Me: Jews and Other Immigrants in Urban America* (New York: Atheneum, 1975), 193.

[10]Quoted in Edward S. Shapiro, "Anti-Semitism Mississippi Style," in *Anti-Semitism in American History*, ed. David A. Gerber (Urbana: University of Illinois Press, 1986), 132–33.

[11]H. R. Haldeman, *The Haldeman Diaries: Inside the Nixon White House* (CD-ROM: New York, 1994).

[12]Adam Gopnik, "The Get-Ready Man," *New Yorker* 76 (June 19 & 26, 2000), 176.

[13]Alan Brinkley, *Liberalism and Its Discontents* (Cambridge, MA: Harvard University Press, 1998), 267; Richard Ostling, "Your Money or His Life," *Time* 129 (26 January 1987), 63.

[14]Leonard W. Levy, *Blasphemy: Verbal Offense against the Sacred, from Moses to Salman Rushdie* (New York: Alfred A. Knopf, 1993), 268, 269; John M. Murrin, "Religion and Politics in America from the First Settlements to the Civil War," in *Religion and American Politics: From the Colonial Period to the 1980s*, ed. Mark A. Noll (New York: Oxford University Press, 1990), 31–35; Peter Gay, *The Party of Humanity: Essays in the French Enlightenment* (New York: W. W. Norton, 1971), 122–26, 270–74, 284, 287–90.

[15]Quoted in John Shelton Reed and Dale Volberg Reed, *1001 Things Everyone Should Know about the South* (New York: Doubleday, 1996), 246.

[16]Alan Mittleman, "Giving Religion Its Due," *Forward*, 15 June 2001, 9.

[17]Jeffrey Rosen, "Is Nothing Secular?", *New York Times Sunday Magazine*, 30 January 2000, 44.

[18]Charles S. Liebman and Steven M. Cohen, *Two Worlds of Judaism: The Israeli and American Experiences* (New Haven, CT: Yale University Press, 1990), 107; Dershowitz, *Vanishing American Jew*, 350, n. 41.

[19]Jane Fritsch, "Holy Cow! Ohio Has a Motto Problem," *New York Times*, 30 April 2000, IV, 2.

[20]Walt Whitman, "Preface, 1855," in *Leaves of Grass and Selected Prose*, ed. John Kouwenhoven (New York: Modern Library, 1950), 441; Werner Sollors, *Beyond Ethnicity: Consent and Descent in American Culture* (New York: Oxford University Press, 1986), 95; Frederick Jackson Turner, "The Significance of the Frontier in American History" (1894), in *Does the Frontier Experience Make America Exceptional*?, ed. Richard Eutalin (Boston: Bedford/St. Martin's, 1999), 30–31.

[21]John Lahr, *Show and Tell: New Yorker Profiles* (New York: Overlook Press, 2000), 258.

[22]Edward S. Shapiro, "World War II and American Jewish Identity," *Modern Judaism* 10 (February 1990), 65.

[23]Lucy S. Dawidowicz, *On Equal Terms: Jews in America, 1881–1981* (New York: Holt, Rinehart and Winston, 1982), 110; Shapiro, "World War II," 71, 74.

[24]Leonard Dinnerstein, *Anti-Semitism in America* (New York: Oxford University Press, 1994), 131–32; Marc Dollinger, *Quest for Inclusion: Jews and Liberalism in Modern America* (Princeton, NJ: Princeton University Press, 2000), 78, 246–47.

[25]Mordecai Richler, *Shovelling Trouble* (London: Quartet Books, 1973), 160.

[26]Frank Newport, "Americans Today Much More Accepting of a Woman, Black, Catholic, or Jew as President," *Gallup News Service*, 29 March 1999 (http://www.gallup.com/poll/releases/ pr990329.asp).

[27]Ted Morgan, *On Becoming American* (Boston: Houghton Mifflin, 1978), 228–29.

[28]Quoted in Howard Pollack, *Aaron Copland: The Life and Work of an Uncommon Man* (New York: Henry Holt, 1999), 17–18.

[29]Morris Raphael Cohen, *A Dreamer's Journey* (Boston: Beacon Press, 1949), 69.

[30]Quoted in Norman Zierold, *The Moguls* (New York: Avon, 1972), 17.

[31]Hollis Alpert, *The Life and Times of Porgy and Bess: The Story of an American Classic* (New York: Alfred A. Knopf, 1990), 92–95; Laurence Bergreen, *As Thousands Cheer: The Life of Irving Berlin* (New York: Viking, 1990), 27, 90–91, 135–36, 258, 365–66; Josh Rubins, "Genius Without Tears," *New York Review of Books* 35 (16 June 1988), 30.

[32]Virgil Thomson, *A Virgil Thomson Reader* (Boston: Houghton Mifflin, 1981), 24, 27.

[33]Quoted in Charles E. Silberman, *A Certain People: American Jews and Their Lives Today* (New York: Summit Books, 1985), 30–31.

[34]Quoted in Susan E. Tifft and Alex S. Jones, *The Trust: The Private and Powerful Family behind* The New York Times (Boston: Little, Brown, 1999), 38.

[35]Tifft and Jones, *The Trust*, 95; Harrison E. Salisbury, *Without Fear or Favor:* The New York Times *and Its Times* (New York: Times Books, 1980), 28–30, 401; Gay Talese, *The Kingdom and the Power* (Cleveland: World, 1969), 59, 91–4, 168–69.

[36]Quoted in Tifft and Jones, *The Trust*, 255.

[37]Tifft and Jones, *The Trust*, 5, 82, 92–93, 94, 95, 96, 97, 120, 155–56.

[38]Quoted in Tifft and Jones, *The Trust*, 25.

[39]Quoted in Jeffrey Potter, *Men, Money and Magic: The Story of Dorothy Schiff* (New York: Signet, 1977), 123.

[40]Tifft and Jones, *The Trust*, 84, 117, 273–74.

[41]Tifft and Jones, *The Trust*, 187–88; Laurel Leff, "A Tragic 'Fight in the Family': *The New York Times*, Reform Judaism and the Holocaust," *American Jewish History* 88 (March 2001), 3–51.

[42]Deborah E. Lipstadt, *Beyond Belief: The American Press and the Coming of the Holocaust, 1933–1945* (New York: Free Press, 1986), 220, 222, 245–47, *passim*; Tifft and Jones, *The Trust*, 217, 218–19, 220, 237, 744.

[43]Quoted in Tifft and Jones, *The Trust*, 237.

[44]Tifft and Jones, *The Trust*, 175–76.

[45]Quoted in Tifft and Jones, *The Trust*, 591.

[46]Quoted in Herbert G. Goldman, *Jolson: The Legend Comes to Life* (New York: Oxford University Press, 1988), 301–02; Jeffrey Melnick, *A Right to Sing the Blues: African Americans, Jews, and American Popular Song* (Cambridge, MA: Harvard University Press, 1999), 262; Michael Rogin, *Blackface, White Noise: Jewish Immigrants in the Hollywood Melting Pot* (Berkeley: University of California Press, 1996), 181.

[47]Ann Douglas, *Terrible Honesty: Mongrel Manhattan in the 1920s* (New York: Farrar, Straus and Giroux, 1995), 145.

[48]Henry Steele Commager, *Jefferson, Nationalism, and the Enlightenment* (New York: George Braziller, 1975), 109–10.

[49]A. Alvarez, *Where Did It All Go Right?: A Memoir* (New York: William Morrow, 1999), 145.

[50]Svetlana Alliluyeva, *Only One Year*, tr. Paul Chavchavadze (New York: Harper and Row, 1969), 354.

[51]Quoted in Julia Reed, "The Case of the Kissing Senator," *New York Review of Books* 43 (1 February 1996), 24.

[52]Abraham Cahan, *The Rise of David Levinsky* (1917; New York: Harper and Row, 1960), 91.

[53]"Dubious Achievement Awards," *Esquire* 91 (2–16 January 1979), 33; Jon Nordheimer, "Miami Bar Mitzvah Has 'Love and Family and Joy'—and Cheerleaders," *New York Times*, 15 May 1978, D10.

[54]Richard Hofstadter, *The Age of Reform: From Bryan to FDR* (New York: Alfred A. Knopf, 1955), 23.

[55]Sigmund Freud, *Civilization and Its Discontents*, tr. and ed. James Strachey (New York: W. W. Norton, 1962), 23.

[56]Singer and Grossman, eds., *American Jewish Year Book 2000*, 246, 491.

[57]Philip Roth, *The Counterlife* (New York: Farrar, Straus, and Giroux, 1986), 146.

CHARLES BERNSTEIN

SIGN UNDER TEST

On an evening in June, alone with anxious mediations, reading by mobbed light, I come again, taste to taste, with my own self-inoculations.

Paying double but taking only half.

As swill becomes saunter.

The sky lies so the dirt can give the boot.

Then again, there are certain things I never understood, yet lately I find myself mesmerized by these blank spots. They have become the sign posts of my consciousness.

The old becomes new again when it arrives after whatever is recent and seems fresh. On the other hand, nothing is so old as that which comes after but seems as if it must have been from before.

It's so quiet you can hear the lint festering in the fog.

I'll give you a hand but only one.

Fighting fire with sugar to make pie while the hay dries in the oysterman's holiday.

Winter tears, summer shadows.

Poetry is patterned thought in search of unpatterned mind.

Love is the messenger not the message.

Till you get to the backside of where you began. Neither round robin nor oblong sparrow.

My faculties are impolitic.

But at least: For two dimes and a nickel you still get something like a quarter.

Sometimes a gust is just a gust.

The ghosts just left.

That still, small voice may not be the root of all evil but it's no innocent bystander either.

There's tackle in the tackle box.

How can you separate the breach from the brook, the branch from the book?

The haze doesn't obscure the view it makes it palpable.

It's not the absence in the presence but the presence in the absence.

When you go away there's no back to come back to. All the addresses have changed and the locks have new combinations.

A husband returns home to find a burning cigar in his ashtray. He soon discovers a man in the broom closet. "What are you doing there?"—"Everybody's got to be somewhere." [Henny Youngman]

Rabbi Eliza asks, "When is a Jew no longer a Jew?"—"When the book is closed."

The pit of the cherry is like the soul of a self-righteous man: when you find it, you want to spit it out.

The slips have become skirts.

The dove cannot find rest for the soul of its foot. Neither can I find peace in the inner worlds beside the nearby.

Inoperative nomenclature.

A series of hints without a question, a slew of clues without a crime.

Why did the turtle cross the road?—To find the chicken.

What you don't know is a far cry from what you do.

Desperately searching for a book that I don't even want to read.

"The world is everything that is the case." But the case is locked in the trunk of a stolen car.

Everything that happens is lost. Even what is recalled is lost in the recalling. Nonetheless, things go on happening.

Memory is to life like a band-aid to a wound.

A girl I once met told me her name rhymed with orange.

Did I just imagine that?

Complexity is a ten-letter word, like difficulty. There's moxie in complexity and tilt in difficulty but what difference does this make?

I'll give you ten minutes and if you don't come out I'll give you ten more minutes.

My cares turned to wares.

Simply stated, there's nothing to state.

It's not what you say that counts nor what you don't say but the relation.

He understated the price of the property to be sure he got less than it was worth. This was the only way he knew for the exchange to have value.

Give me a place to sit and I will look for a place to put up my feet.

TILT

Everything in the world exists in order to end up as an opera. An opera without music is what we call everyday life. Poetry is opera without the story, score, costumes, make-up, or staging. It's a libretto set to its own music. The reader is both the conductor and lead singer. The audience gathers at the unconscious. Tickets are sold only on the morning of the performance; students pay half but often stand. Unsatisfied customers may claim refunds for twice the cost of admission; these are paid directly by the poet.

"You've got a lot of moxie."

The "double silly" consists of making two complete turns with another person while walking in the street.

I've got my next few years of work mapped out for me: figuring out what to do over the next few years.

When you say baroque you're barking up the wrong tree, which suits me.

The station wagon stayed stationary at the station.

Stunned he put down his gun and started to run.

The Jew stops being the Jew when the movie's over.

No horizon on the horizon.

Going to sleep to continue the story.

Third eye hindsighted.

Making another patch for the patch.

There's no business like no business like no business I know.

Blue is no longer blue when it loses its hue.

Terrible day to start the way. (Terrible way to start to stray.)

If language could talk we would refuse to understand it.

Hue is a property of optics not objects.

As to "avant garde": I am not in advance of anything but perhaps close, in the neighborhood, around.

Better to come up from behind than to lead. If you lead you'd have to know where you are going whereas I only know where I am not going.

The politics in a poem has to do with how it enters the world, how it makes its meaning, how its forms work in social contexts. The politics in a poem is specific to poetry not politics.

Now I am getting weary of ideology and would like to give it up entirely but it seems the more I give it up the more it has me by the throat. I write so I can breathe.

And better artificial respiration than no respiration. Better imaging reparation than silence.

Or let's say trying to re-imagine the possibilities of sentience through the material sentience of language.

Don't ask me to be frank. I don't even know if I can be myself.

You never know what invention will look like or else it wouldn't be invention.

We see each other as if with hidden sensors. Those not tuned in miss the action entirely, even when it's right before their eyes.

The Greeks had an idea of *nostos,* which is not quite what we call nostalgia. *Nostos* suggests the political and ethical responsibility of the human being, in orienting herself or himself. You can't go home again but you can stay tuned to your senses of responsibility.

So much depends upon what you are expecting.

The chicken she is cooked but the liver is raw.

As for we who love to be admonished. . . .

Certain that this satin would intoxicate even Satan; the trips of the trade, the lisps of the frayed.

If that's the price I will pay it but not gladly.

Like I told her, you can add up all the zeros in the world but it will never amount to anything. Whereas two plus two, while barely four, suggests progress.

If progress is a process, what is the purpose of purpose or the allure of allure?

You see I told you so but you weren't listening or maybe I forgot to press SEND.

It is equally problematic to shout "Theater!" at a crowded fire.

I break for speed bumps.

Eugene Ormandy wore organdy. George Solti speaks in sotte voce. Toscanini dons a bikini. Neville Marriner slides down the banister. Herbert von Karajan had two carry-ons. Kurt Mazur abhors clamor.

Everything that happens in life exists to be reflected on in Boca.

"Do you see that? Those people came in after us and they're being served first."

It takes a village to read a poem.

The patter of petunias in the marmalade.

Everybody's got to be somewhere.

Save the last chance for me.

CONTRIBUTORS

PEARL ABRAHAM is the author of the novels *The Romance Reader* (1995) and *Giving Up America* (1998), both from Penguin/Putnam, and the editor of the anthology in Dutch *Een sterke vrouw: Jewish Heroines in Literature* (Meulenhoff, 2000).

MARTHA BANTA is Professor Emeritus, University of California, Los Angeles; past president of the American Studies Association, and 2002 recipient of the Bode-Pearson Award for Lifetime Achievement and Service to the ASA. Her most recent book is *Barbaric Intercourse: Caricature and the Culture of Conduct.*

LEONARD BARKAN is the Arthur W. Marks '19 Professor of Comparative Literature and Director of the Society of Fellows at Princeton University. He is the author most recently of *Transuming Passion: Ganymede and the Erotics of Humanism* (Stanford University Press, 1991) and *Unearthing the Past: Archaeology and Aesthetics in the Making of Renaissance Culture* (Yale University Press, 1999).

CHARLES BERNSTEIN's most recent books are *With Strings* (2002) and *My Way: Speeches and Poems* (1999), both from the University of Chicago Press, and *Republics of Reality: 1975–1995* (2000), from Sun & Moon Press, and, as editor, *Close Listening: Poetry and the Performed Word* (Oxford University Press, 1998) and *99 Poets / 1999: An International Poetics Symposium* (boundary2/Duke University Press, 1999).

SARA BLAIR teaches English and American studies at the University of Michigan. She is the author of *Henry James and the Writing of Race and Nation* (1996) and of numerous essays on modernism, modernity, and visual culture. Her current project, *Harlem and the Image of Afterlife*, explores collaborations between writers and photographers in post-Renaissance Harlem; part of this work will appear in "Ralph Ellison, Photographer," forthcoming in winter 2005 in the journal *Raritan.*

CHANA BLOCH is the author of three books of poems, most recently *Mrs. Dumpty*, winner of the 1998 Felix Pollak Prize in

Poetry. She is co-translator of the biblical Song of Songs, and four books by Israeli poets: *A Dress of Fire* and *The Window* by Dahlia Ravikovitch, *The Selected Poetry of Yehuda Amichai*, and Amichai's magnum opus, *Open Closed Open*. She has also published a critical study, *Spelling the Word: George Herbert and the Bible*. She teaches in the creative writing program at Mills College.

JONATHAN BOYARIN is a lawyer and anthropologist who lives on the Lower East Side of New City. His writings are concerned with problems of the transmission of East European Jewish culture and the theoretical questions that surround these problems, such as the role of text in culture, the politics of memory, and the comparative dynamics of diaspora. Of the ten books he has written or edited, the first was *From a Ruined Garden: The Memorial Books of Polish Jewry* (University of Indiana Press, 1998) and the most recent is *Powers of Diaspora* (with Daniel Boyarin; University of Minnesota Press, 2002).

DANIEL MARK EPSTEIN's seventh book of poems is *The Traveler's Calendar* (Overlook Press, 2002). He is the author of biographies of Aimee Semple McPherson, Nat King Cole, and, most recently, Edna St. Vincent Millay, as well as a translation of Euripides's *The Bacchae*.

JONATHAN FREEDMAN is Professor of English and American Studies at the University of Michigan. He is the author of *Professions of Taste: Henry James, British Aestheticism and Commodity Culture* (Stanford University Press, 1991) and, most recently, *The Temple of Culture: Assimilation, Anti-Semitism, and the Making of Literary Anglo-America* (Oxford University Press, 2000). In addition, he has edited collections of essays on Henry James, Oscar Wilde, and Alfred Hitchcock. He has held a Guggenheim Fellowship and been a fellow at the National Humanities Center and has also taught at Yale, Caltech, Oxford, and the Bread Loaf School of English. He is currently working on a book on ethnicity and perversion.

BONNIE FRIEDMAN is the author of *The Thief of Happiness: The Story of an Extraordinary Psychotherapy* (Beacon Press, 2002) and *Writing Past Dark: Envy, Fear, Distraction, and Other Dilemmas in the Writer's Life* (HarperCollins, 1993). She lives in Brooklyn, New York.

LAURENCE GOLDSTEIN, editor of *MQR* and Professor of English at the University of Michigan, is the author most recently of *The American Poet at the Movies: A Critical History* (University of Michigan Press, 1994) and a volume of poems, *Cold Reading* (Copper Beech Press, 1995). He coedited (with Robert Chrisman) *Robert Hayden: Essays on the Poetry* (University of Michigan Press, 2001).

STEPHEN GREENBLATT, the Cogan University Professor of the Humanities at Harvard University, is the author, most recently, of *Hamlet in Purgatory* (Princeton University Press, 2001). He is currently the President of the Modern Language Association and is at work on *Will in the World*, a biographical study of Shakespeare.

RICK HILLES has poems recently published or forthcoming in *Poetry*, *The Nation*, *The New Republic*, and *The Paris Review*. He teaches creative writing and poetry at the University of Michigan but will be on leave for the 2002/3 academic year and living in eastern and southern Europe as the Amy Lowell Travelling Scholar.

RODGER KAMENETZ is the author of three books of poetry, including *The Missing Jew: New and Selected Poems* (1992) and *Stuck: Poems Midlife* (1997), both from Time Being Books. His works in prose include *The Jew in the Lotus* (HarperSanFrancisco, 1994) and *Stalking Elijah* (HarperSanFrancisco, 1997), which won the National Jewish Book Award in 1997. He writes a monthly column for the *Forward*, "Psalm 151."

RICHARD KOSTELANETZ is the author or editor of numerous books, including most recently *Wordworks: Poems Selected and New* (BOA Editions, 1993), *Writings on Glass: Essays, Interviews, Criticism* (Schirmer Books, 1997), *AnOther E.E. Cummings* (Liveright, 1998), and *A Dictionary of the Avant-gardes* (Schirmer Books, 2000). Full biographical entries can be found in *The HarperCollins Reader's Encyclopedia of American Literature* and the Encyclopedia Britannica, among other directories.

JOANNE LEONARD is a professor of Art and Design and of Women's Studies at the University of Michigan. Her work is published and exhibited nationally and internationally. Look for her essay at *The Feminist Scholar: Changing Focus—Family Photography and American Jewish Identity* at http://www.barnard.columbia.edu/sfonline/ and a book about her art and life forthcoming in 2005 from the University of Michigan Press.

JULIAN LEVINSON is the Samuel Shetzer Assistant Professor of American Jewish Studies and English Literature at the University of Michigan. He is currently completing a book entitled *Jewish Self-Fashioning: American Literature and the Art of De-Assimilation.*

JOHN LIMON, Professor of English at Williams College, is the author most recently of *Writing After War: American War Fiction from Realism to Postmodernism* (Oxford University Press, 1994) and *Stand-up Comedy in Theory, or, Abjection in America* (Duke University Press, 2000).

BERNARD MENDOZA started his career as a photographer in London during the cultural revolution of the '60s. His introduction to Dr. Roman Vishniac's *A Vanished World* and a desire to work on his own projects led to his photo-essay on Hassidic communities in America, *From Generation to Generation* (now in the permanent collection of The Museum of Fine Art in Houston). This, together with some of his other projects, has been exhibited and published around the world, including showings at The Smithsonian and The National Portrait Gallery.

GREGORY ORFALEA, a descendant of the first immigrant Arab family in America (1878), is the author of *Before the Flames: A Quest for the History of Arab Americans* (University of Texas Press, 1988) and *Messengers of the Lost Battalion: The Heroic 551st and the Turning of the Tide at the Battle of the Bulge* (The Free Press, 1995).

JACQUELINE OSHEROW is Professor of English at the University of Utah, where she teaches poetry workshops as well as courses in the Hebrew Bible and English literature. Recent volumes of poetry include *Conversations with Survivors* (University of Georgia Press, 1994), *With a Moon in Transit* (Grove Press, 1996), and *Dead Men's Praise* (Grove Press, 1999). She is the recipient of Guggenheim (1997–8) and NEA (1999–2000) fellowships.

ROBERT PINSKY, a former Poet Laureate of the United States, is the author of *The Figured Wheel: New and Collected Poems 1966–1996* (1996) and a subsequent volume, *Jersey Rain* (2000), both from Farrar, Straus & Giroux. He teaches in the graduate writing program at Boston University.

SHARON POMERANTZ is a graduate of the Unversity of Michigan MFA program. Her short fiction has appeared in *Ploughshares*, *The Black Warrior Review*, *The Colorado Review*, *The Massachusetts Review*, and the Penguin/Plume anthology *Nice Jewish Girls: Growing Up in America*. She is currently working on a novel.

NANCY REISMAN is the author of *House Fires*, which won the Iowa Short Fiction Award for 1999. Her stories have appeared in *Tin House*, *New England Review*, *The Kenyon Review*, *Glimmer Train*, and other journals, as well as in *The Best American Short Stories 2001*. She is the Helen Herzog Zell Professor at the University of Michigan.

GRACE SCHULMAN's newest poetry collection is *Days of Wonder: New and Selected Poems* (Houghton Mifflin, 2002).

LOUIS SIMPSON is the author of seventeen books of verse as well as works of literary criticism and memoirs. His most recent publication is a translation, *François Villon: The Legacy & The Testament* (Story Line Press). *The Owner of the House: New and Collected Poems* is scheduled for publication in the fall of 2003. He resides in Stony Brook, New York.

ALISA SOLOMON is Professor of English and Journalism at Baruch College/City University of New York and of English and Theater in the Ph.D. program of the CUNY Graduate Center, where she also serves as director of the Center for Lesbian and Gay Studies. She is Staff Writer for *The Village Voice*, where she writes theater criticism as well as political features on such subjects as U.S. immigration policy, Jewish community affairs, the Israeli-Palestinian conflict, and women's sports. Her book *Re-dressing the Canon: Essays on Theatre and Gender* (Routledge) won the George Jean Nathan Award for Dramatic Criticism in 1998.

STEPHEN J. WHITFIELD holds the Max Richter Chair in American Civilization at Brandeis University. He is the author of books about Hannah Arendt and Dwight Macdonald, as well as *American Space, Jewish Time* (Archon Books, 1988), *The Culture of the Cold War* (Johns Hopkins University Press, 1991), and most recently, *In Search of American Jewish Culture* (University Press of New England, 1999).

SHIRA WOLOSKY was Associate Professor of Comparative Literature at Yale University before moving to the Hebrew University of Jerusalem, where she is Professor of English and American Literature. Her publications include *Emily Dickinson: A Voice of War* (Yale University Press, 1984), *Language Mysticism* (Stanford University Press, 1995), *The Art of Poetry* (Oxford University Press, 2001), and *Poetry and Public Discourse*, the forthcoming fifth volume of *The Cambridge History of American Literature*. She was a Guggenheim fellow in 2000.

Bernard Mendoza, *The Tap Lesson,* Denver, 1999